OUT OF THE BLUE

A COLLECTION OF STRANGE STORIES

EDITED BY
COREY FRYIA
AND
MARTA TANRIKULU

STACHE

Production

Creative Team

Corey Fryia, Co-Editor
Marta Tanrikulu, Co-Editor
Marcus Muller, Story Editor
Claire Connelly, Cover Artist
Jason Moning, Designer

 STACHE PUBLISHING LLC

Alice Harvey @MilkandHoney618
Anthony Mathenia @armathenia
David Tickner @outgrownstache
Drew Rose @DrewAntonRose

Jordan Williams @JOrdanWilliam5
Lauren Ousley @LaurenOusely
Ryan Lawson @RyanLawson87
Shane Fulgham @shanecrash

ISBN 978-0-692-32087-7

S-2 SECTION
GENERAL HEADQUARTERS,
CENTER FOR ODD RESEARCH,
SAINT LOUIS, MO,
OCTOBER 26, 1952

FILE CONTENTS

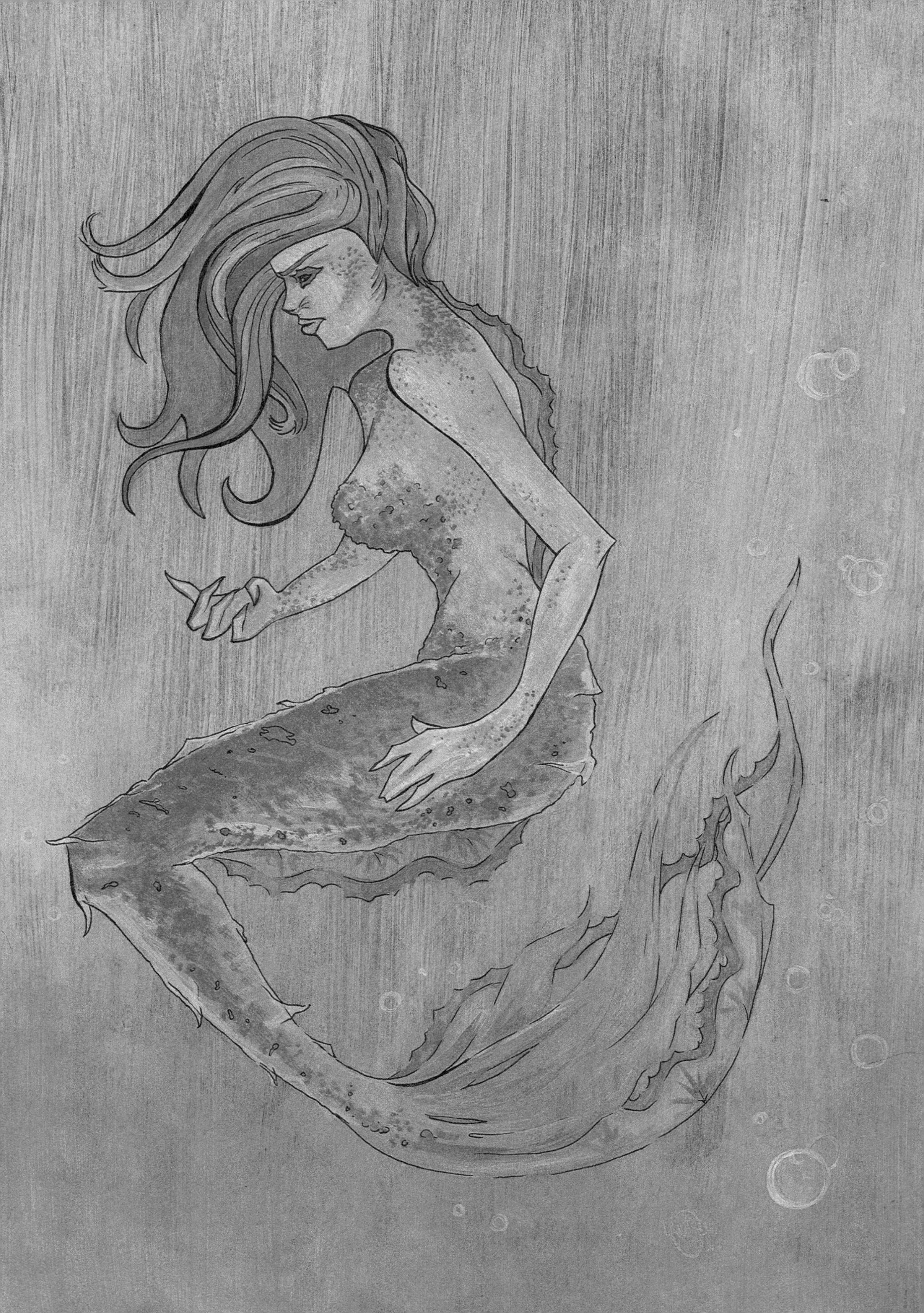

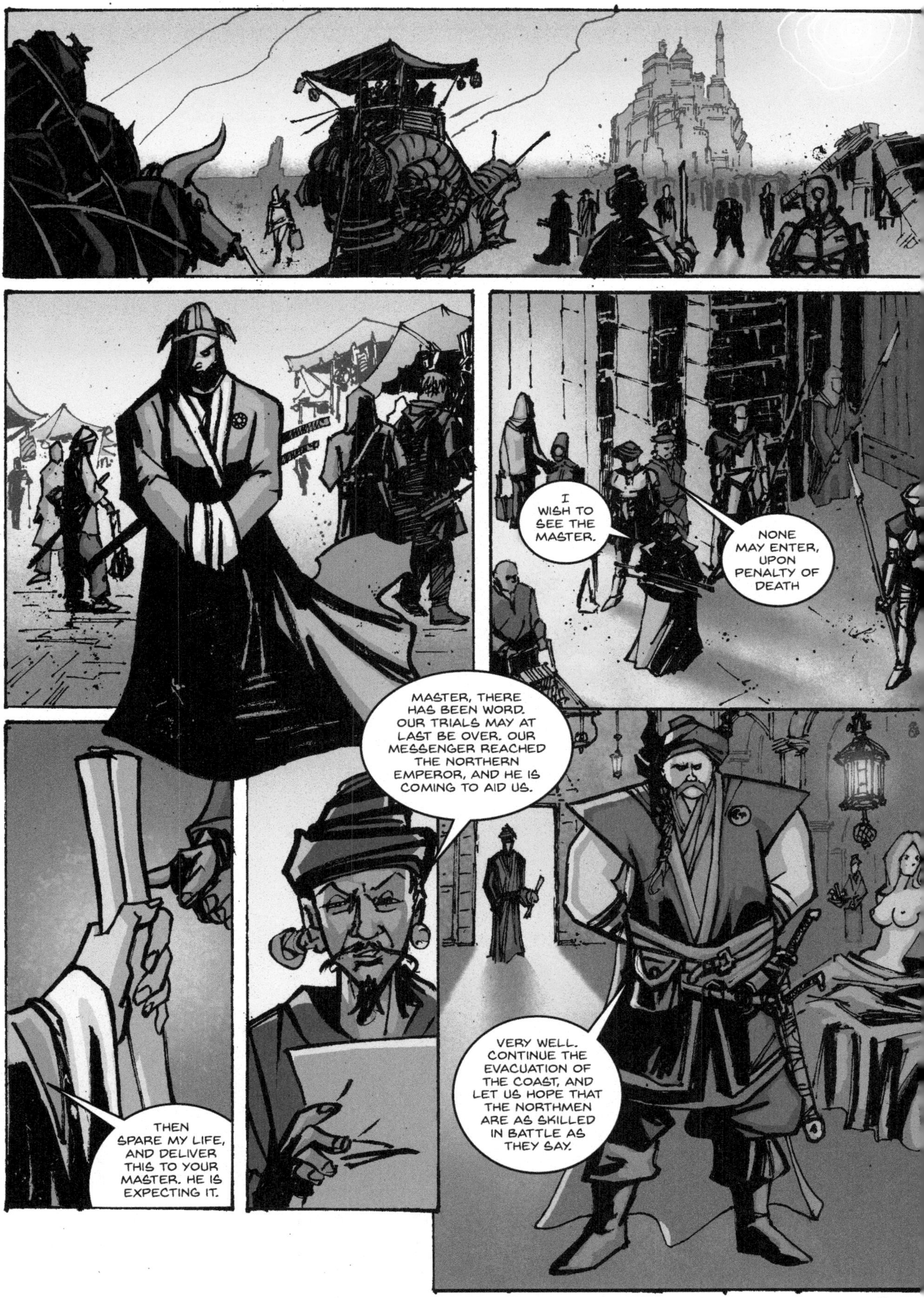
I WISH TO SEE THE MASTER.
NONE MAY ENTER, UPON PENALTY OF DEATH
THEN SPARE MY LIFE, AND DELIVER THIS TO YOUR MASTER. HE IS EXPECTING IT.
MASTER, THERE HAS BEEN WORD. OUR TRIALS MAY AT LAST BE OVER. OUR MESSENGER REACHED THE NORTHERN EMPEROR, AND HE IS COMING TO AID US.
VERY WELL. CONTINUE THE EVACUATION OF THE COAST, AND LET US HOPE THAT THE NORTHMEN ARE AS SKILLED IN BATTLE AS THEY SAY.

MIKE EXNER III ~ WRITER

DAVID NEWBOLD ~ PENCILS/INKS

JOSEPH BAKER ~ COLORS
BIG PANTS! ME W/JOE SIMMONS ~ LETTERS

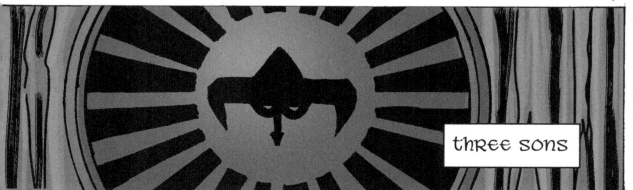

THREE SONS

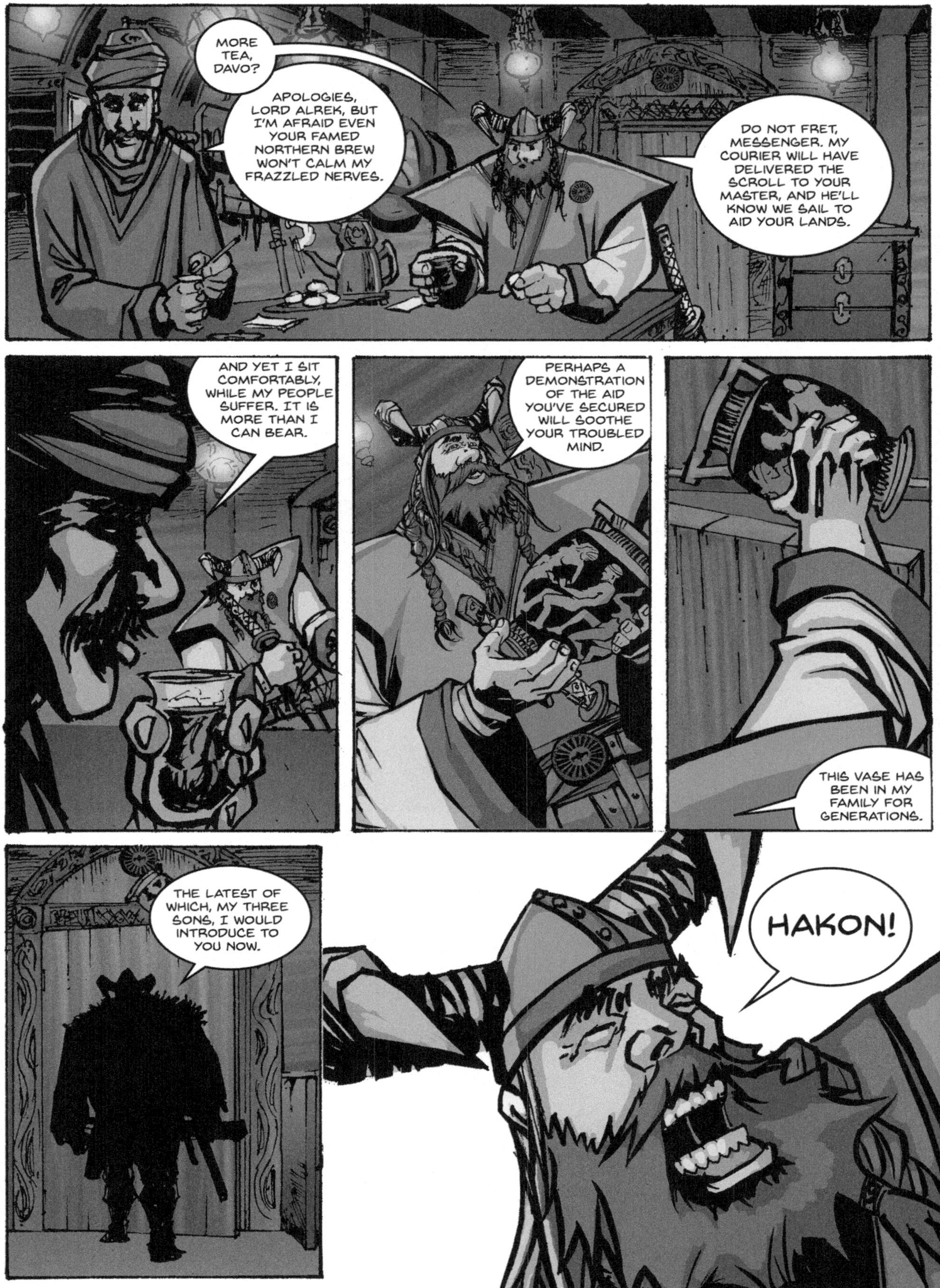
MORE TEA, DAVO?
APOLOGIES, LORD ALREK, BUT I'M AFRAID EVEN YOUR FAMED NORTHERN BREW WON'T CALM MY FRAZZLED NERVES.
DO NOT FRET, MESSENGER. MY COURIER WILL HAVE DELIVERED THE SCROLL TO YOUR MASTER, AND HE'LL KNOW WE SAIL TO AID YOUR LANDS.
AND YET I SIT COMFORTABLY, WHILE MY PEOPLE SUFFER. IT IS MORE THAN I CAN BEAR.
PERHAPS A DEMONSTRATION OF THE AID YOU'VE SECURED WILL SOOTHE YOUR TROUBLED MIND.
THIS VASE HAS BEEN IN MY FAMILY FOR GENERATIONS.
THE LATEST OF WHICH, MY THREE SONS, I WOULD INTRODUCE TO YOU NOW.
HAKON!

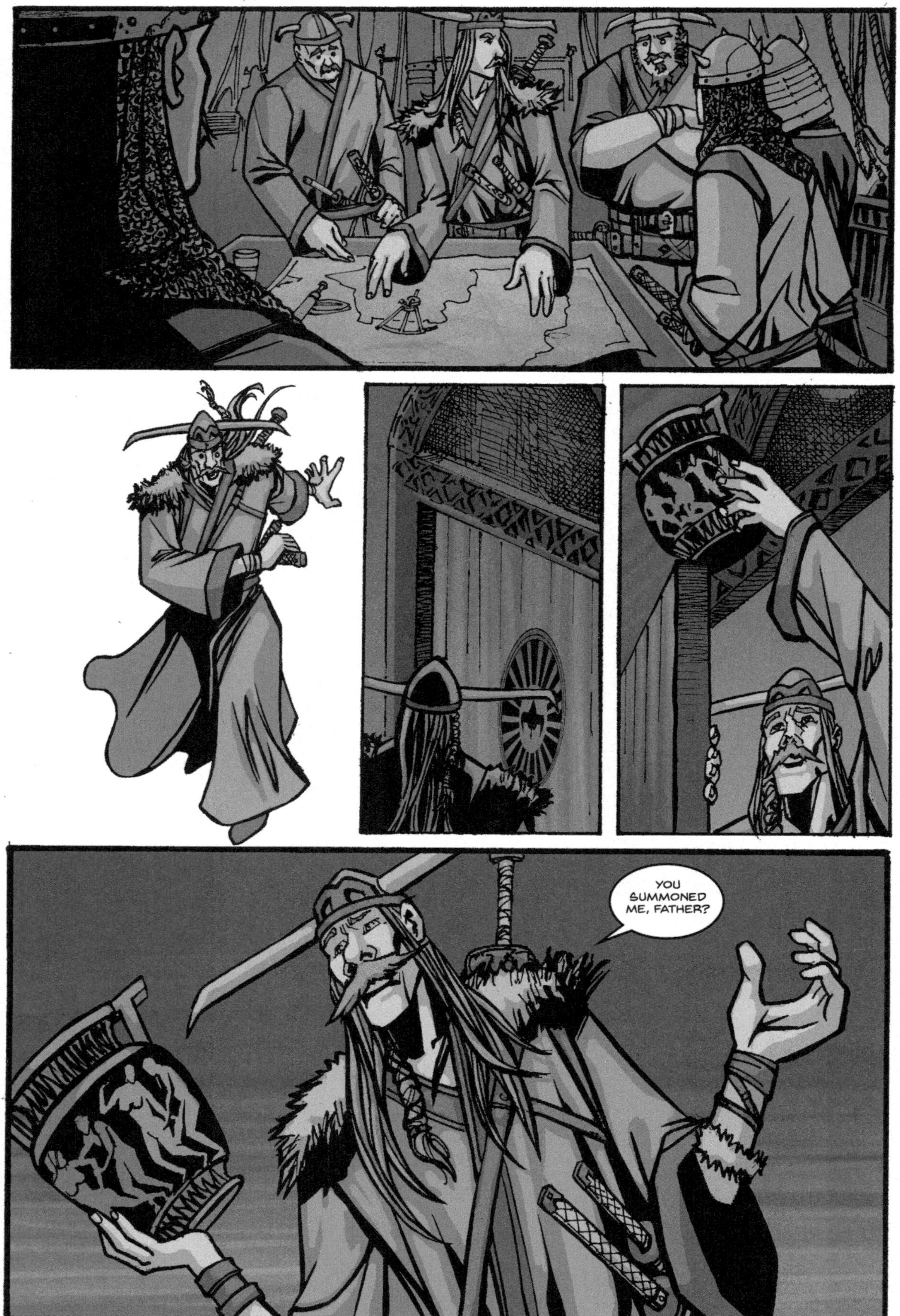
YOU SUMMONED ME, FATHER?

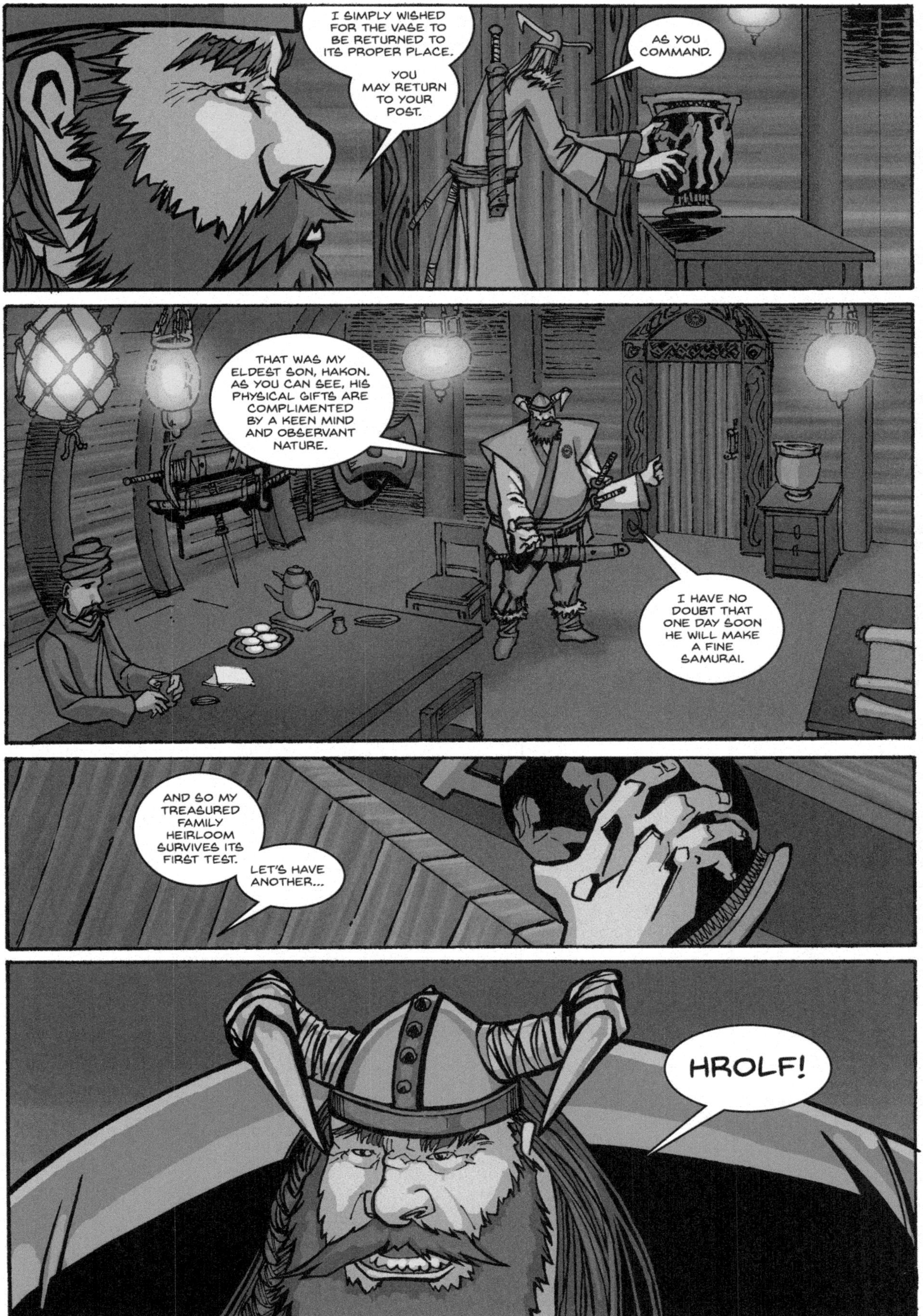
I SIMPLY WISHED FOR THE VASE TO BE RETURNED TO ITS PROPER PLACE.
YOU MAY RETURN TO YOUR POST.
AS YOU COMMAND.
THAT WAS MY ELDEST SON, HAKON. AS YOU CAN SEE, HIS PHYSICAL GIFTS ARE COMPLIMENTED BY A KEEN MIND AND OBSERVANT NATURE.
I HAVE NO DOUBT THAT ONE DAY SOON HE WILL MAKE A FINE SAMURAI.
AND SO MY TREASURED FAMILY HEIRLOOM SURVIVES ITS FIRST TEST.
LET'S HAVE ANOTHER...
HROLF!

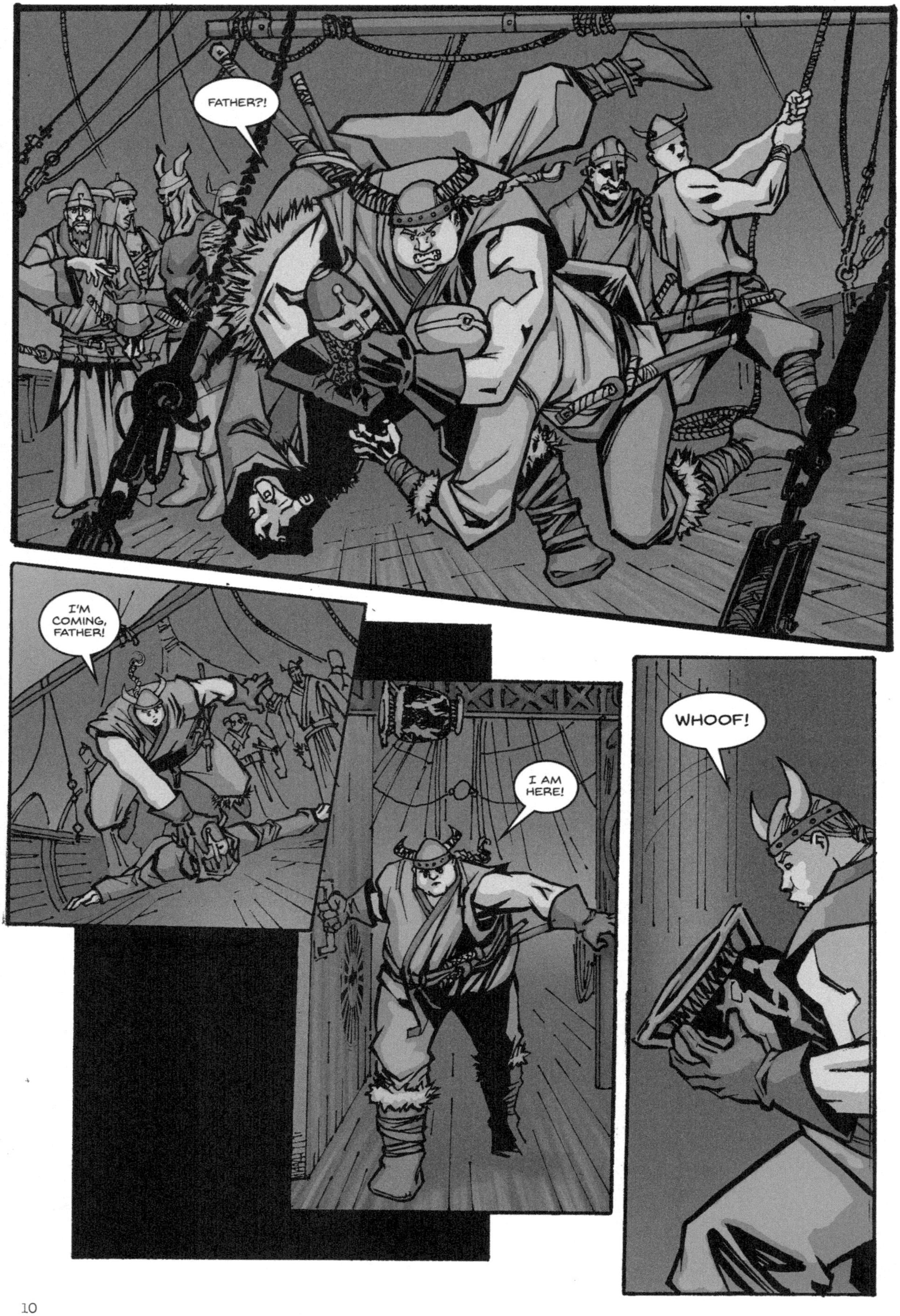
FATHER?!
I'M COMING, FATHER!
I AM HERE!
WHOOF!

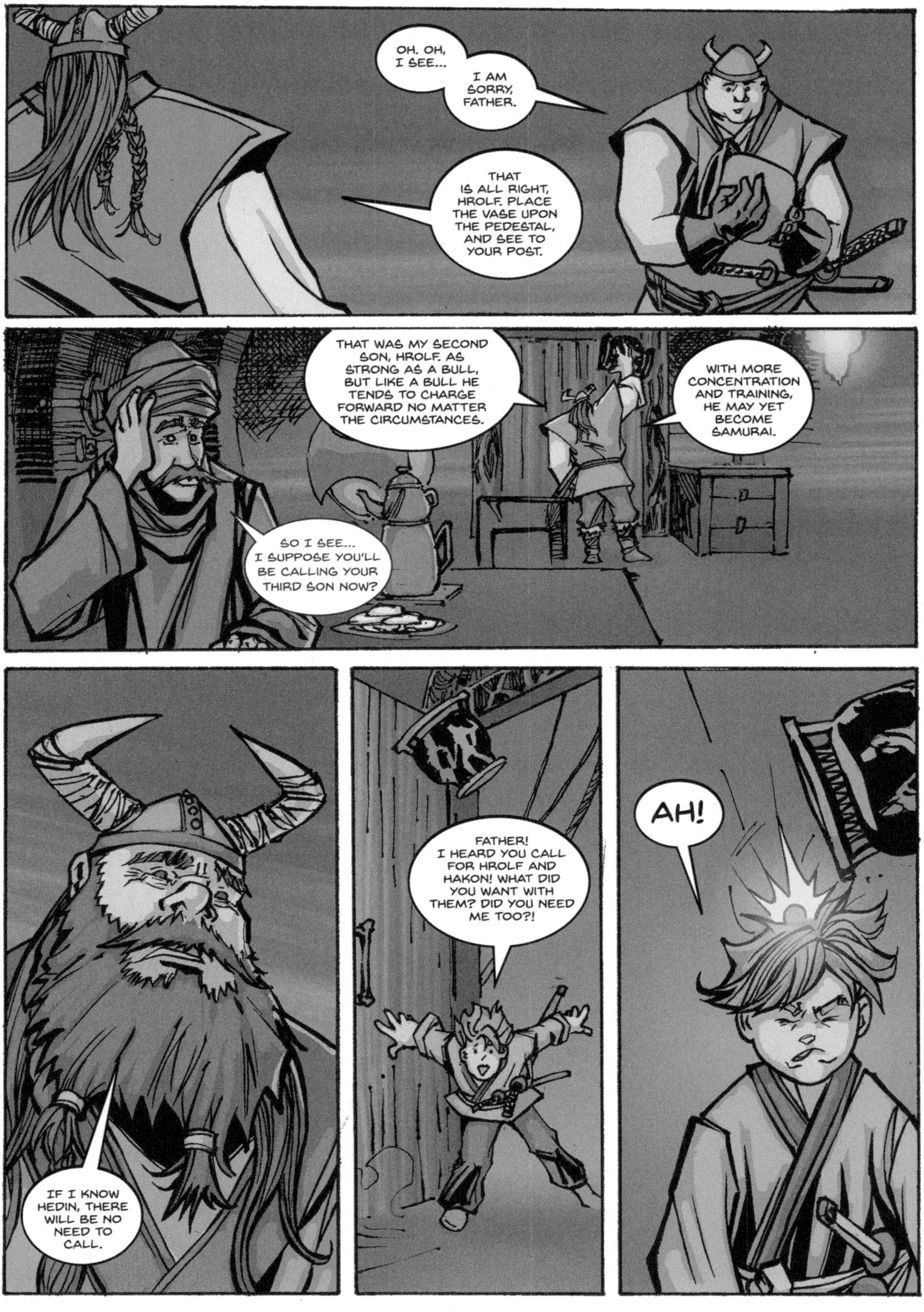
OH. OH, I SEE...
I AM SORRY, FATHER.
THAT IS ALL RIGHT, HROLF. PLACE THE VASE UPON THE PEDESTAL, AND SEE TO YOUR POST.
THAT WAS MY SECOND SON, HROLF. AS STRONG AS A BULL, BUT LIKE A BULL HE TENDS TO CHARGE FORWARD NO MATTER THE CIRCUMSTANCES.
WITH MORE CONCENTRATION AND TRAINING, HE MAY YET BECOME SAMURAI.
SO I SEE... I SUPPOSE YOU'LL BE CALLING YOUR THIRD SON NOW?
IF I KNOW HEDIN, THERE WILL BE NO NEED TO CALL.
FATHER! I HEARD YOU CALL FOR HROLF AND HAKON! WHAT DID YOU WANT WITH THEM? DID YOU NEED ME TOO?!
AH!

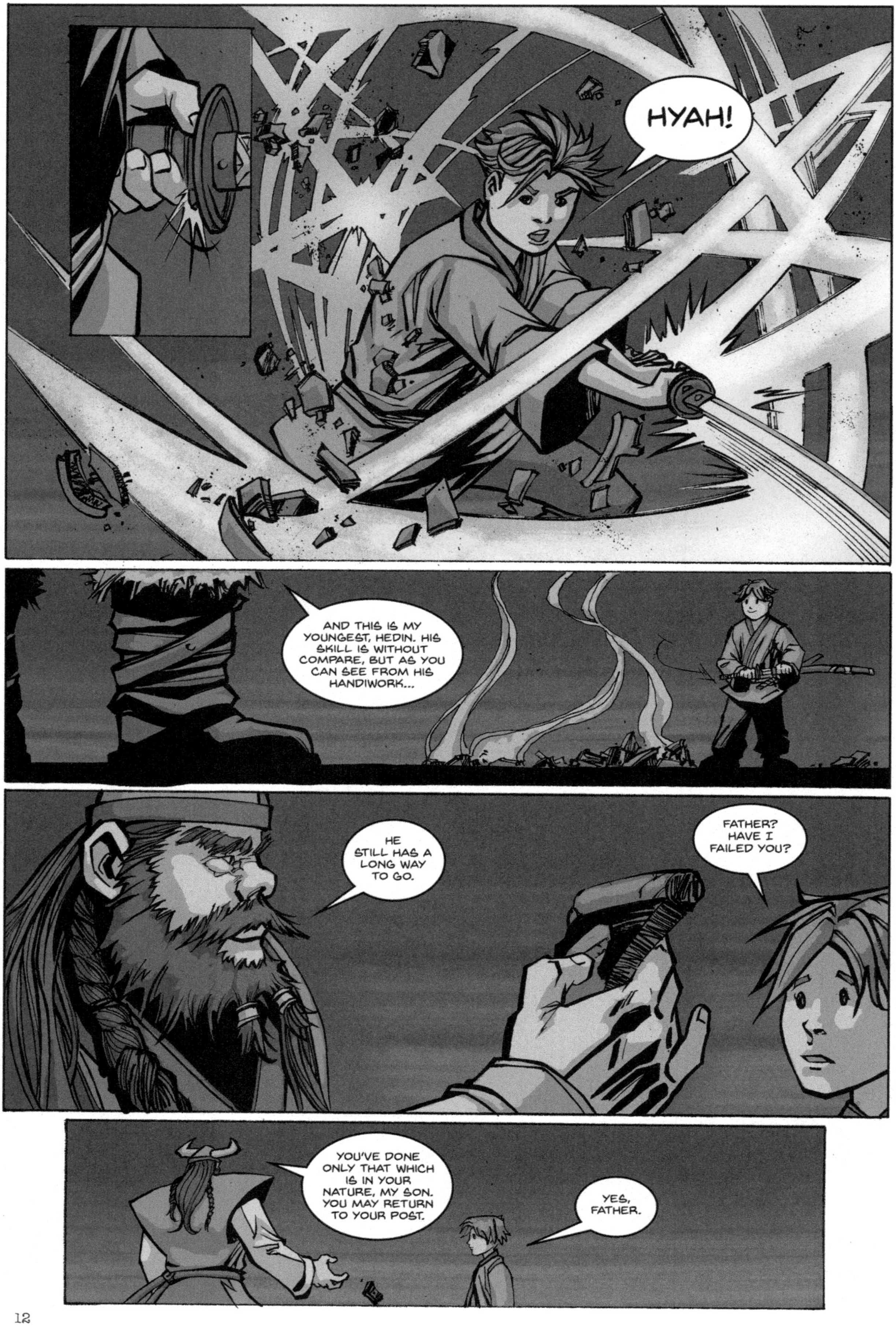
HYAH!
AND THIS IS MY YOUNGEST, HEDIN. HIS SKILL IS WITHOUT COMPARE, BUT AS YOU CAN SEE FROM HIS HANDIWORK...
HE STILL HAS A LONG WAY TO GO.
FATHER? HAVE I FAILED YOU?
YOU'VE DONE ONLY THAT WHICH IS IN YOUR NATURE, MY SON. YOU MAY RETURN TO YOUR POST.
YES, FATHER.

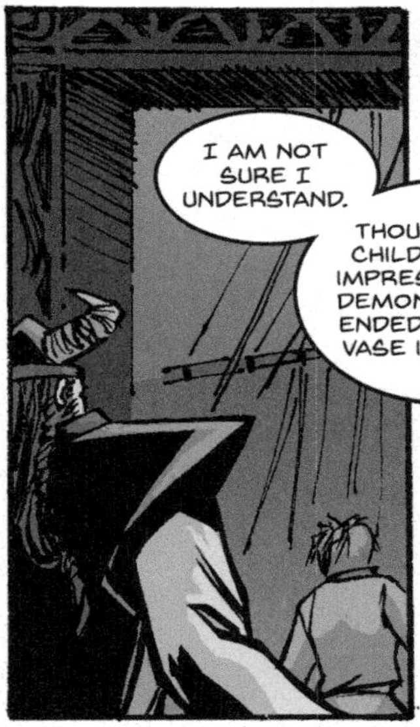
I AM NOT SURE I UNDERSTAND.

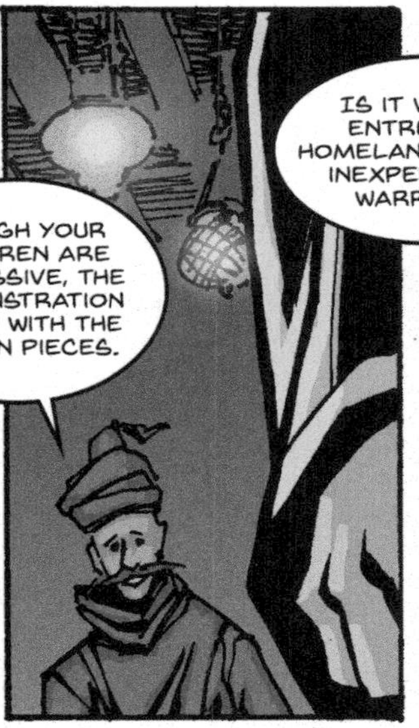
THOUGH YOUR CHILDREN ARE IMPRESSIVE, THE DEMONSTRATION ENDED WITH THE VASE IN PIECES.

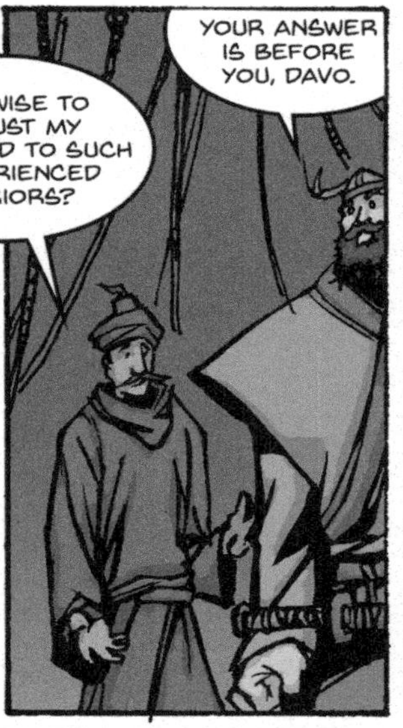
IS IT WISE TO ENTRUST MY HOMELAND TO SUCH INEXPERIENCED WARRIORS?
YOUR ANSWER IS BEFORE YOU, DAVO.

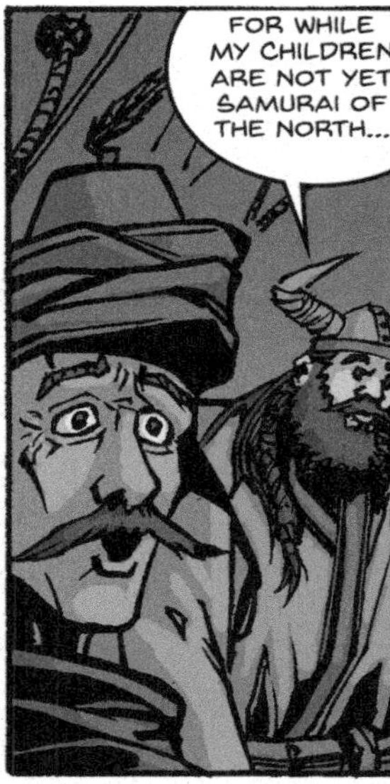
FOR WHILE MY CHILDREN ARE NOT YET SAMURAI OF THE NORTH...

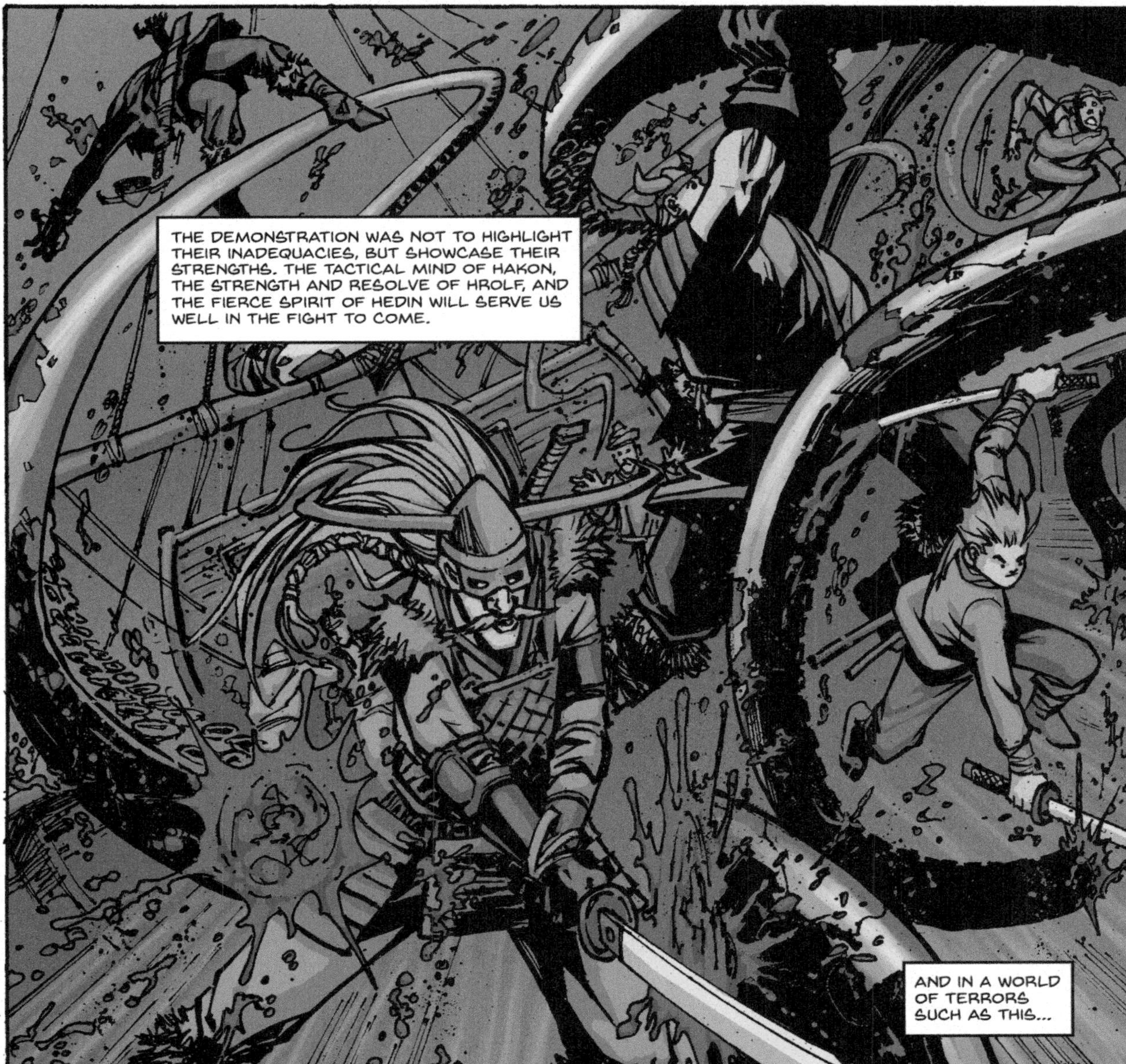
THE DEMONSTRATION WAS NOT TO HIGHLIGHT THEIR INADEQUACIES, BUT SHOWCASE THEIR STRENGTHS. THE TACTICAL MIND OF HAKON, THE STRENGTH AND RESOLVE OF HROLF, AND THE FIERCE SPIRIT OF HEDIN WILL SERVE US WELL IN THE FIGHT TO COME.
AND IN A WORLD OF TERRORS SUCH AS THIS...

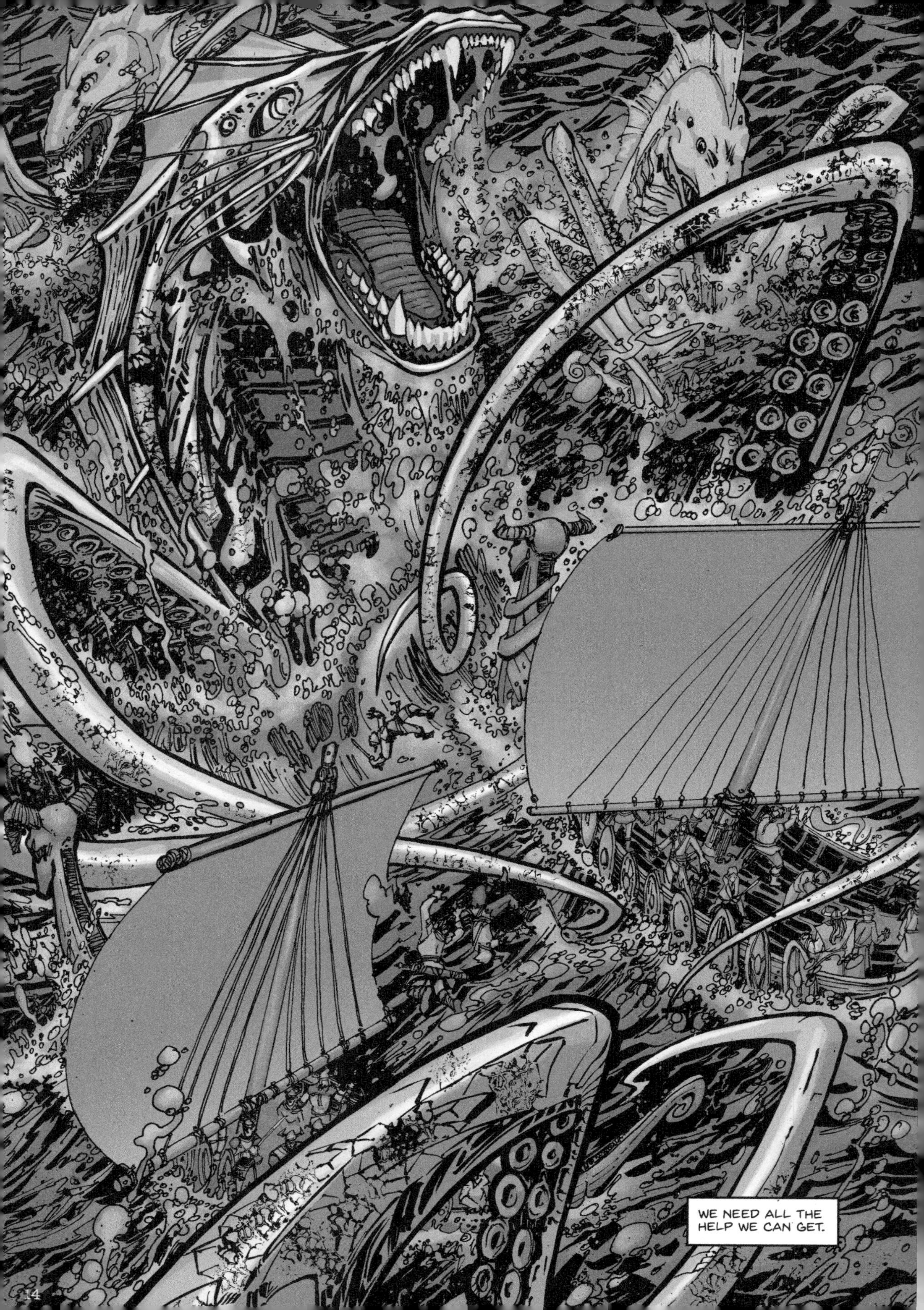
WE NEED ALL THE
HELP WE CAN GET.

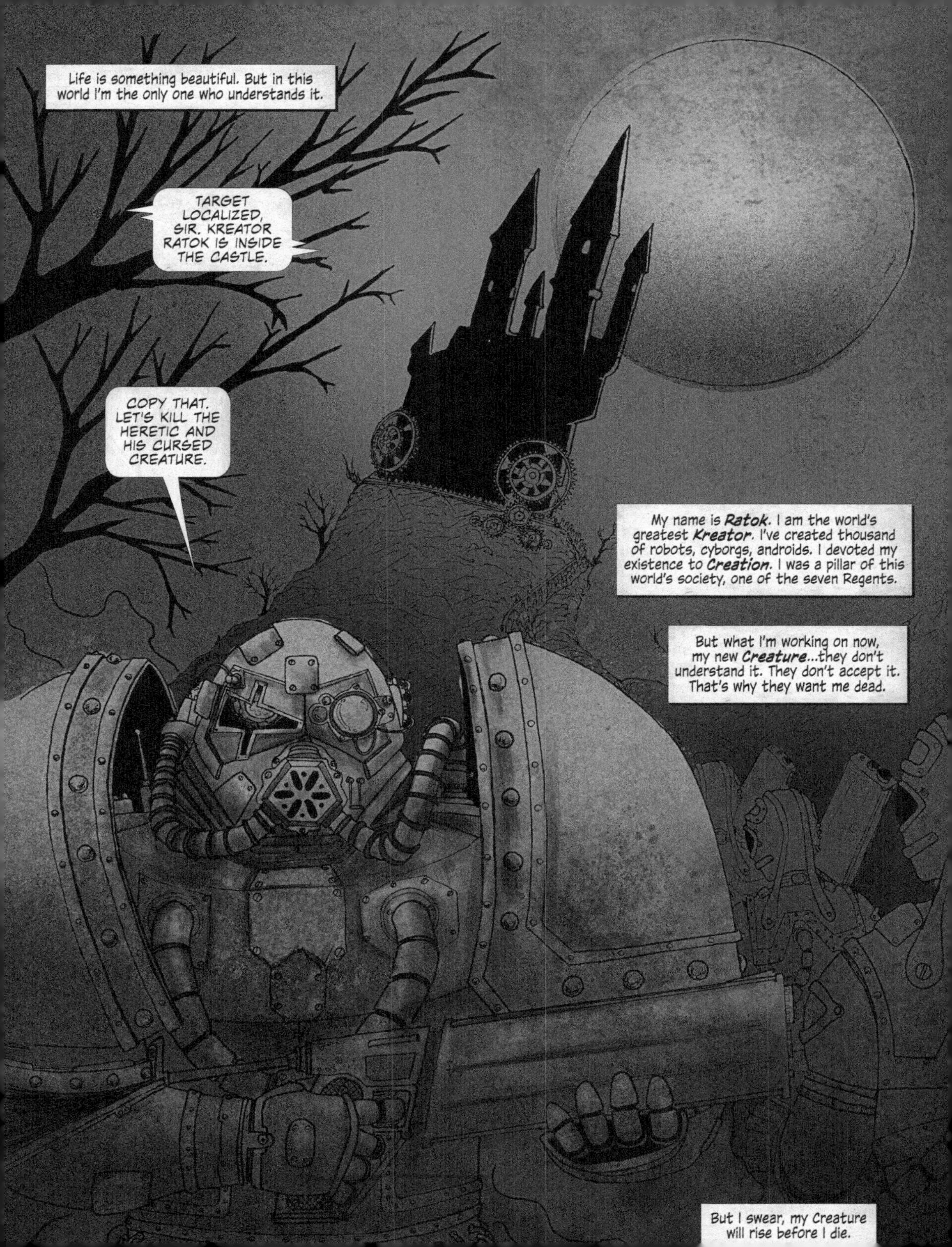

Life is something beautiful. But in this world I'm the only one who understands it.
TARGET LOCALIZED, SIR. KREATOR RATOK IS INSIDE THE CASTLE.
COPY THAT. LET'S KILL THE HERETIC AND HIS CURSED CREATURE.
My name is Ratok. I am the world's greatest Kreator. I've created thousand of robots, cyborgs, androids. I devoted my existence to Creation. I was a pillar of this world's society, one of the seven Regents.
But what I'm working on now, my new Creature...they don't understand it. They don't accept it. That's why they want me dead.
But I swear, my Creature will rise before I die.

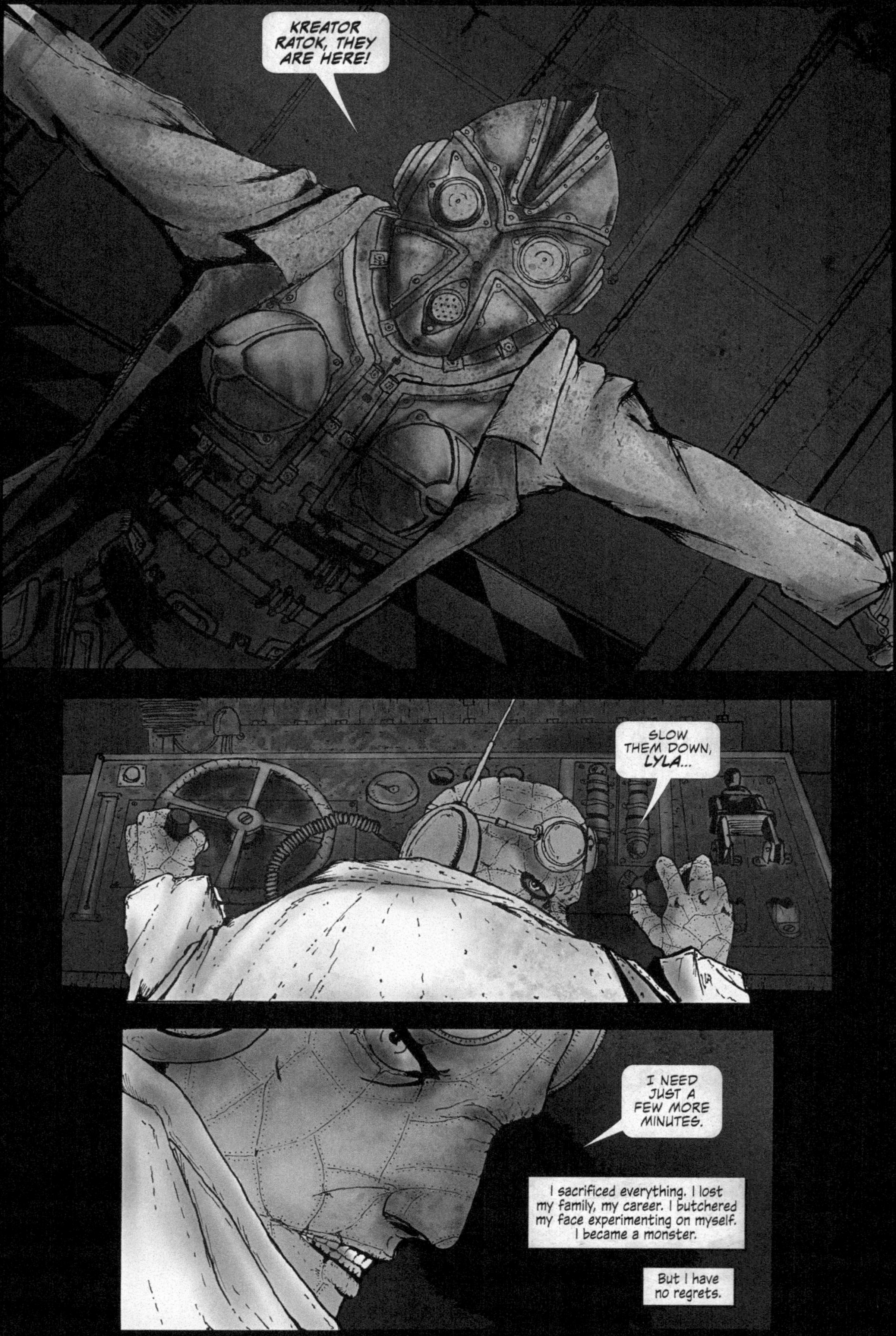
KREATOR RATOK, THEY ARE HERE!
SLOW THEM DOWN, LYLA...
I NEED JUST A FEW MORE MINUTES.
I sacrificed everything. I lost my family, my career. I butchered my face experimenting on myself. I became a monster.
But I have no regrets.

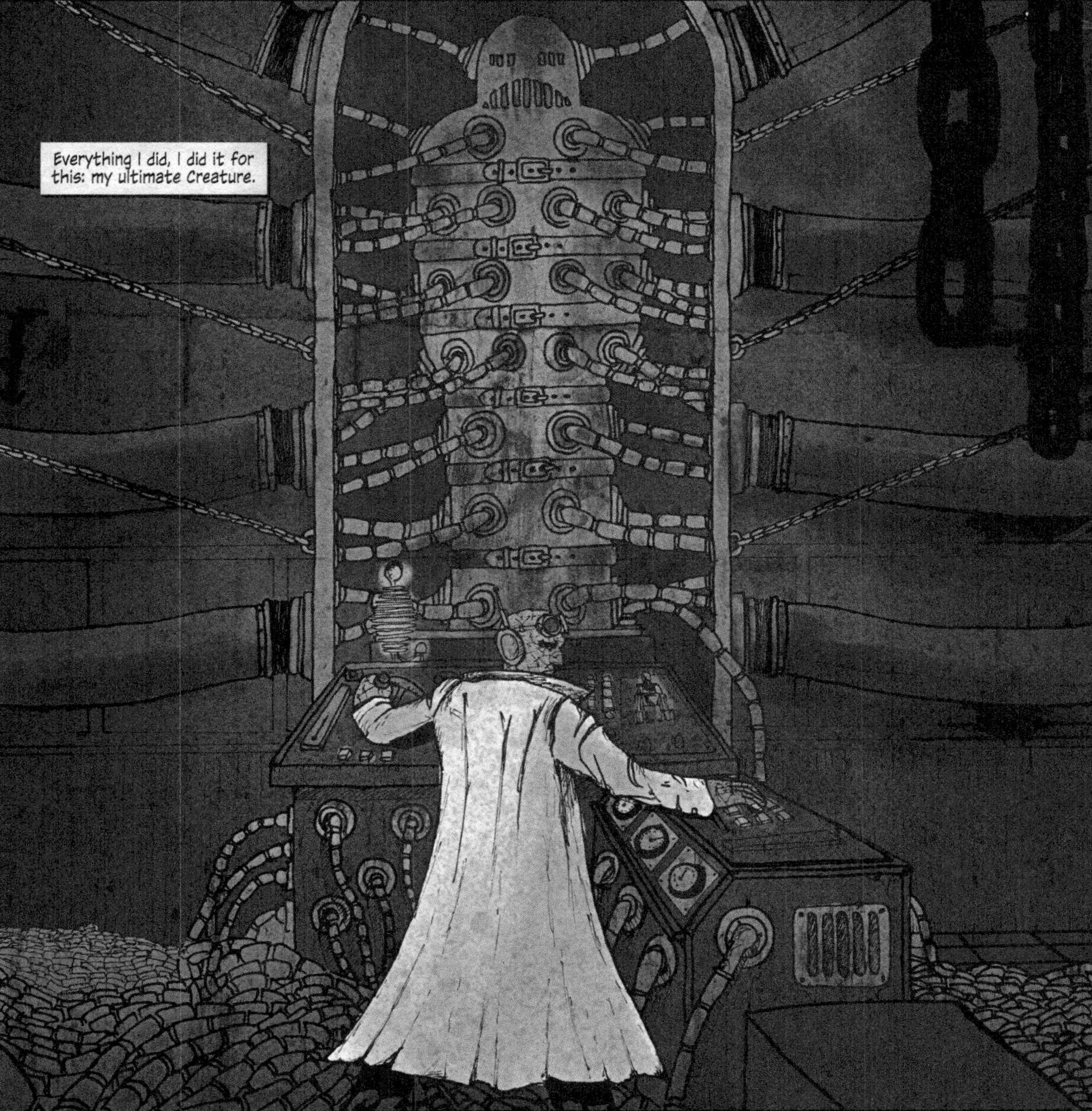
Everything I did, I did it for this: my ultimate Creature.
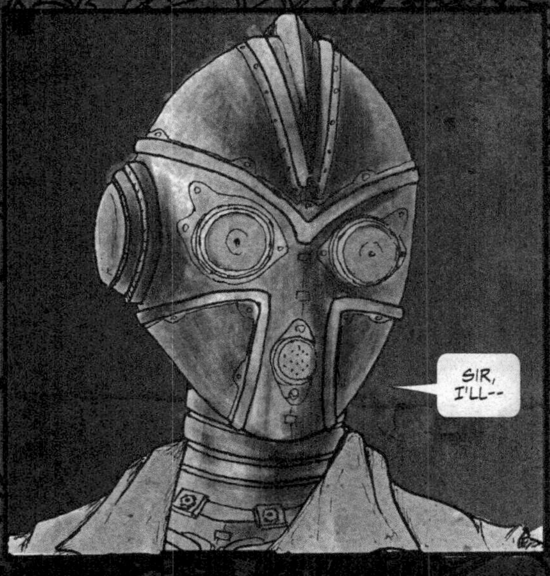
SIR, I'LL--
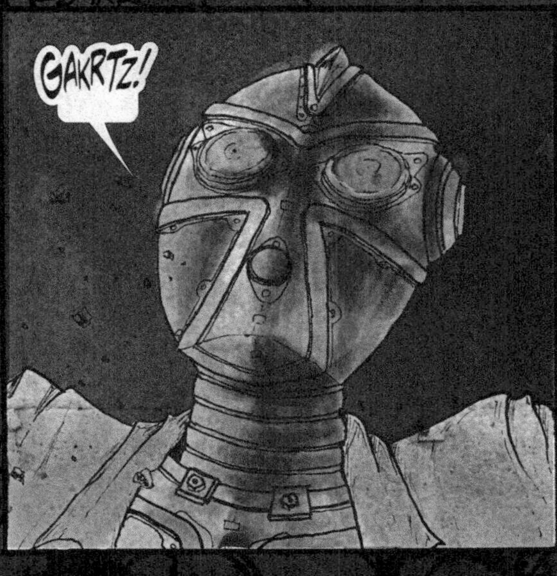
GAKRTZ!

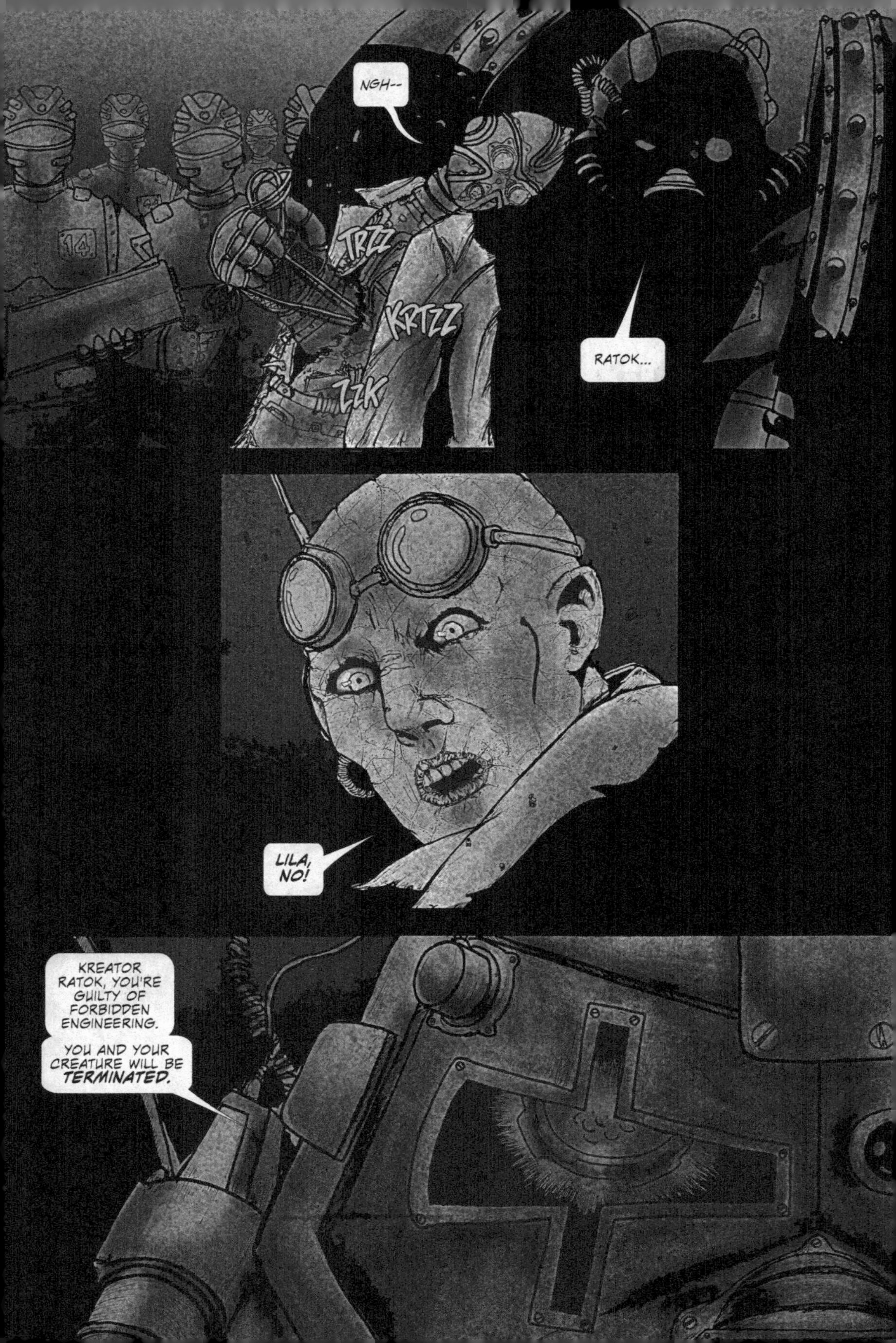
NGH--
TRZZ
KRTZZ
ZZK
RATOK...
LILA, NO!
KREATOR RATOK, YOU'RE GUILTY OF FORBIDDEN ENGINEERING.
YOU AND YOUR CREATURE WILL BE **TERMINATED.**

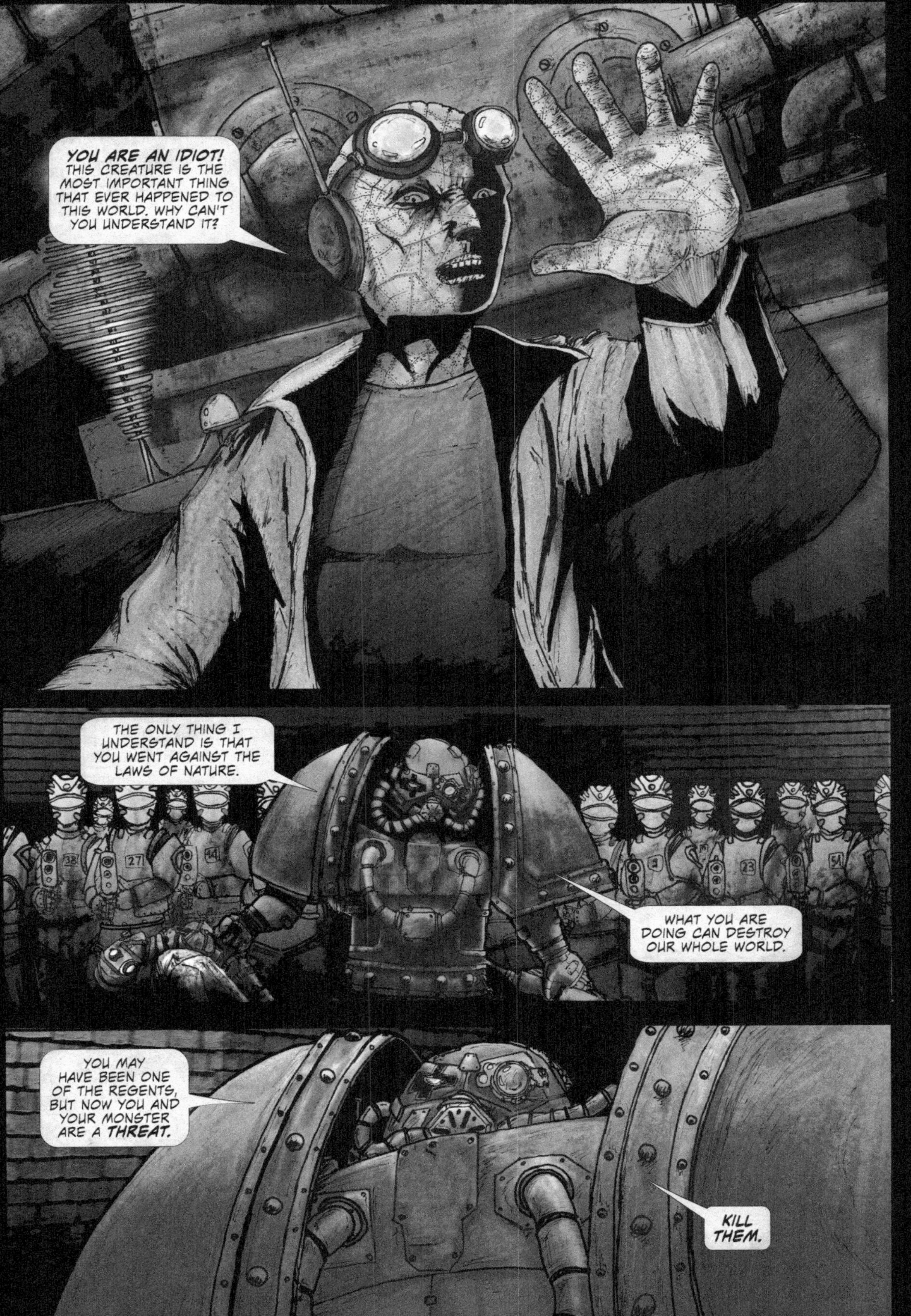
YOU ARE AN IDIOT! THIS CREATURE IS THE MOST IMPORTANT THING THAT EVER HAPPENED TO THIS WORLD. WHY CAN'T YOU UNDERSTAND IT?
THE ONLY THING I UNDERSTAND IS THAT YOU WENT AGAINST THE LAWS OF NATURE.
WHAT YOU ARE DOING CAN DESTROY OUR WHOLE WORLD.
YOU MAY HAVE BEEN ONE OF THE REGENTS, BUT NOW YOU AND YOUR MONSTER ARE A THREAT.
KILL THEM.

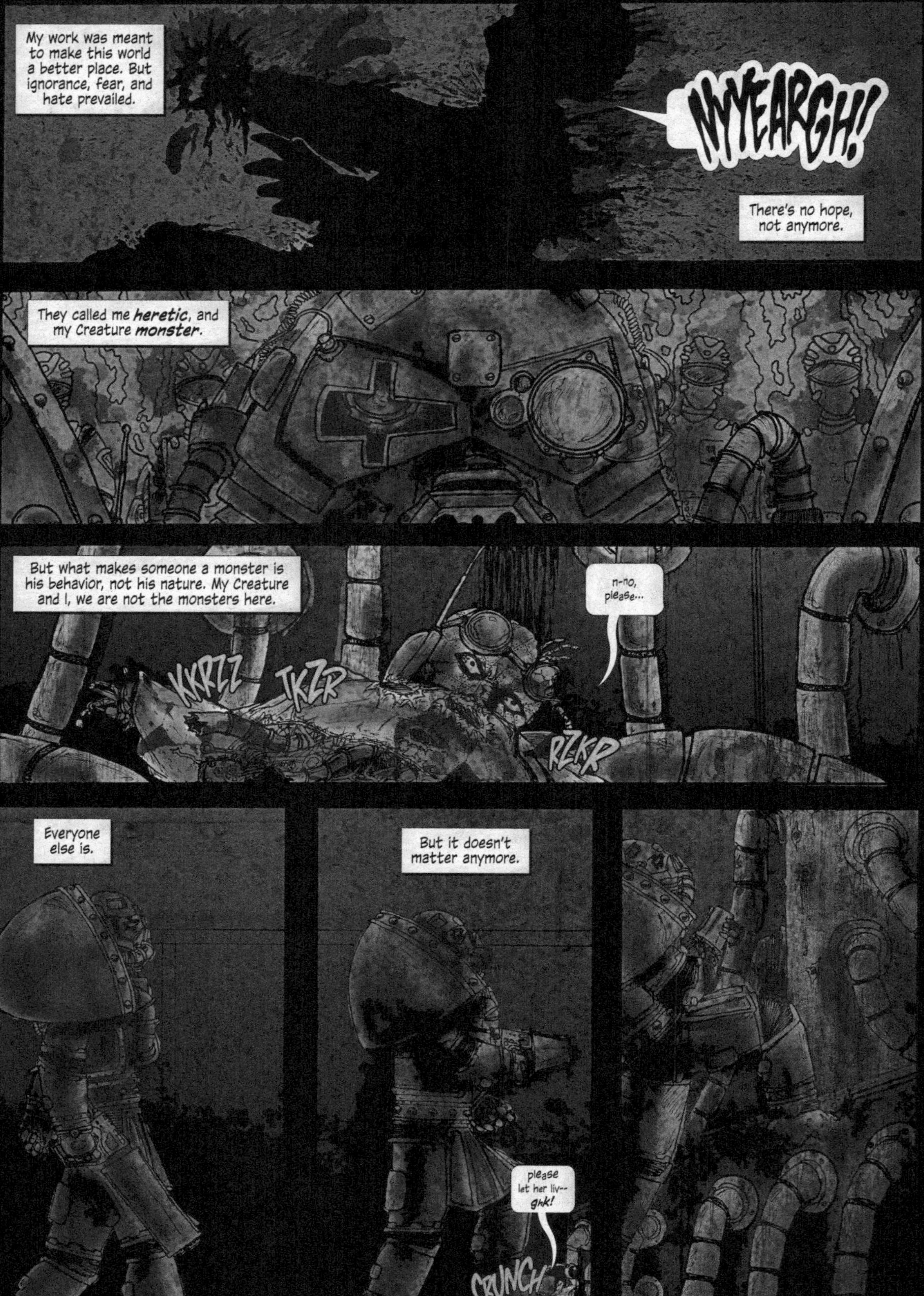
My work was meant to make this world a better place. But ignorance, fear, and hate prevailed.
MYYEARGH!
There's no hope, not anymore.
They called me ***heretic***, and my Creature ***monster***.
But what makes someone a monster is his behavior, not his nature. My Creature and I, we are not the monsters here.
n-no, please...
KKRZZ
TKZR
RZKR
Everyone else is.
But it doesn't matter anymore.
please let her liv-- ***ghk!***
CRUNCH

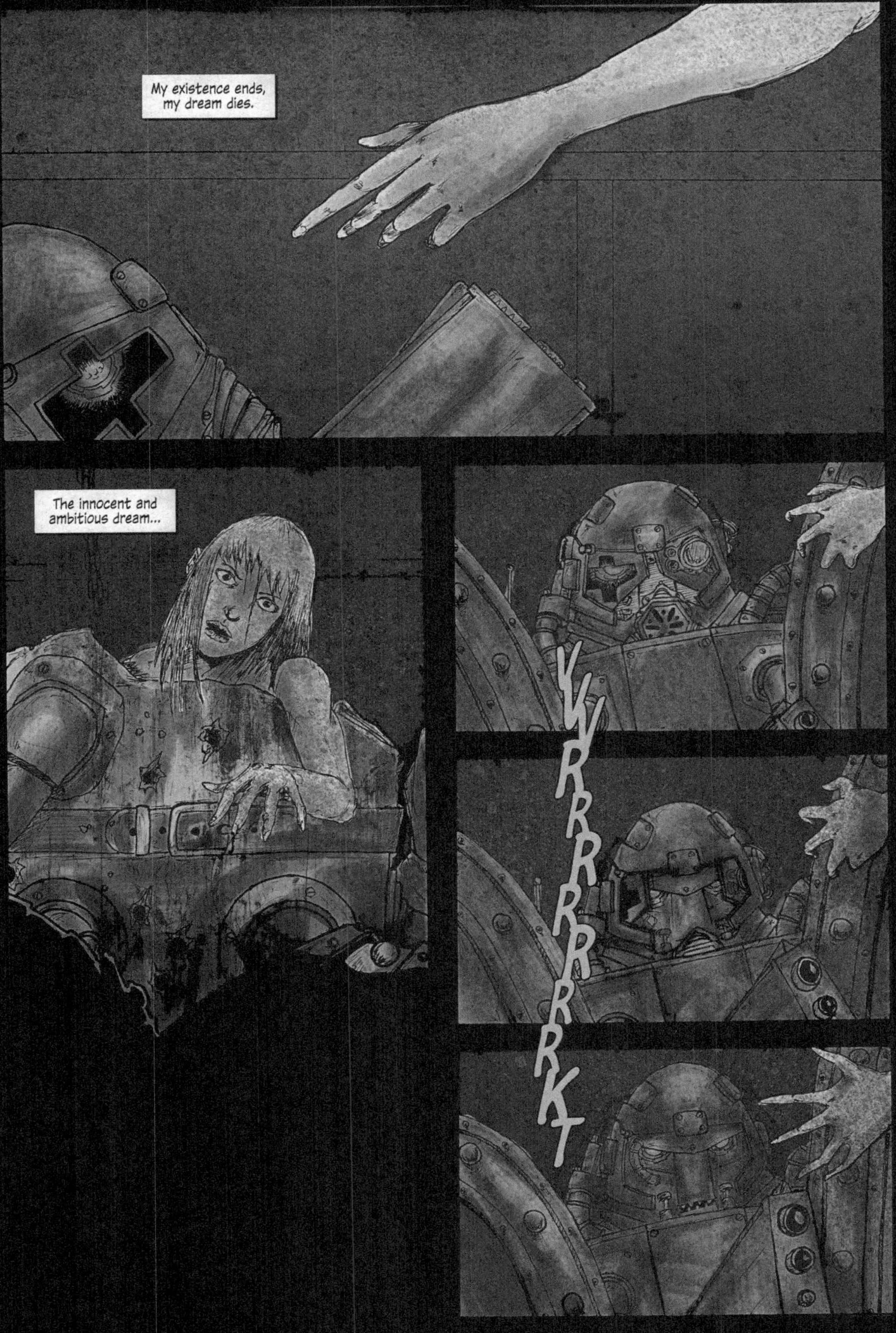

My existence ends, my dream dies.
The innocent and ambitious dream...
VVRRRRRRRKT

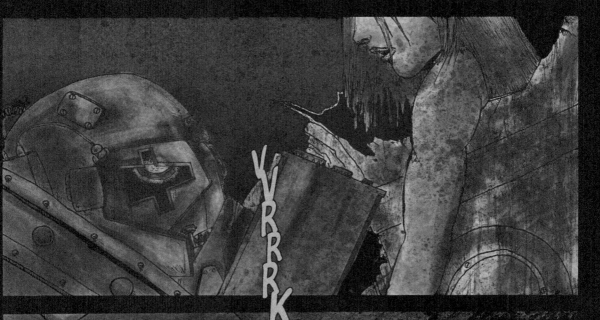

...of bringing real
life into this iron world.

VVRRRKT

BLAM

KREATOR

Written by Marco Della Verde
Illustrated by Fausto Carotti
Colored by Fabio Angelini

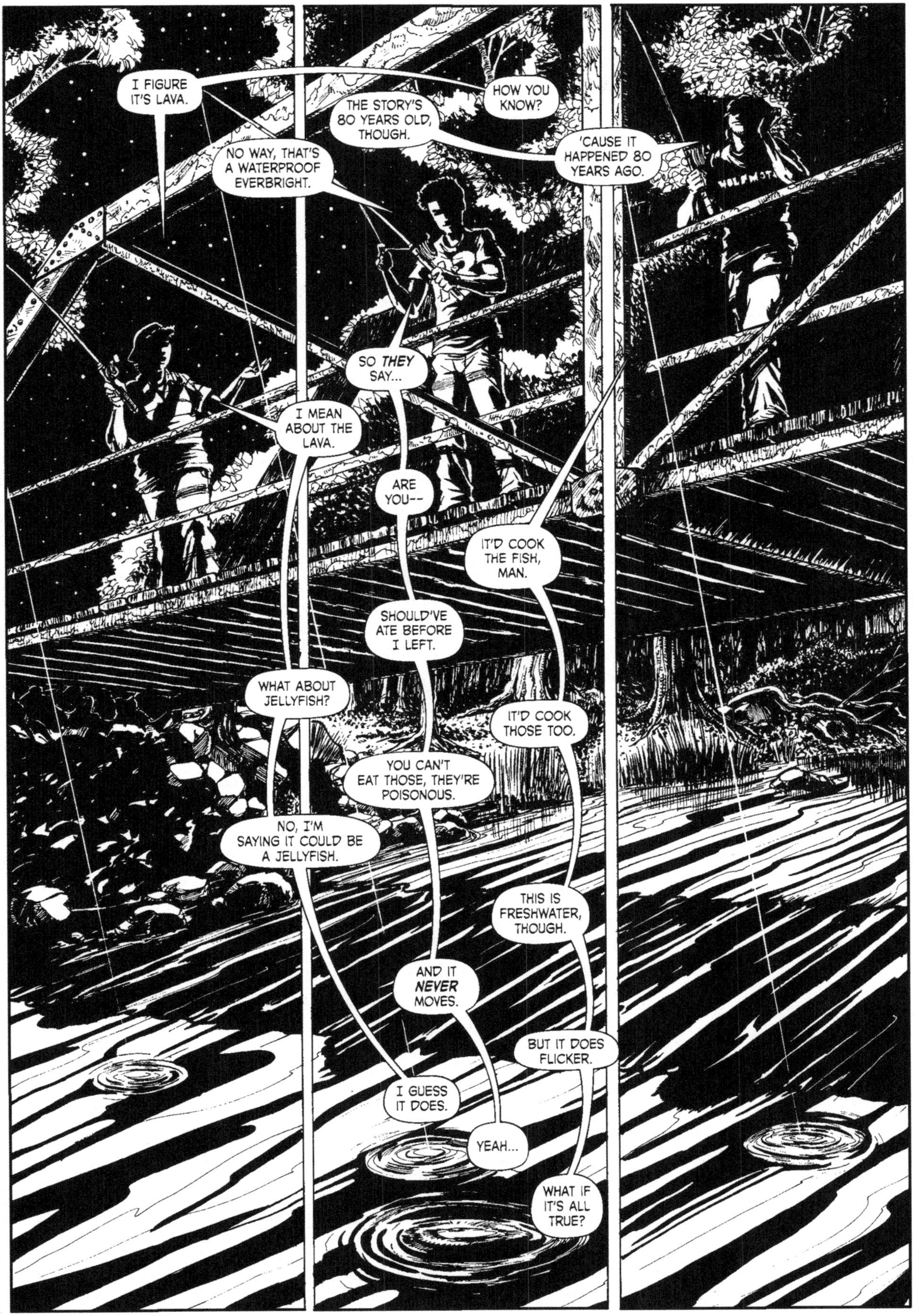

I FIGURE IT'S LAVA.
HOW YOU KNOW?
THE STORY'S 80 YEARS OLD, THOUGH.
'CAUSE IT HAPPENED 80 YEARS AGO.
NO WAY, THAT'S A WATERPROOF EVERBRIGHT.
SO *THEY* SAY...
I MEAN ABOUT THE LAVA.
ARE YOU--
IT'D COOK THE FISH, MAN.
SHOULD'VE ATE BEFORE I LEFT.
WHAT ABOUT JELLYFISH?
IT'D COOK THOSE TOO.
YOU CAN'T EAT THOSE, THEY'RE POISONOUS.
NO, I'M SAYING IT COULD BE A JELLYFISH.
THIS IS FRESHWATER, THOUGH.
AND IT ***NEVER*** MOVES.
BUT IT DOES FLICKER.
I GUESS IT DOES.
YEAH...
WHAT IF IT'S ALL TRUE?

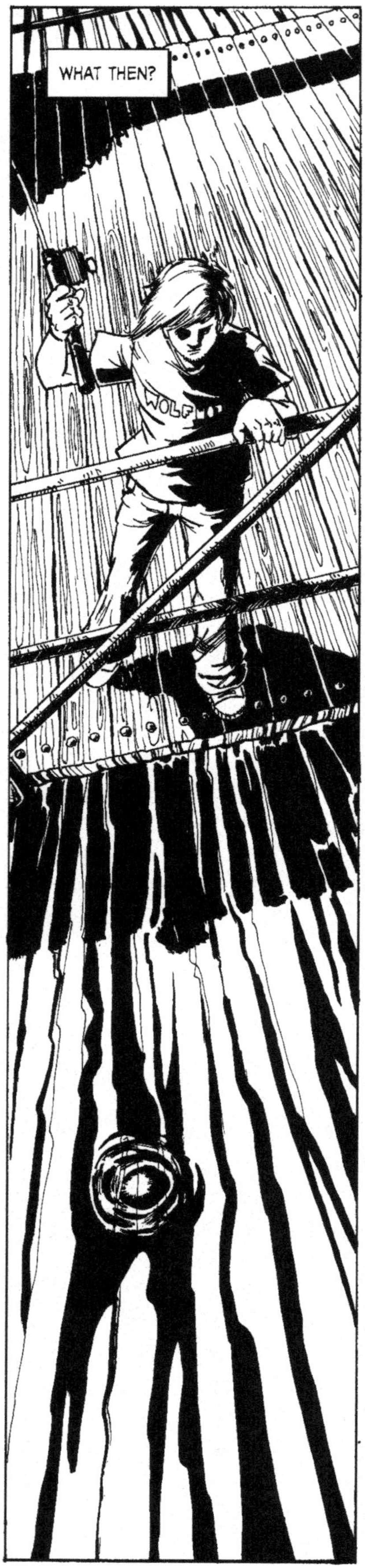
WHAT THEN?
WOLF

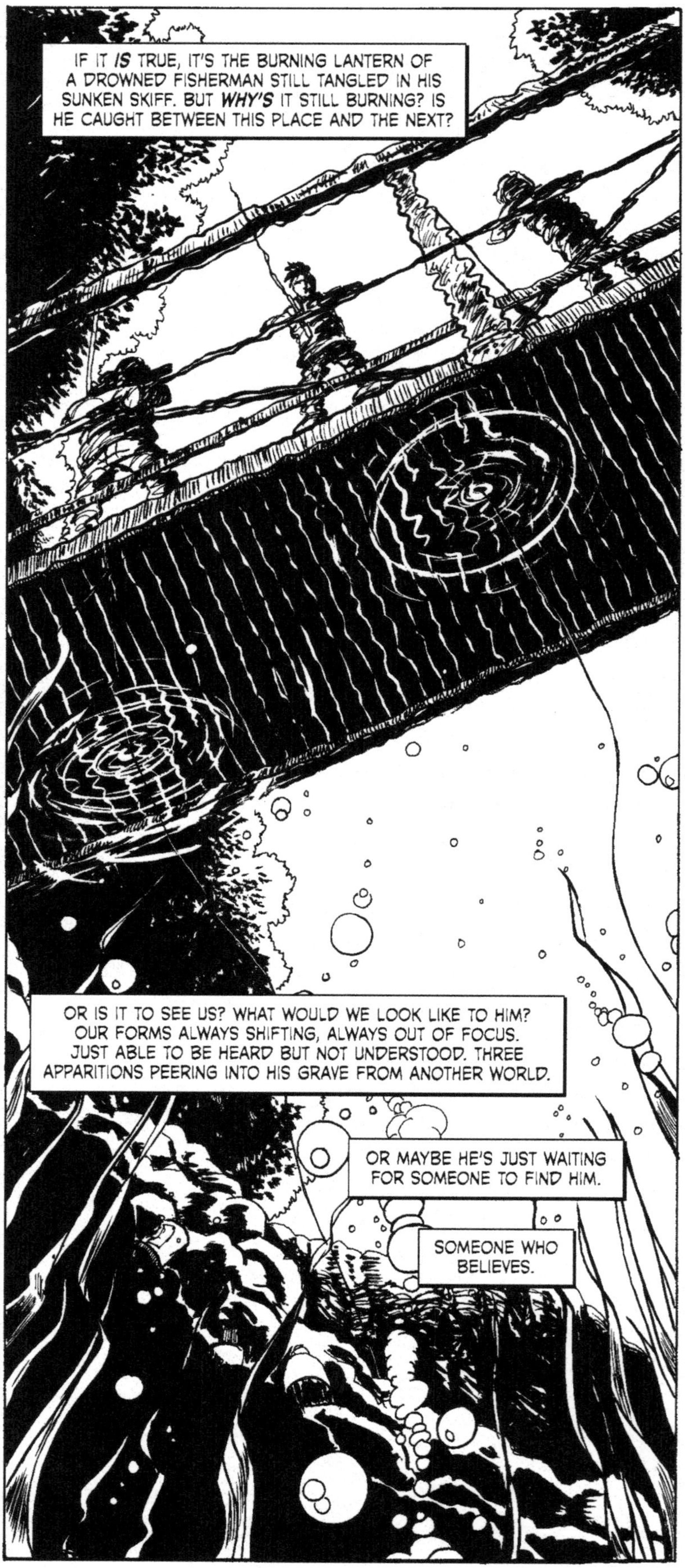
IF IT *IS* TRUE, IT'S THE BURNING LANTERN OF A DROWNED FISHERMAN STILL TANGLED IN HIS SUNKEN SKIFF. BUT *WHY'S* IT STILL BURNING? IS HE CAUGHT BETWEEN THIS PLACE AND THE NEXT?
OR IS IT TO SEE US? WHAT WOULD WE LOOK LIKE TO HIM? OUR FORMS ALWAYS SHIFTING, ALWAYS OUT OF FOCUS. JUST ABLE TO BE HEARD BUT NOT UNDERSTOOD. THREE APPARITIONS PEERING INTO HIS GRAVE FROM ANOTHER WORLD.
OR MAYBE HE'S JUST WAITING FOR SOMEONE TO FIND HIM.
SOMEONE WHO BELIEVES.

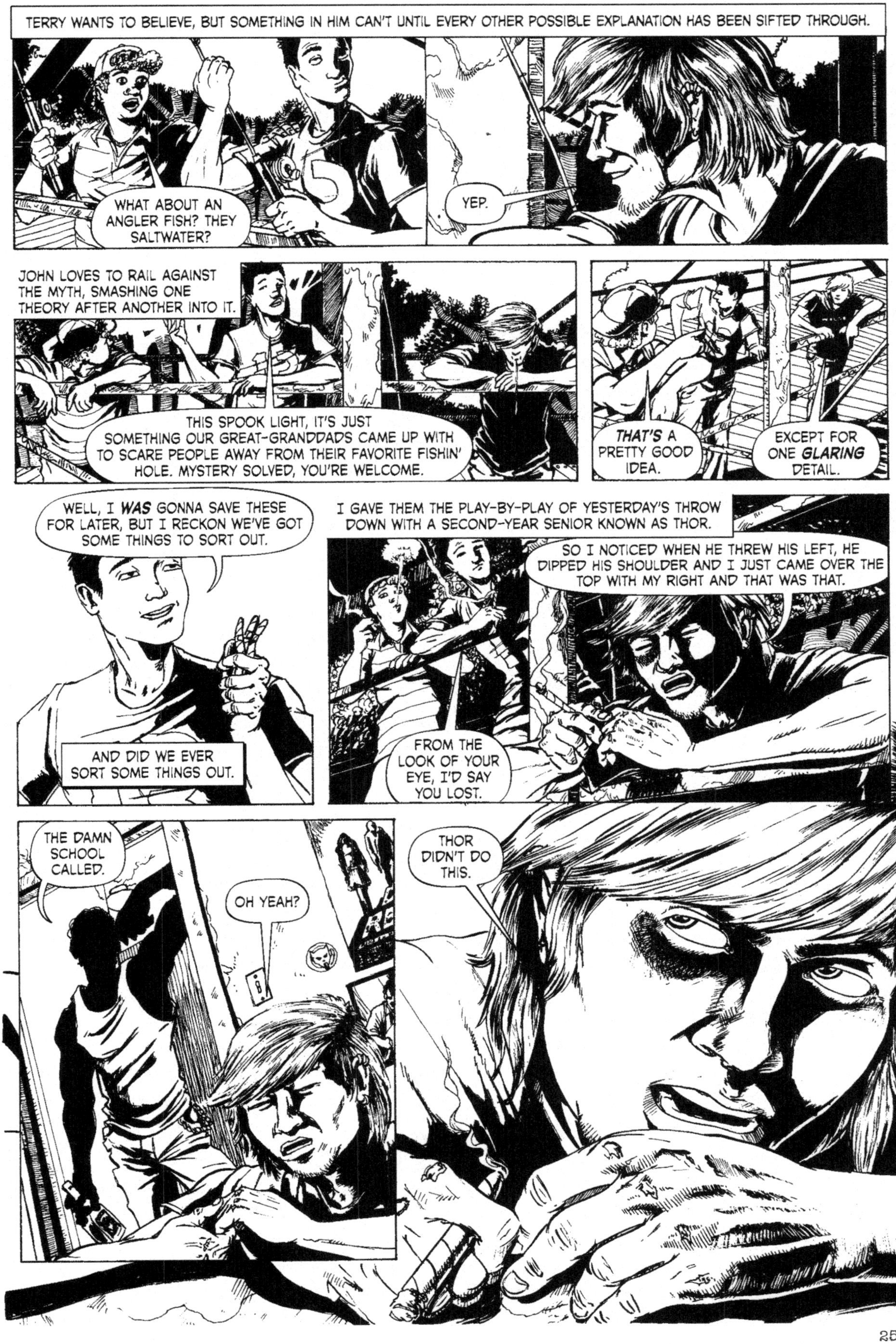
TERRY WANTS TO BELIEVE, BUT SOMETHING IN HIM CAN'T UNTIL EVERY OTHER POSSIBLE EXPLANATION HAS BEEN SIFTED THROUGH.
WHAT ABOUT AN ANGLER FISH? THEY SALTWATER?
YEP.
JOHN LOVES TO RAIL AGAINST THE MYTH, SMASHING ONE THEORY AFTER ANOTHER INTO IT.
THIS SPOOK LIGHT, IT'S JUST SOMETHING OUR GREAT-GRANDDADS CAME UP WITH TO SCARE PEOPLE AWAY FROM THEIR FAVORITE FISHIN' HOLE. MYSTERY SOLVED, YOU'RE WELCOME.
THAT'S A PRETTY GOOD IDEA.
EXCEPT FOR ONE GLARING DETAIL.
WELL, I WAS GONNA SAVE THESE FOR LATER, BUT I RECKON WE'VE GOT SOME THINGS TO SORT OUT.
AND DID WE EVER SORT SOME THINGS OUT.
I GAVE THEM THE PLAY-BY-PLAY OF YESTERDAY'S THROW DOWN WITH A SECOND-YEAR SENIOR KNOWN AS THOR.
SO I NOTICED WHEN HE THREW HIS LEFT, HE DIPPED HIS SHOULDER AND I JUST CAME OVER THE TOP WITH MY RIGHT AND THAT WAS THAT.
FROM THE LOOK OF YOUR EYE, I'D SAY YOU LOST.
THE DAMN SCHOOL CALLED.
OH YEAH?
THOR DIDN'T DO THIS.

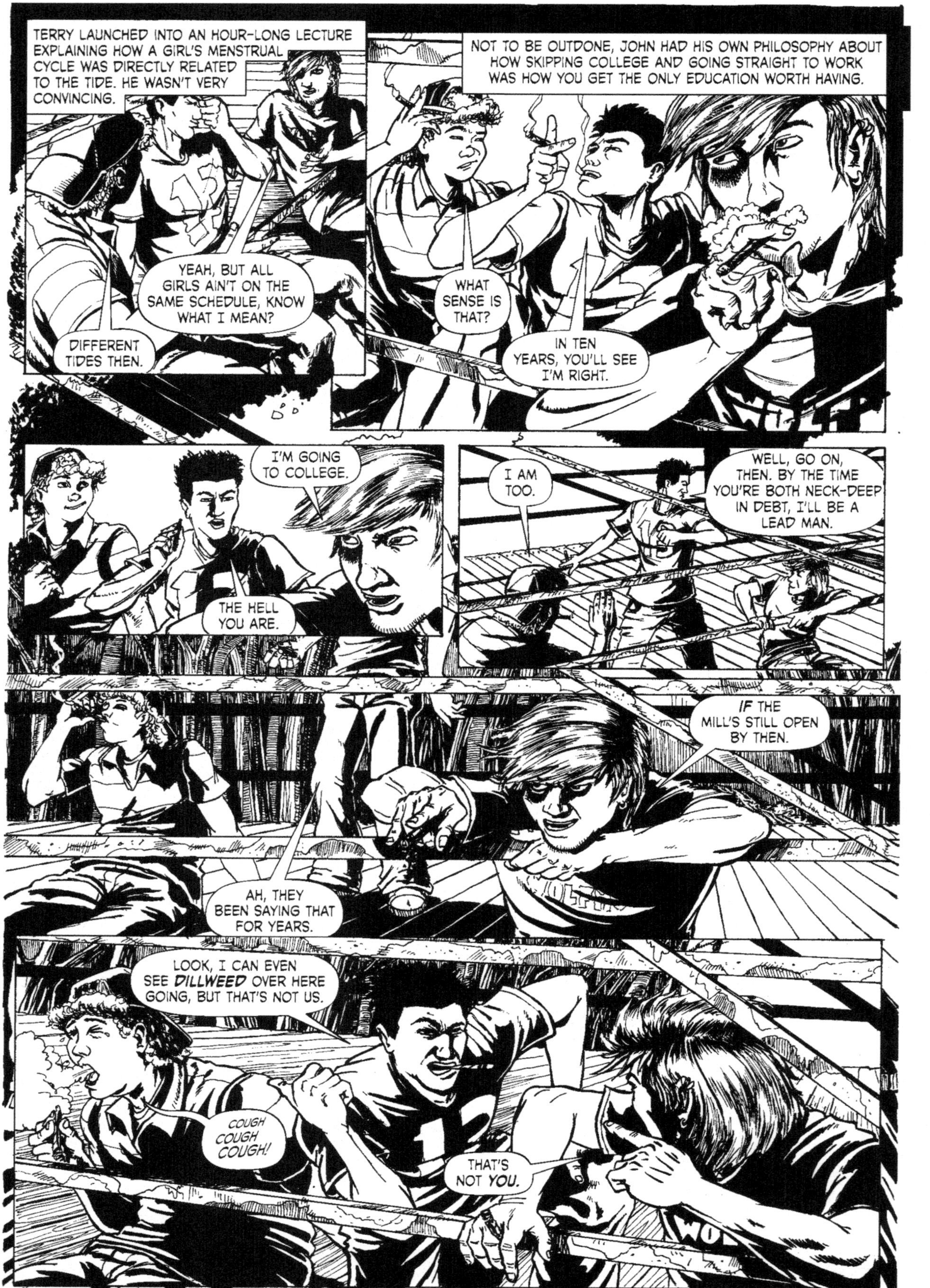
TERRY LAUNCHED INTO AN HOUR-LONG LECTURE EXPLAINING HOW A GIRL'S MENSTRUAL CYCLE WAS DIRECTLY RELATED TO THE TIDE. HE WASN'T VERY CONVINCING.
YEAH, BUT ALL GIRLS AIN'T ON THE SAME SCHEDULE, KNOW WHAT I MEAN?
DIFFERENT TIDES THEN.
NOT TO BE OUTDONE, JOHN HAD HIS OWN PHILOSOPHY ABOUT HOW SKIPPING COLLEGE AND GOING STRAIGHT TO WORK WAS HOW YOU GET THE ONLY EDUCATION WORTH HAVING.
WHAT SENSE IS THAT?
IN TEN YEARS, YOU'LL SEE I'M RIGHT.
I'M GOING TO COLLEGE.
THE HELL YOU ARE.
I AM TOO.
WELL, GO ON, THEN. BY THE TIME YOU'RE BOTH NECK-DEEP IN DEBT, I'LL BE A LEAD MAN.
IF THE MILL'S STILL OPEN BY THEN.
AH, THEY BEEN SAYING THAT FOR YEARS.
LOOK, I CAN EVEN SEE DILLWEED OVER HERE GOING, BUT THAT'S NOT US.
COUGH COUGH COUGH!
THAT'S NOT YOU.

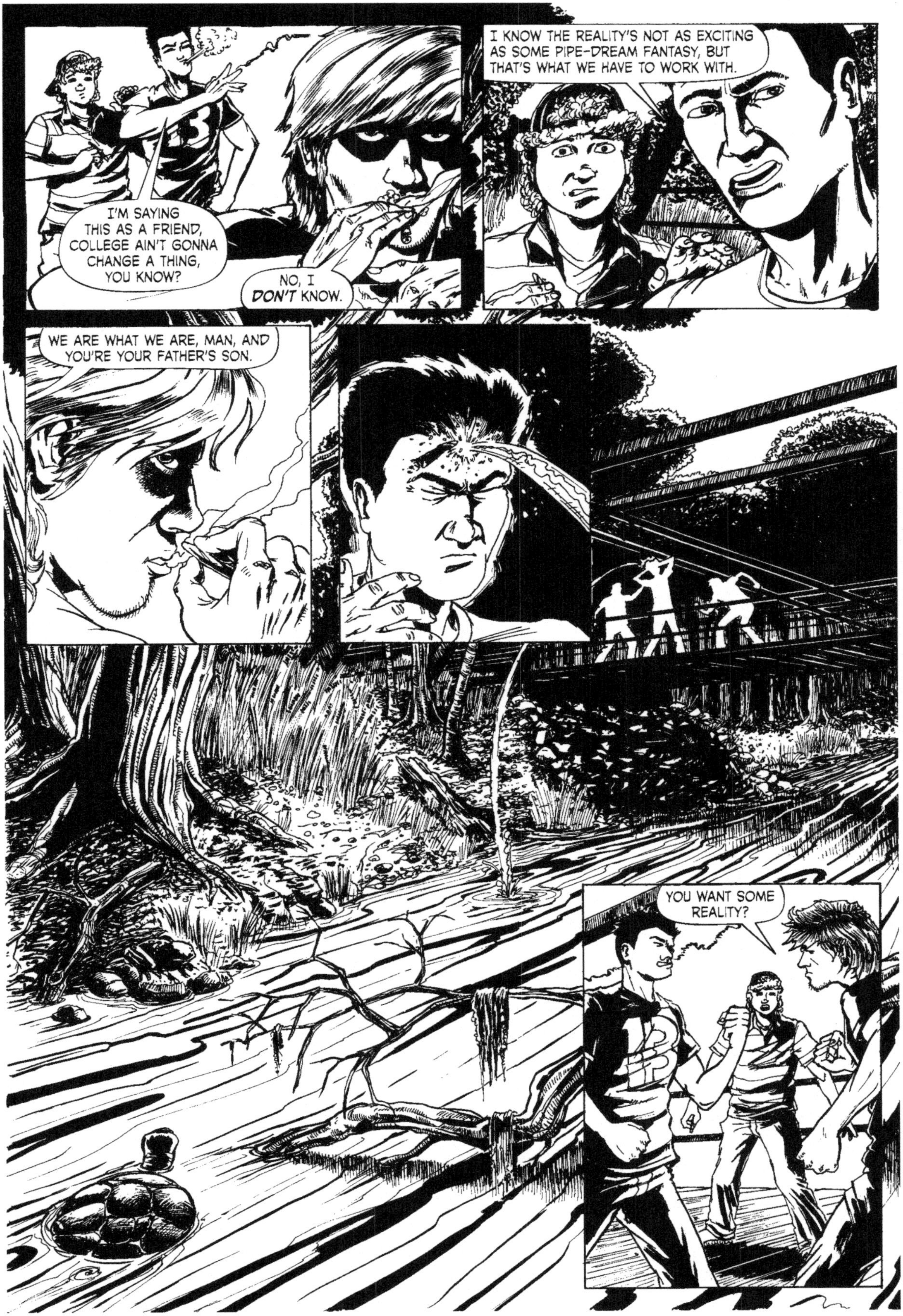
I'M SAYING THIS AS A FRIEND, COLLEGE AIN'T GONNA CHANGE A THING, YOU KNOW?
NO, I *DON'T* KNOW.
I KNOW THE REALITY'S NOT AS EXCITING AS SOME PIPE-DREAM FANTASY, BUT THAT'S WHAT WE HAVE TO WORK WITH.
WE ARE WHAT WE ARE, MAN, AND YOU'RE YOUR FATHER'S SON.
YOU WANT SOME REALITY?

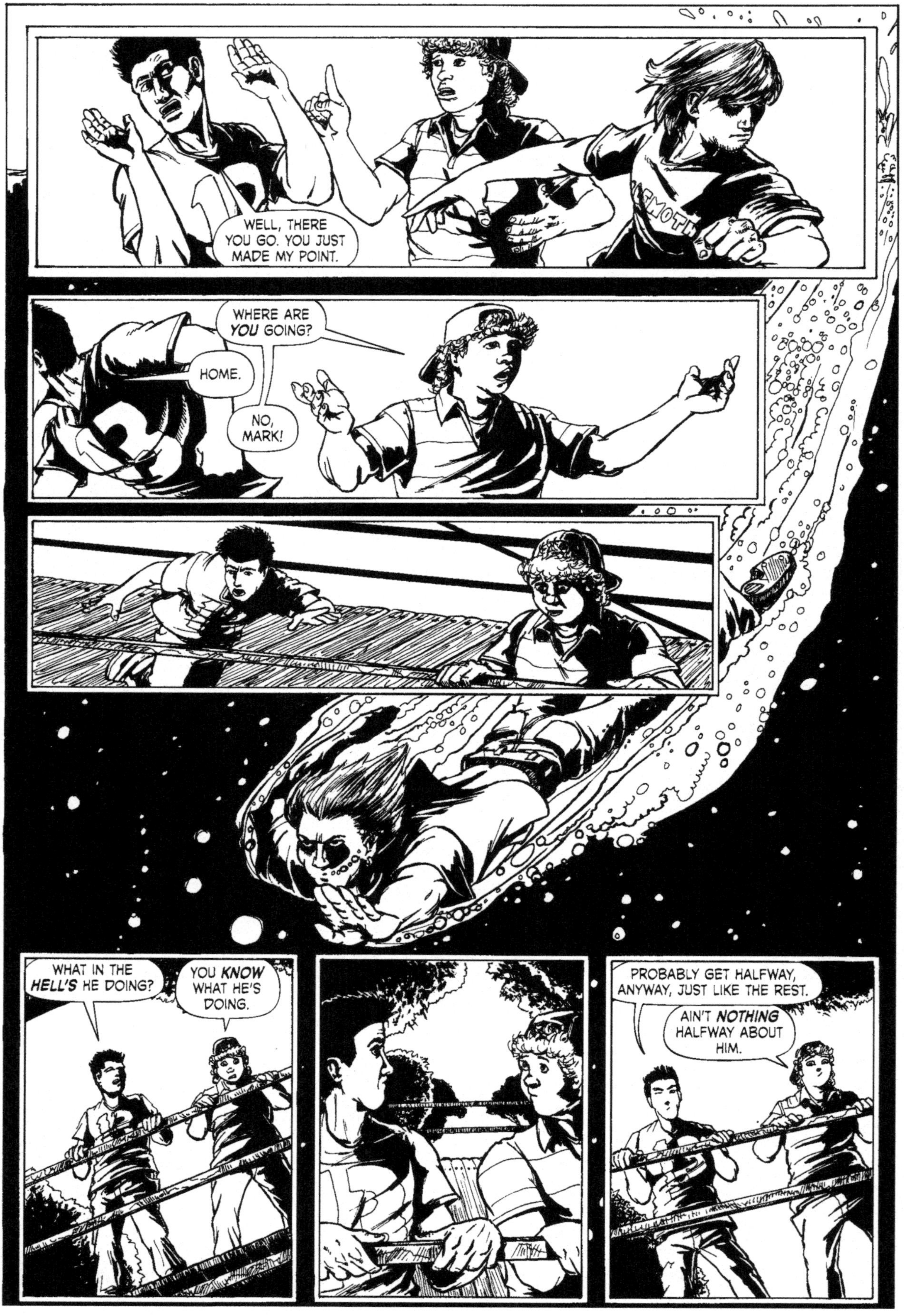
WELL, THERE YOU GO. YOU JUST MADE MY POINT.
WHERE ARE YOU GOING?
HOME.
NO, MARK!
WHAT IN THE HELL'S HE DOING?
YOU KNOW WHAT HE'S DOING.
PROBABLY GET HALFWAY, ANYWAY, JUST LIKE THE REST.
AIN'T NOTHING HALFWAY ABOUT HIM.

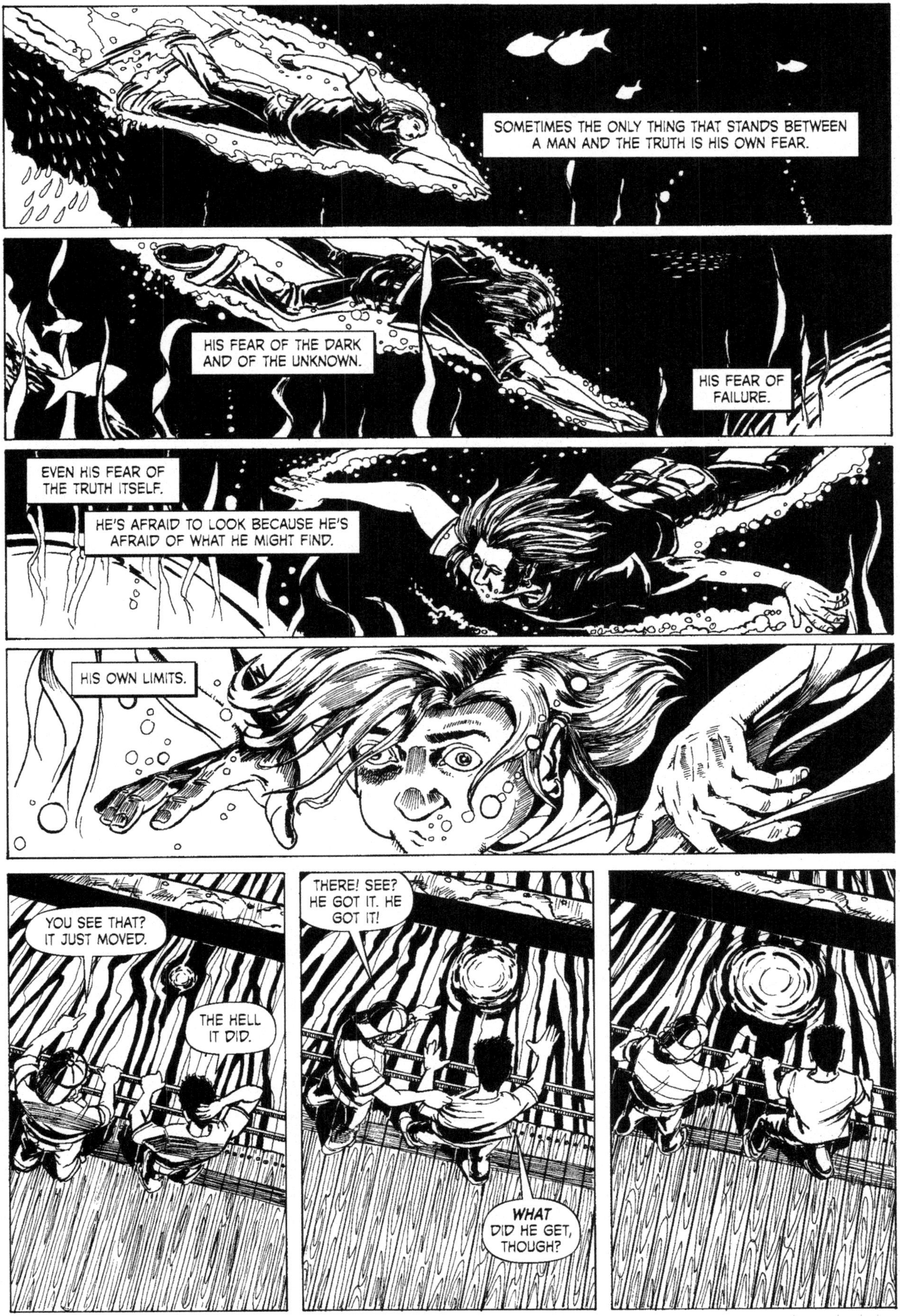
SOMETIMES THE ONLY THING THAT STANDS BETWEEN A MAN AND THE TRUTH IS HIS OWN FEAR.
HIS FEAR OF THE DARK AND OF THE UNKNOWN.
HIS FEAR OF FAILURE.
EVEN HIS FEAR OF THE TRUTH ITSELF.
HE'S AFRAID TO LOOK BECAUSE HE'S AFRAID OF WHAT HE MIGHT FIND.
HIS OWN LIMITS.
YOU SEE THAT? IT JUST MOVED.
THE HELL IT DID.
THERE! SEE? HE GOT IT. HE GOT IT!
WHAT DID HE GET, THOUGH?

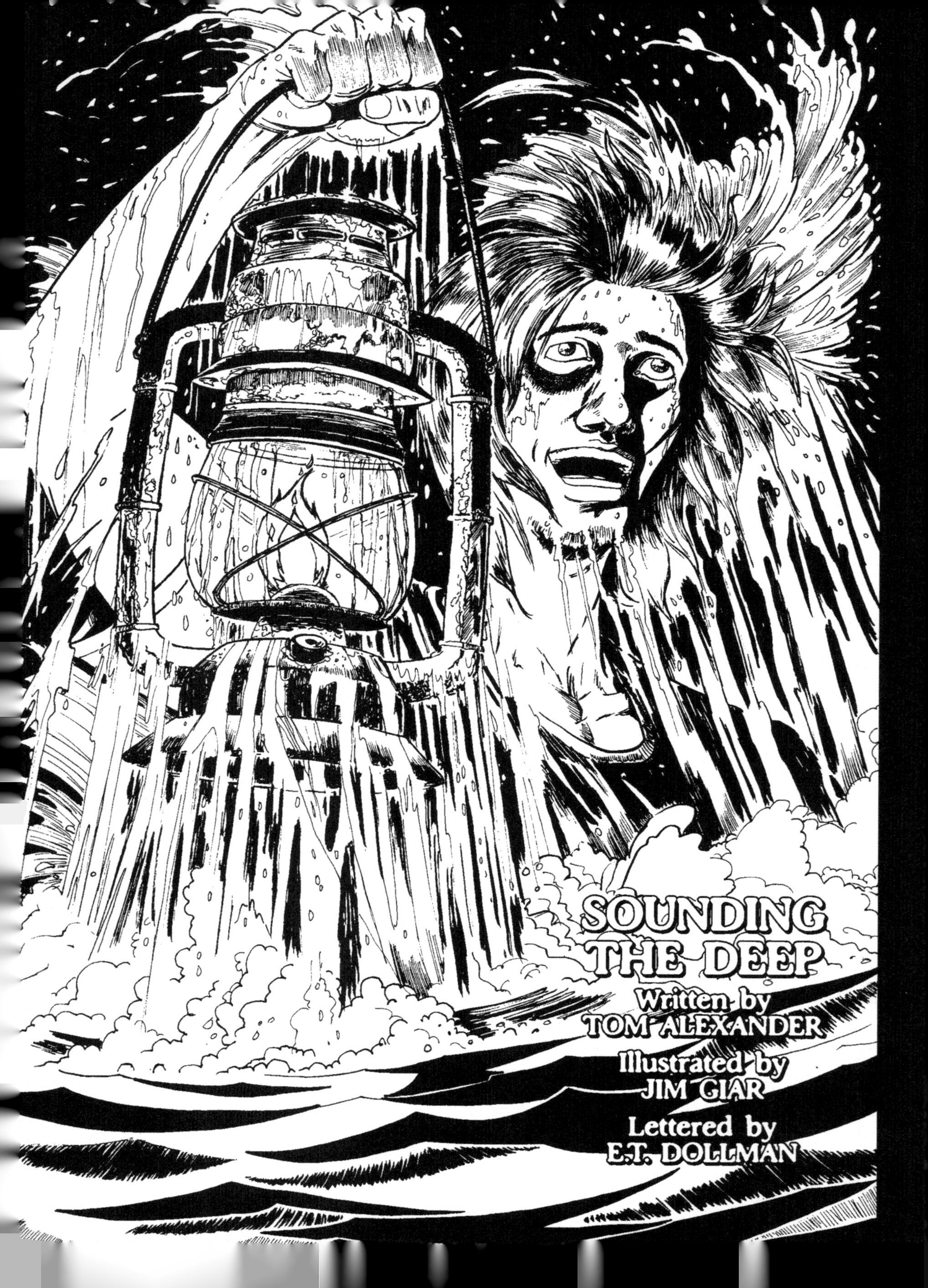
SOUNDING THE DEEP
Written by TOM ALEXANDER
Illustrated by JIM GIAR
Lettered by E.T. DOLLMAN

In His Image

Story and art: JE

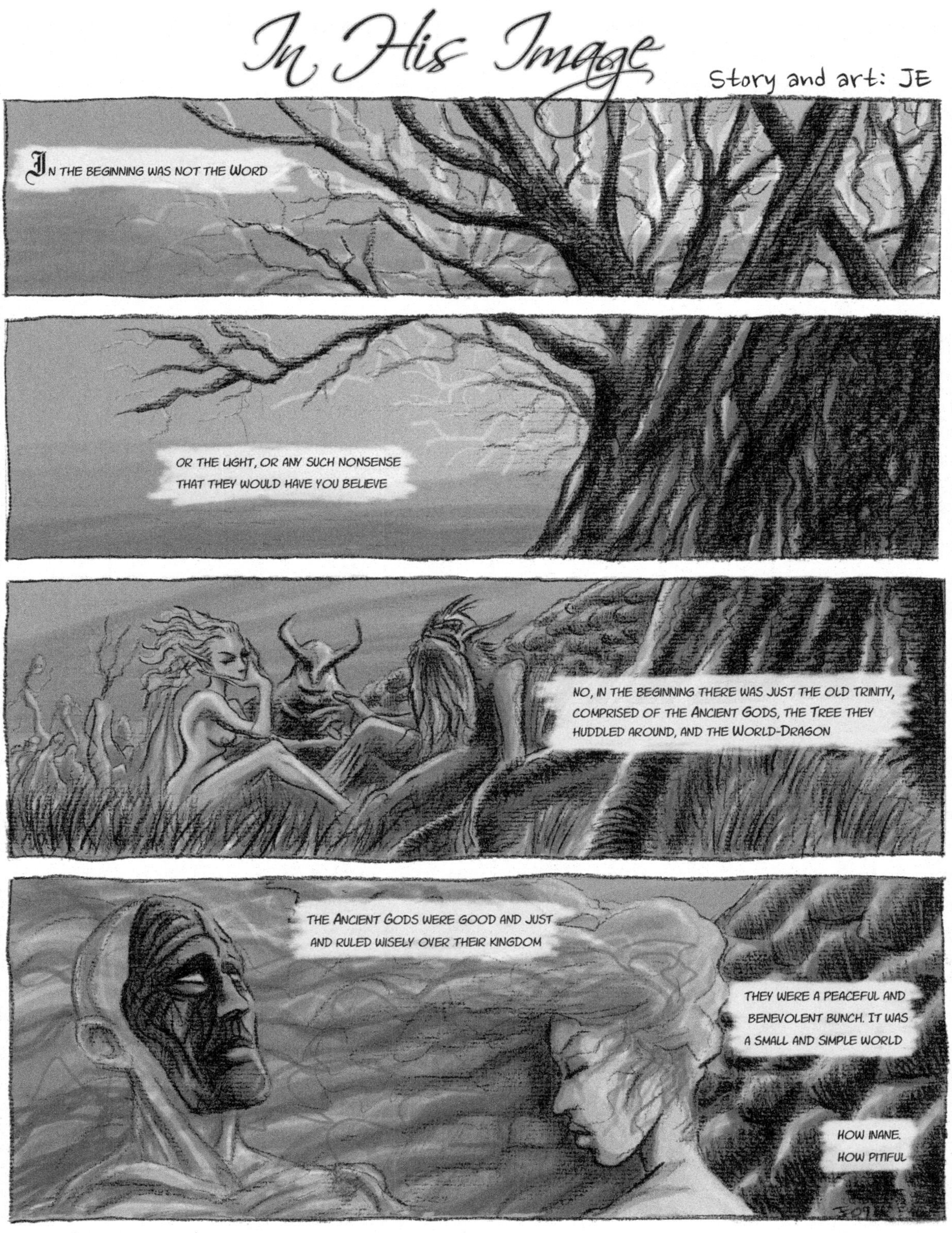
In the beginning was not the Word
Or the light, or any such nonsense that they would have you believe
No, in the beginning there was just the old trinity, comprised of the Ancient Gods, the Tree they huddled around, and the World-Dragon
The Ancient Gods were good and just and ruled wisely over their kingdom
They were a peaceful and benevolent bunch. It was a small and simple world
How inane. How pitiful

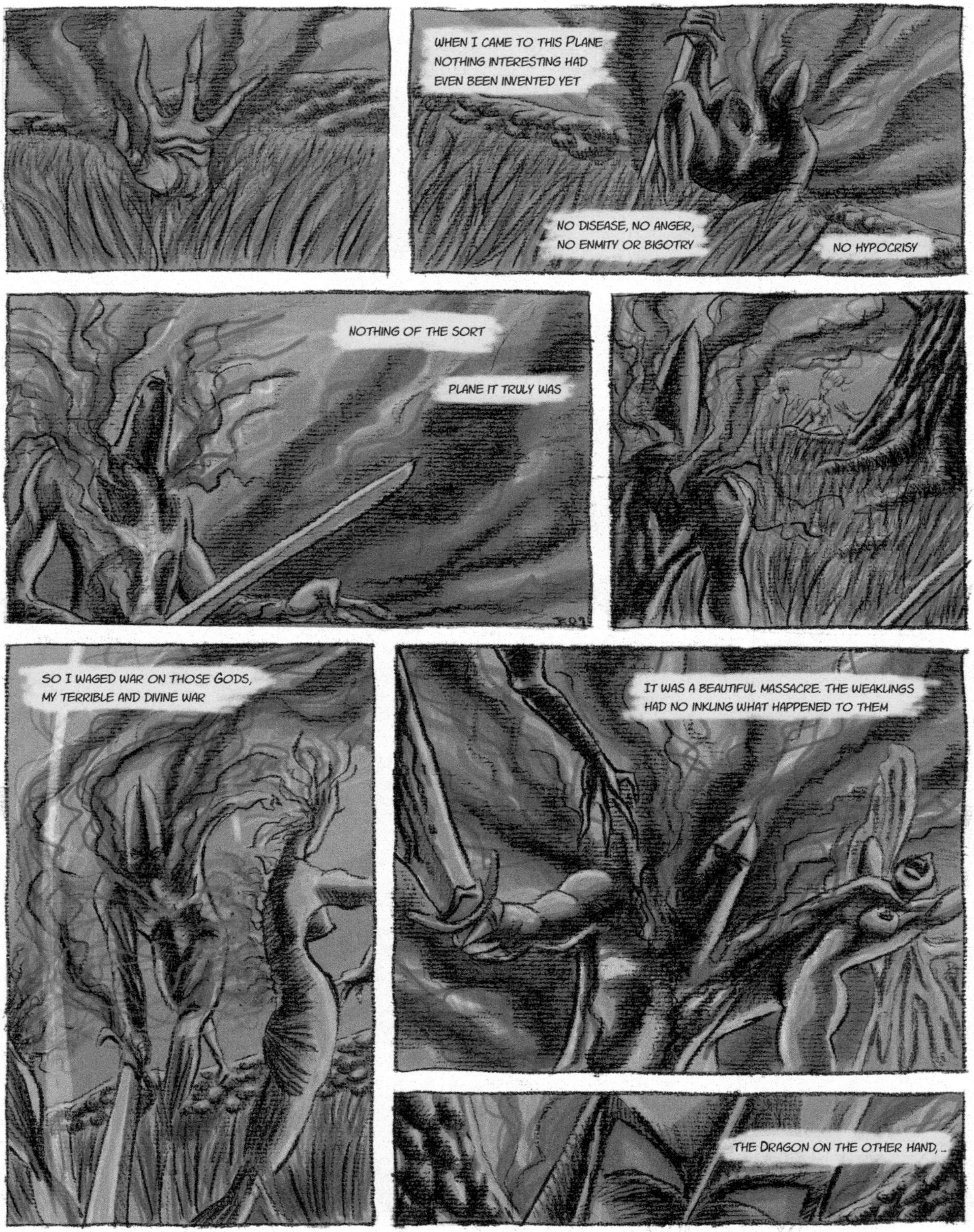
WHEN I CAME TO THIS PLANE NOTHING INTERESTING HAD EVEN BEEN INVENTED YET
NO DISEASE, NO ANGER, NO ENMITY OR BIGOTRY
NO HYPOCRISY
NOTHING OF THE SORT
PLANE IT TRULY WAS
SO I WAGED WAR ON THOSE GODS, MY TERRIBLE AND DIVINE WAR
IT WAS A BEAUTIFUL MASSACRE. THE WEAKLINGS HAD NO INKLING WHAT HAPPENED TO THEM
THE DRAGON ON THE OTHER HAND, ...

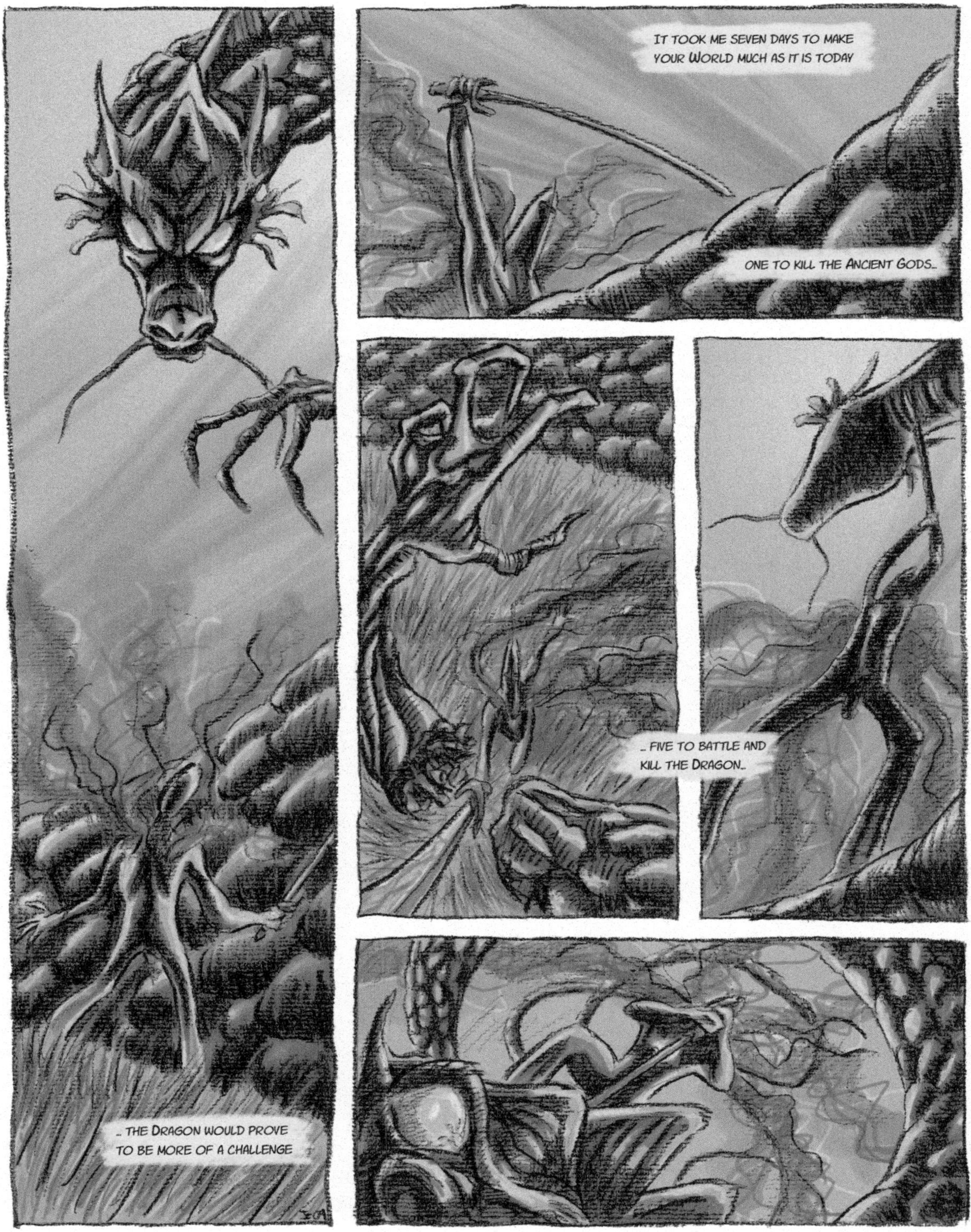
It took me seven days to make your World much as it is today
one to kill the Ancient Gods..
.. five to battle and kill the Dragon..
.. the Dragon would prove to be more of a challenge

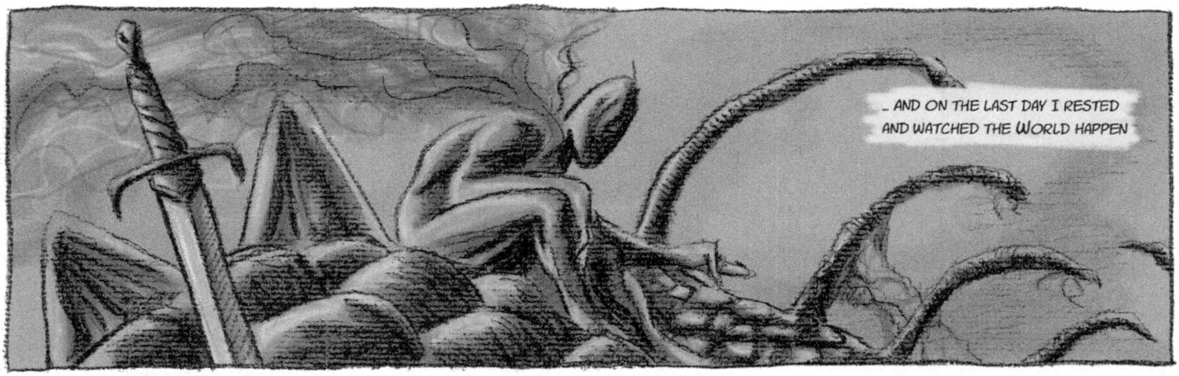
.. AND ON THE LAST DAY I RESTED AND WATCHED THE WORLD HAPPEN

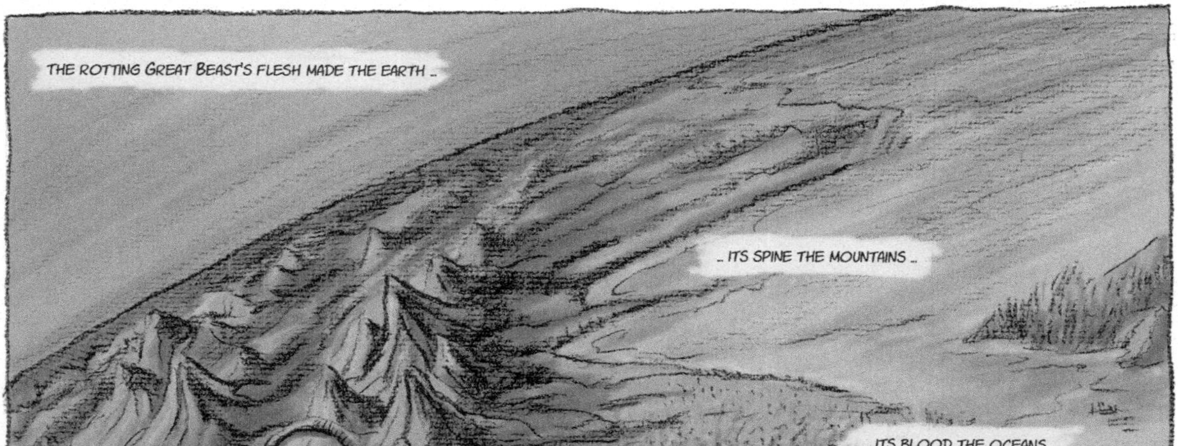
THE ROTTING GREAT BEAST'S FLESH MADE THE EARTH ..
.. ITS SPINE THE MOUNTAINS ..
.. ITS BLOOD THE OCEANS ..
.. AND ITS LAST BREATH THE AIR YOU NOW BREATHE

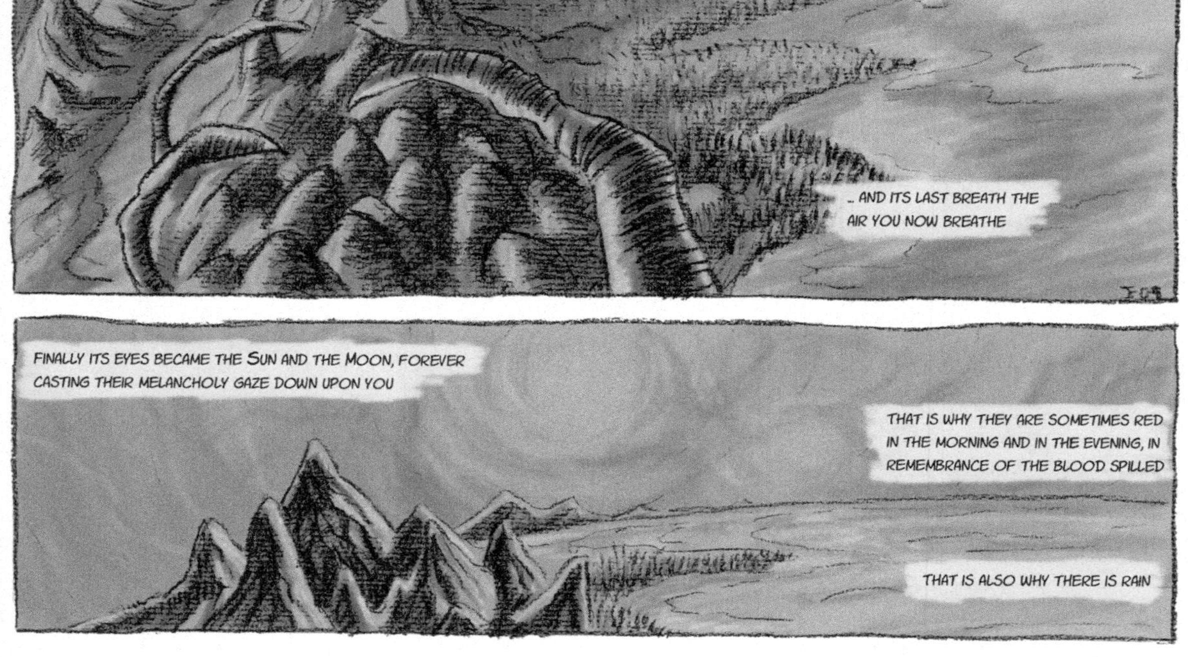
FINALLY ITS EYES BECAME THE SUN AND THE MOON, FOREVER CASTING THEIR MELANCHOLY GAZE DOWN UPON YOU
THAT IS WHY THEY ARE SOMETIMES RED IN THE MORNING AND IN THE EVENING, IN REMEMBRANCE OF THE BLOOD SPILLED
THAT IS ALSO WHY THERE IS RAIN

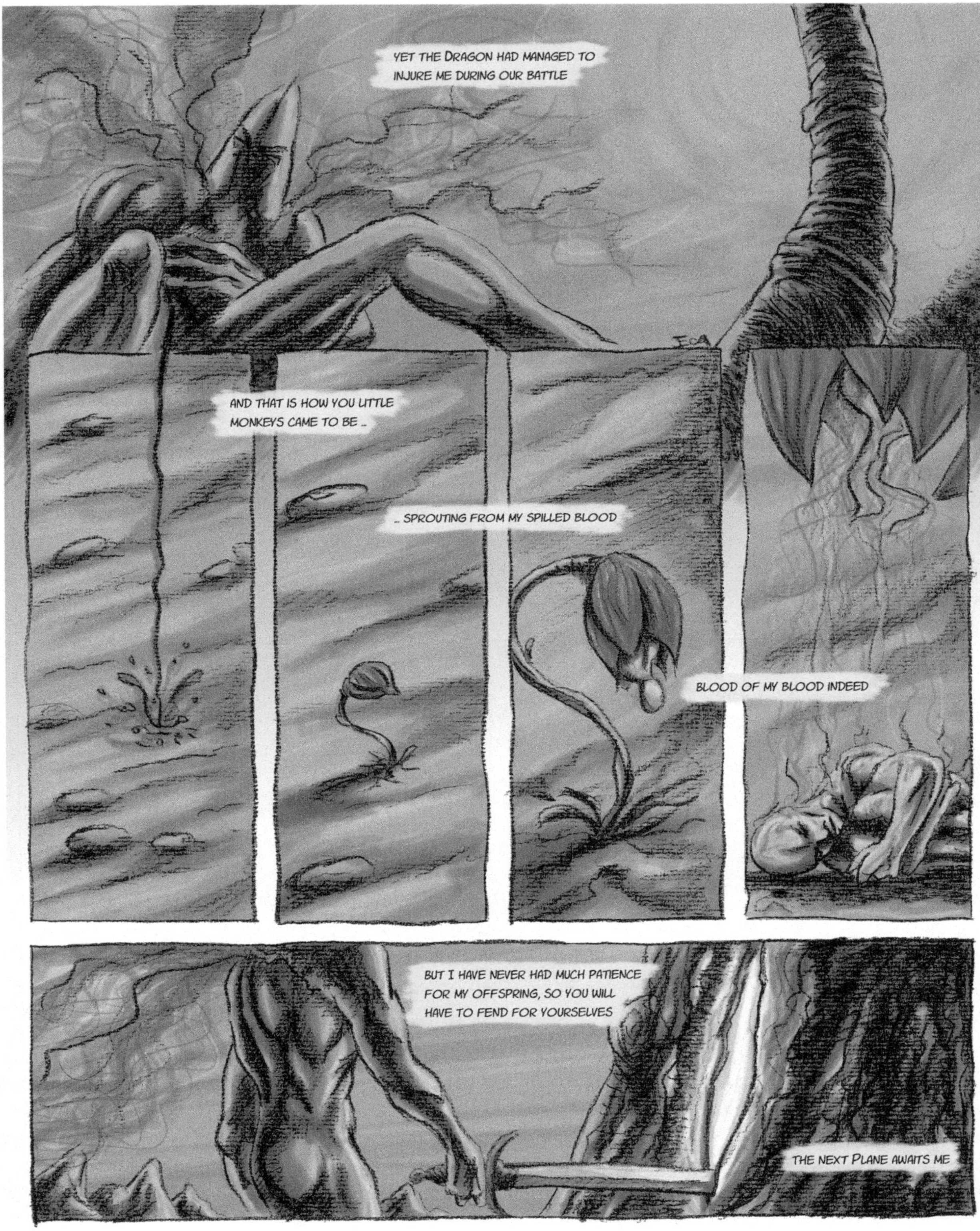
YET THE DRAGON HAD MANAGED TO INJURE ME DURING OUR BATTLE
AND THAT IS HOW YOU LITTLE MONKEYS CAME TO BE ..
.. SPROUTING FROM MY SPILLED BLOOD
BLOOD OF MY BLOOD INDEED
BUT I HAVE NEVER HAD MUCH PATIENCE FOR MY OFFSPRING, SO YOU WILL HAVE TO FEND FOR YOURSELVES
THE NEXT PLANE AWAITS ME

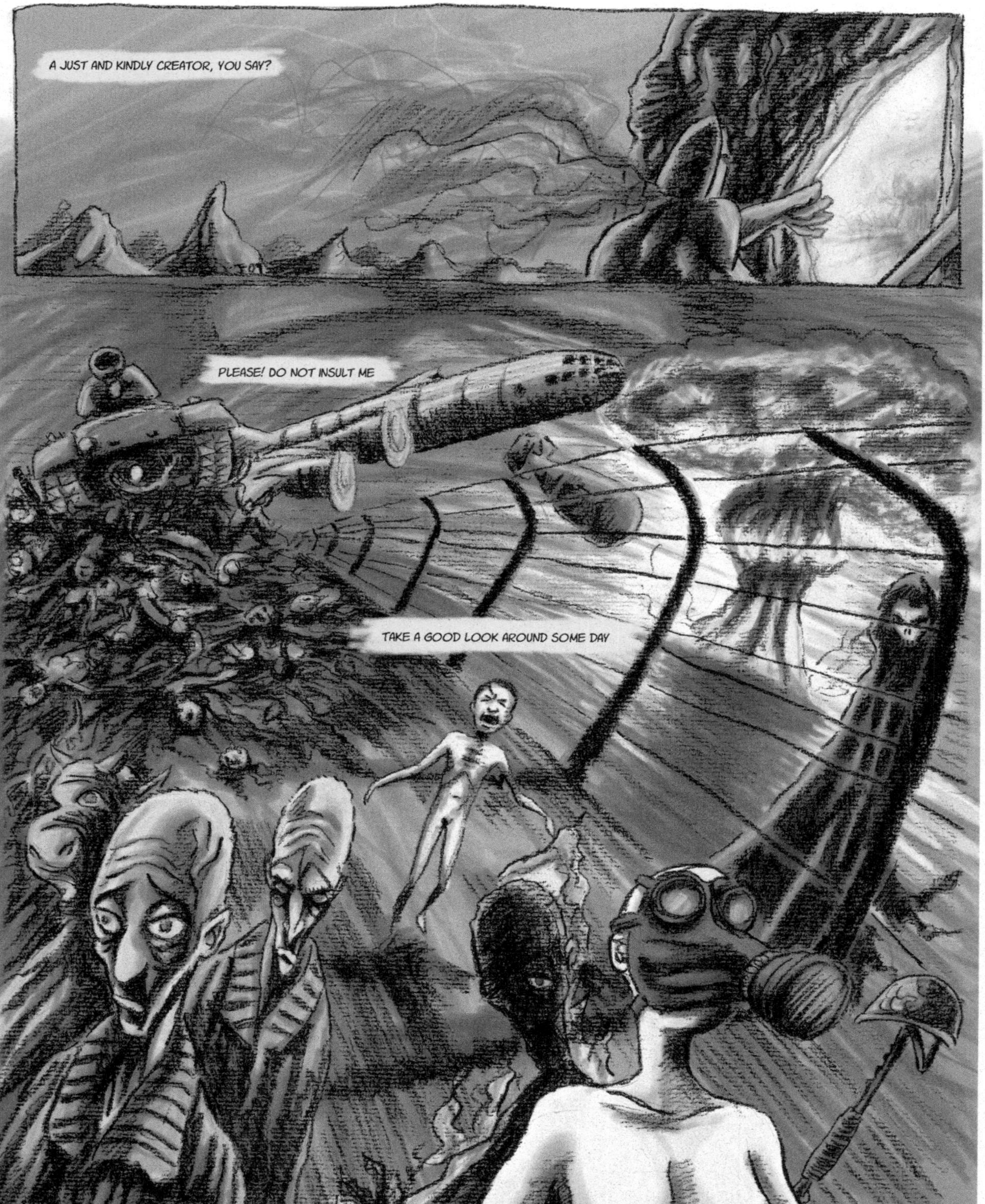
A JUST AND KINDLY CREATOR, YOU SAY?
PLEASE! DO NOT INSULT ME
TAKE A GOOD LOOK AROUND SOME DAY

AS A FAMILY

Writer
Glenn Møane
Artist
Tomasz Witas
Letterer
E.T. Dollman

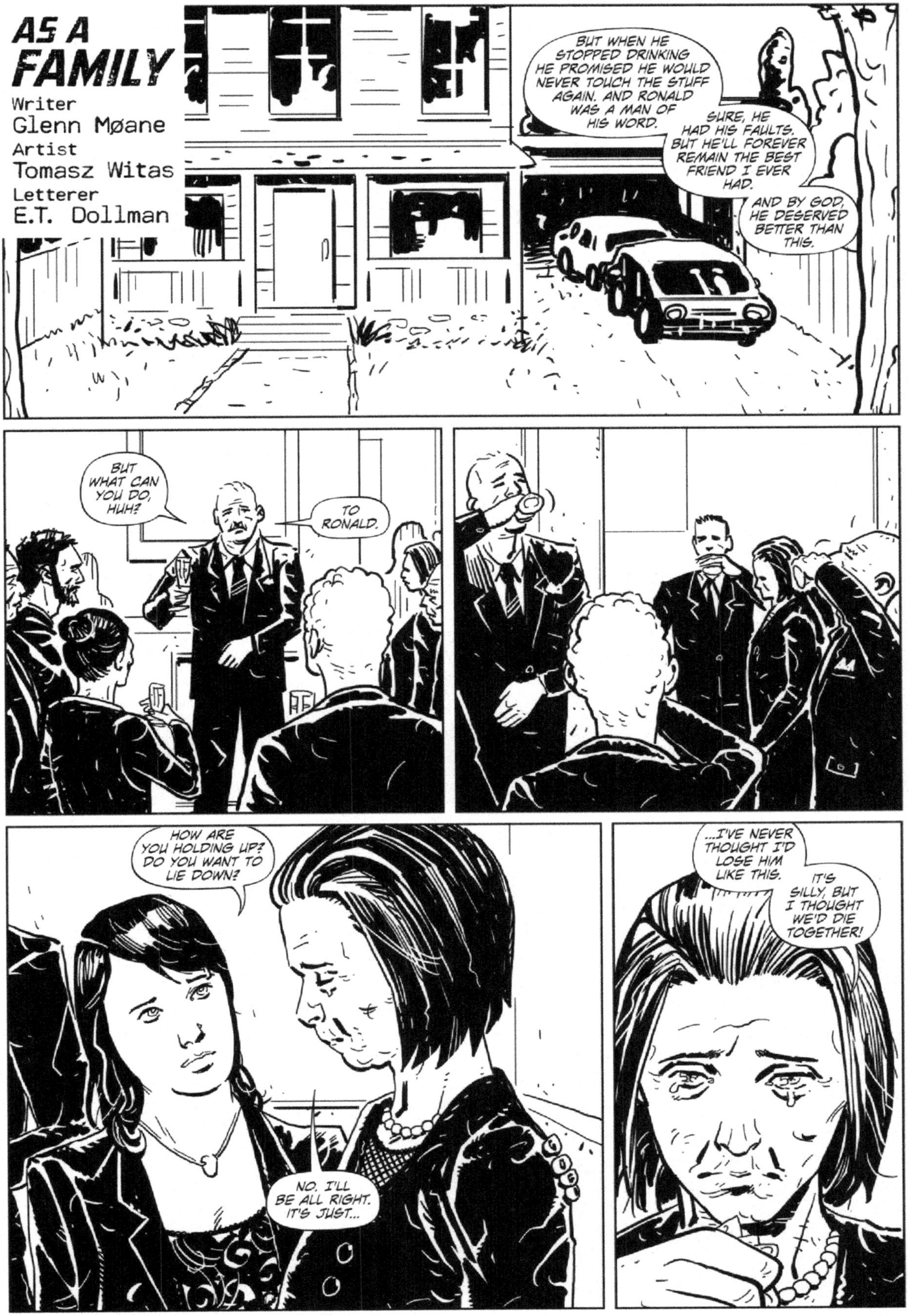

BUT WHEN HE STOPPED DRINKING HE PROMISED HE WOULD NEVER TOUCH THE STUFF AGAIN. AND RONALD WAS A MAN OF HIS WORD.
SURE, HE HAD HIS FAULTS. BUT HE'LL FOREVER REMAIN THE BEST FRIEND I EVER HAD.
AND BY GOD, HE DESERVED BETTER THAN THIS.
BUT WHAT CAN YOU DO, HUH?
TO RONALD.
HOW ARE YOU HOLDING UP? DO YOU WANT TO LIE DOWN?
NO. I'LL BE ALL RIGHT. IT'S JUST...
...I'VE NEVER THOUGHT I'D LOSE HIM LIKE THIS.
IT'S SILLY, BUT I THOUGHT WE'D DIE TOGETHER!

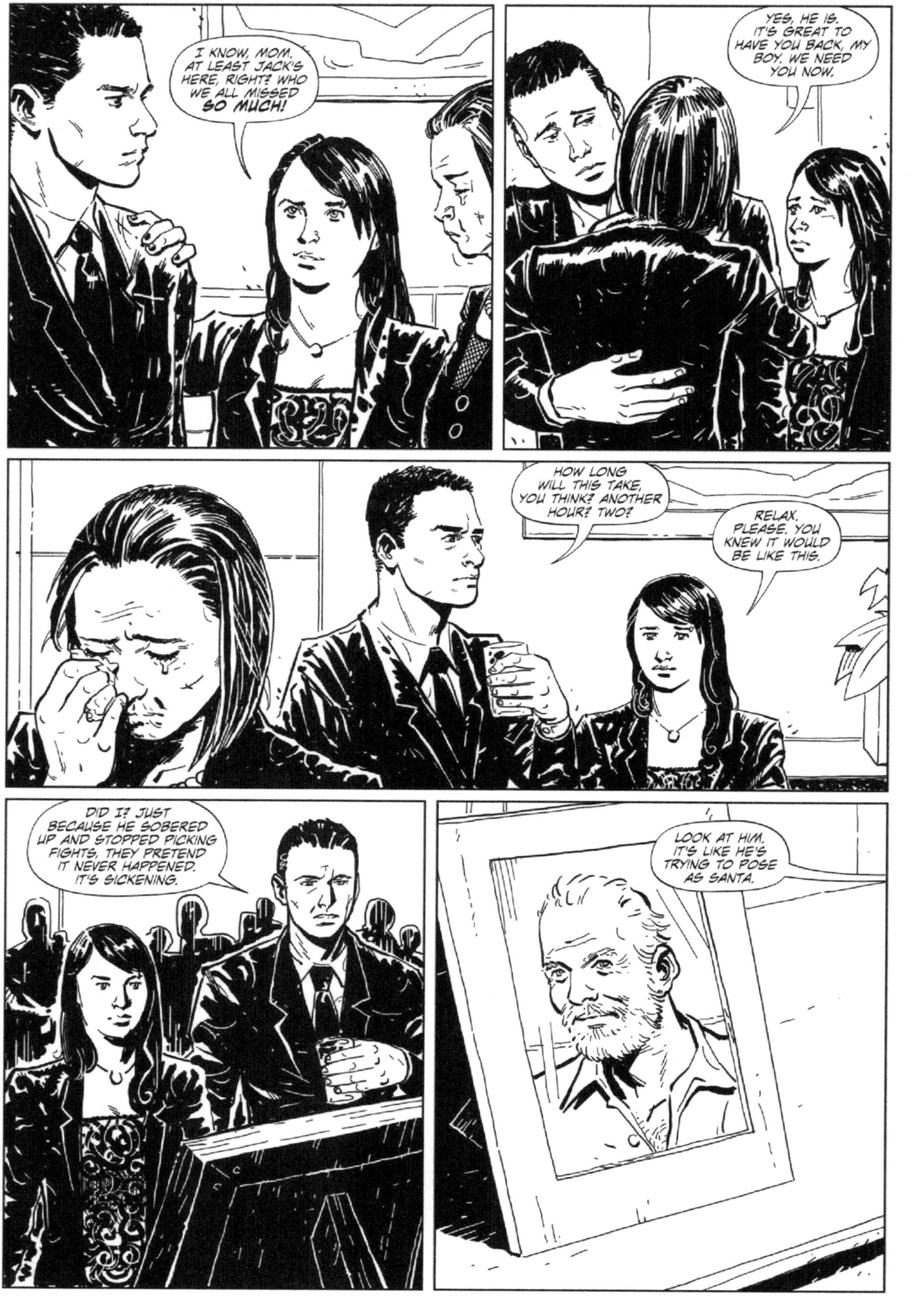
I KNOW, MOM. AT LEAST JACK'S HERE, RIGHT? WHO WE ALL MISSED SO MUCH!
YES, HE IS. IT'S GREAT TO HAVE YOU BACK, MY BOY. WE NEED YOU NOW.
HOW LONG WILL THIS TAKE, YOU THINK? ANOTHER HOUR? TWO?
RELAX. PLEASE. YOU KNEW IT WOULD BE LIKE THIS.
DID I? JUST BECAUSE HE SOBERED UP AND STOPPED PICKING FIGHTS, THEY PRETEND IT NEVER HAPPENED. IT'S SICKENING.
LOOK AT HIM. IT'S LIKE HE'S TRYING TO POSE AS SANTA.

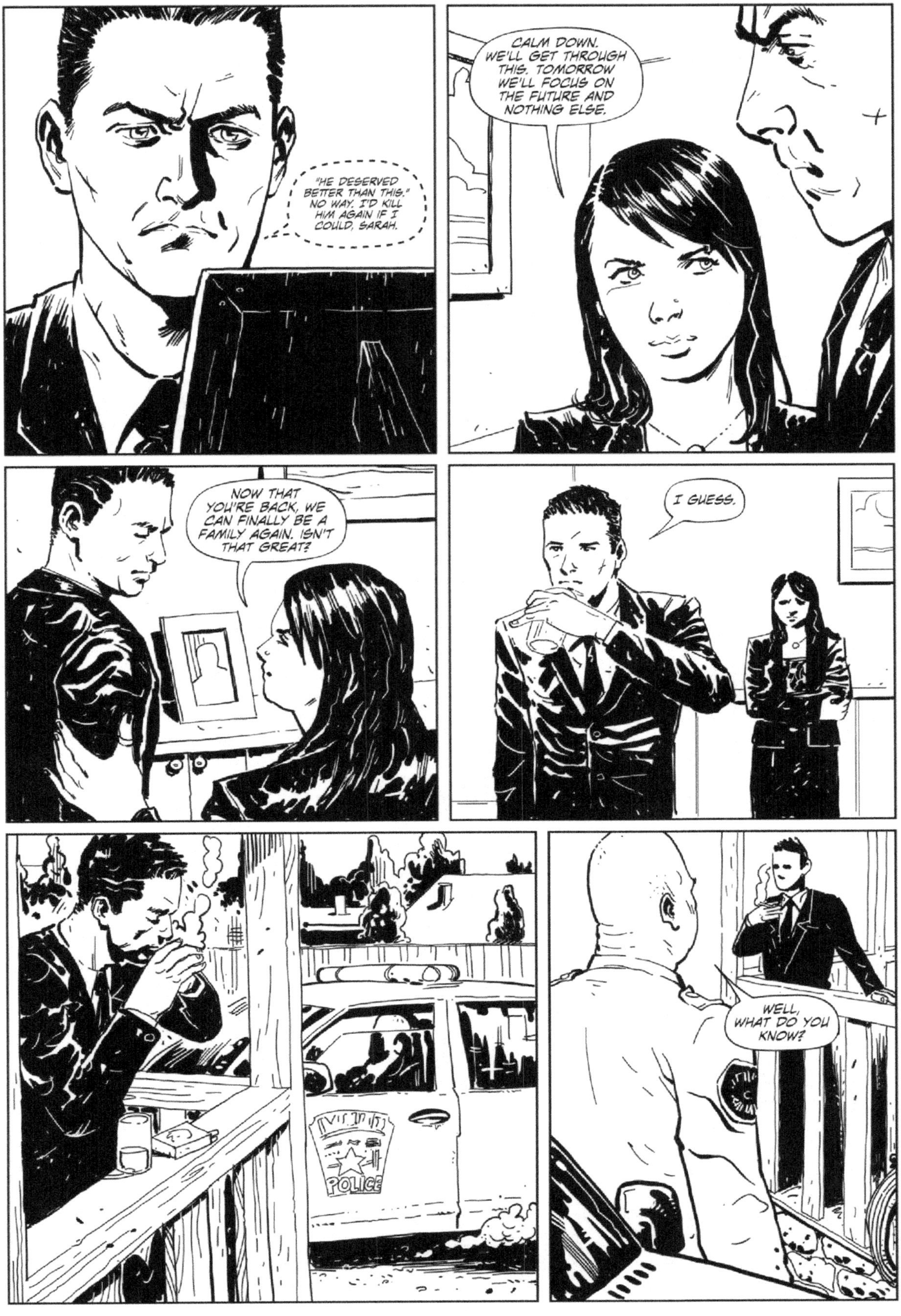
"HE DESERVED BETTER THAN THIS." NO WAY. I'D KILL HIM AGAIN IF I COULD, SARAH.
CALM DOWN. WE'LL GET THROUGH THIS. TOMORROW WE'LL FOCUS ON THE FUTURE AND NOTHING ELSE.
NOW THAT YOU'RE BACK, WE CAN FINALLY BE A FAMILY AGAIN. ISN'T THAT GREAT?
I GUESS.
POLICE
WELL, WHAT DO YOU KNOW?

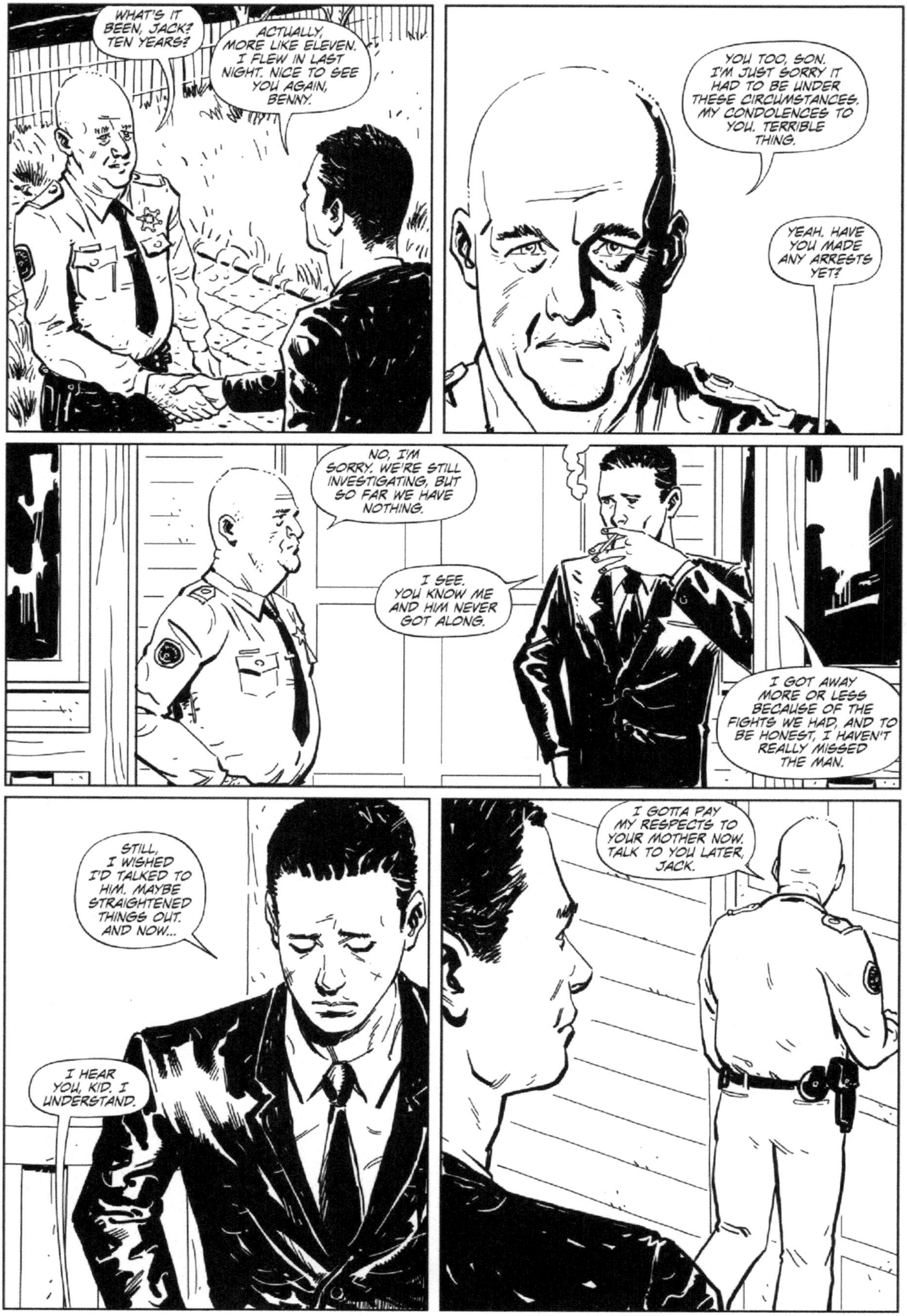
WHAT'S IT BEEN, JACK? TEN YEARS?
ACTUALLY, MORE LIKE ELEVEN. I FLEW IN LAST NIGHT. NICE TO SEE YOU AGAIN, BENNY.
YOU TOO, SON. I'M JUST SORRY IT HAD TO BE UNDER THESE CIRCUMSTANCES. MY CONDOLENCES TO YOU. TERRIBLE THING.
YEAH. HAVE YOU MADE ANY ARRESTS YET?
NO, I'M SORRY. WE'RE STILL INVESTIGATING, BUT SO FAR WE HAVE NOTHING.
I SEE. YOU KNOW ME AND HIM NEVER GOT ALONG.
I GOT AWAY MORE OR LESS BECAUSE OF THE FIGHTS WE HAD, AND TO BE HONEST, I HAVEN'T REALLY MISSED THE MAN.
STILL, I WISHED I'D TALKED TO HIM. MAYBE STRAIGHTENED THINGS OUT. AND NOW...
I HEAR YOU, KID. I UNDERSTAND.
I GOTTA PAY MY RESPECTS TO YOUR MOTHER NOW. TALK TO YOU LATER, JACK.

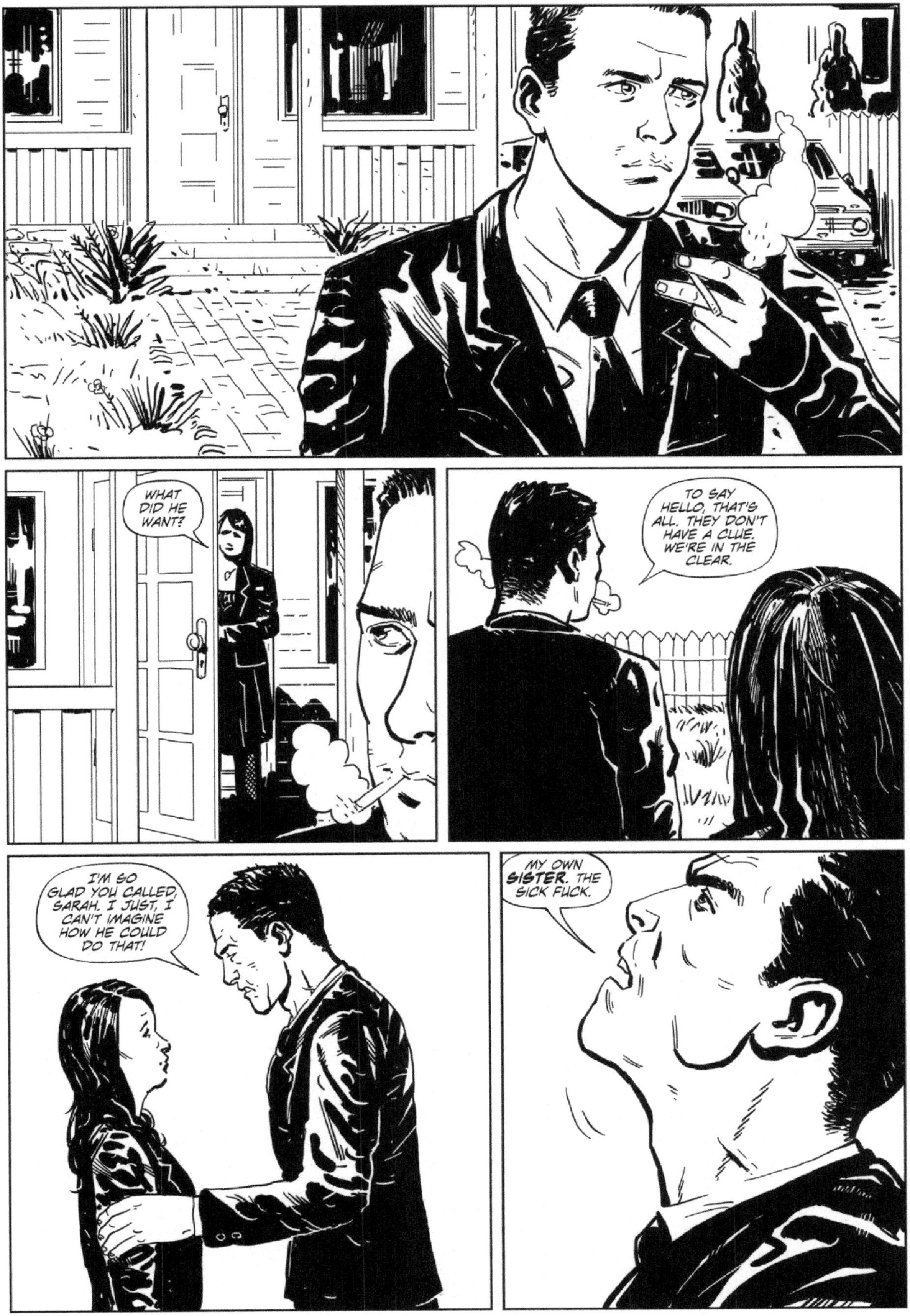
WHAT DID HE WANT?
TO SAY HELLO, THAT'S ALL. THEY DON'T HAVE A CLUE. WE'RE IN THE CLEAR.
I'M SO GLAD YOU CALLED, SARAH. I JUST, I CAN'T IMAGINE HOW HE COULD DO THAT!
MY OWN **SISTER**. THE SICK FUCK.

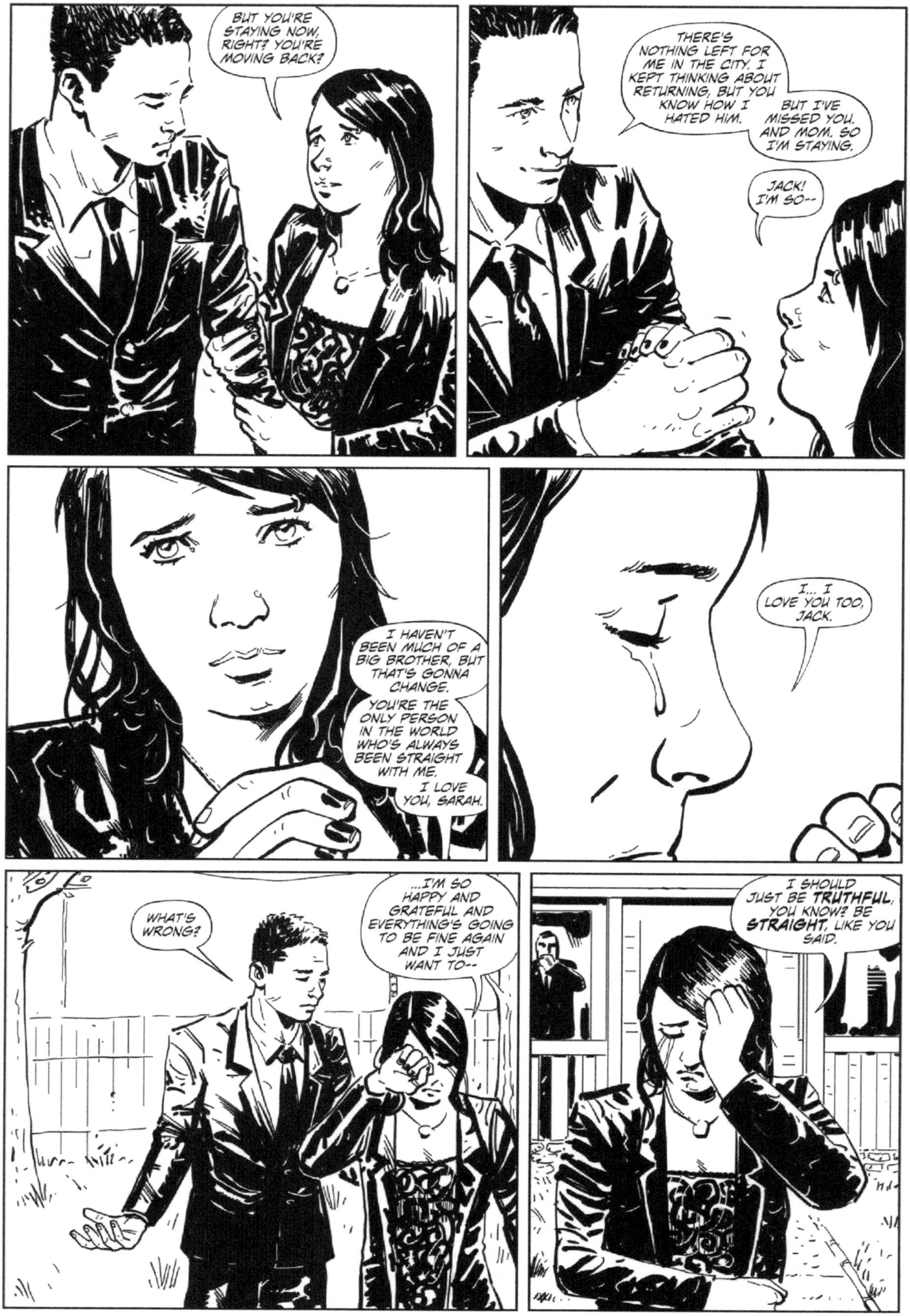
BUT YOU'RE STAYING NOW, RIGHT? YOU'RE MOVING BACK?
THERE'S NOTHING LEFT FOR ME IN THE CITY. I KEPT THINKING ABOUT RETURNING, BUT YOU KNOW HOW I HATED HIM.
BUT I'VE MISSED YOU. AND MOM. SO I'M STAYING.
JACK! I'M SO--
I HAVEN'T BEEN MUCH OF A BIG BROTHER, BUT THAT'S GONNA CHANGE.
YOU'RE THE ONLY PERSON IN THE WORLD WHO'S ALWAYS BEEN STRAIGHT WITH ME.
I LOVE YOU, SARAH.
I... I LOVE YOU TOO, JACK.
WHAT'S WRONG?
...I'M SO HAPPY AND GRATEFUL AND EVERYTHING'S GOING TO BE FINE AGAIN AND I JUST WANT TO--
I SHOULD JUST BE **TRUTHFUL**, YOU KNOW? BE **STRAIGHT**, LIKE YOU SAID.

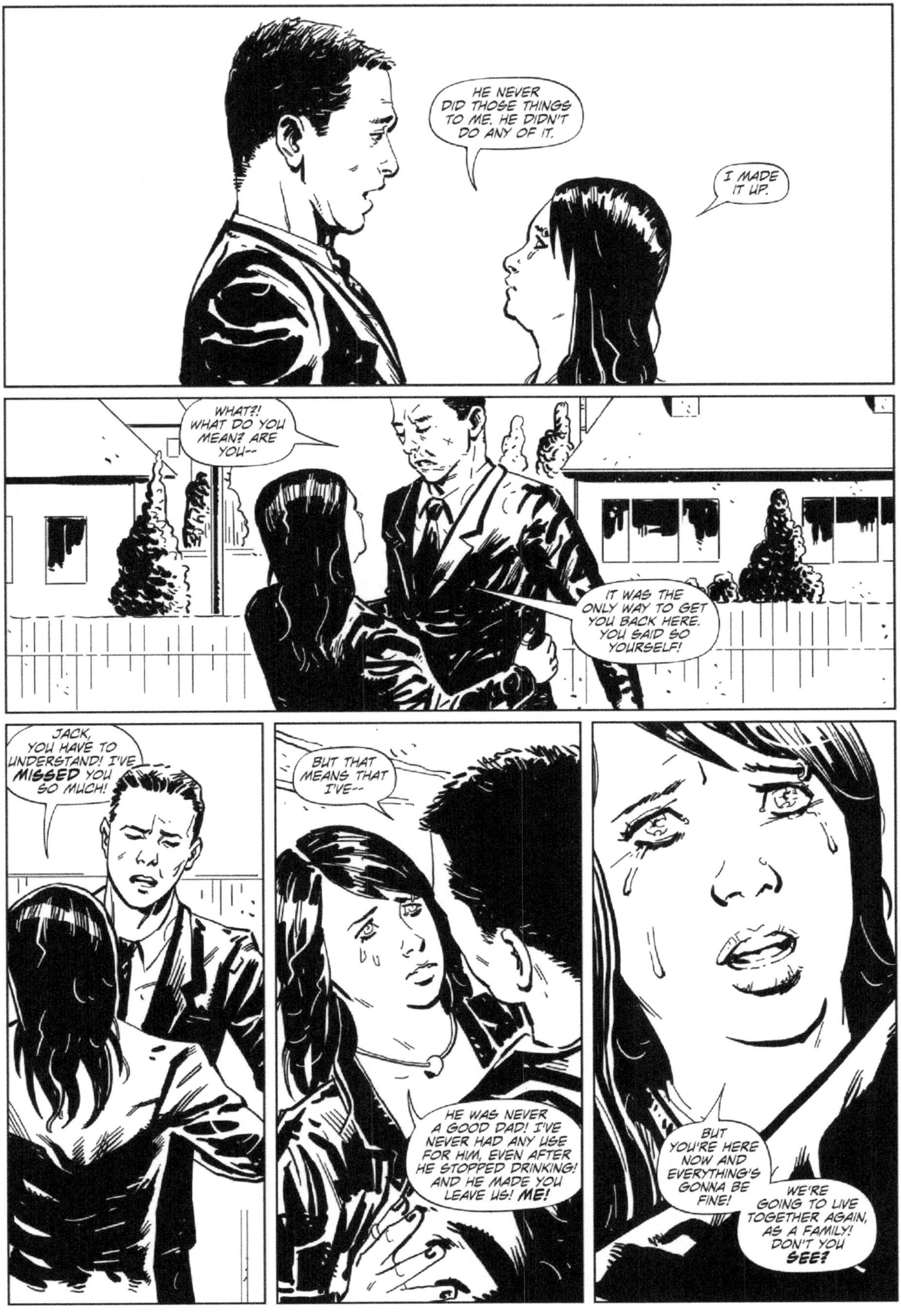
HE NEVER DID THOSE THINGS TO ME. HE DIDN'T DO ANY OF IT.
I MADE IT UP.
WHAT?! WHAT DO YOU MEAN? ARE YOU--
IT WAS THE ONLY WAY TO GET YOU BACK HERE. YOU SAID SO YOURSELF!
JACK, YOU HAVE TO UNDERSTAND! I'VE MISSED YOU SO MUCH!
BUT THAT MEANS THAT I'VE--
HE WAS NEVER A GOOD DAD! I'VE NEVER HAD ANY USE FOR HIM, EVEN AFTER HE STOPPED DRINKING! AND HE MADE YOU LEAVE US! ME!
BUT YOU'RE HERE NOW AND EVERYTHING'S GONNA BE FINE!
WE'RE GOING TO LIVE TOGETHER AGAIN, AS A FAMILY! DON'T YOU SEE?

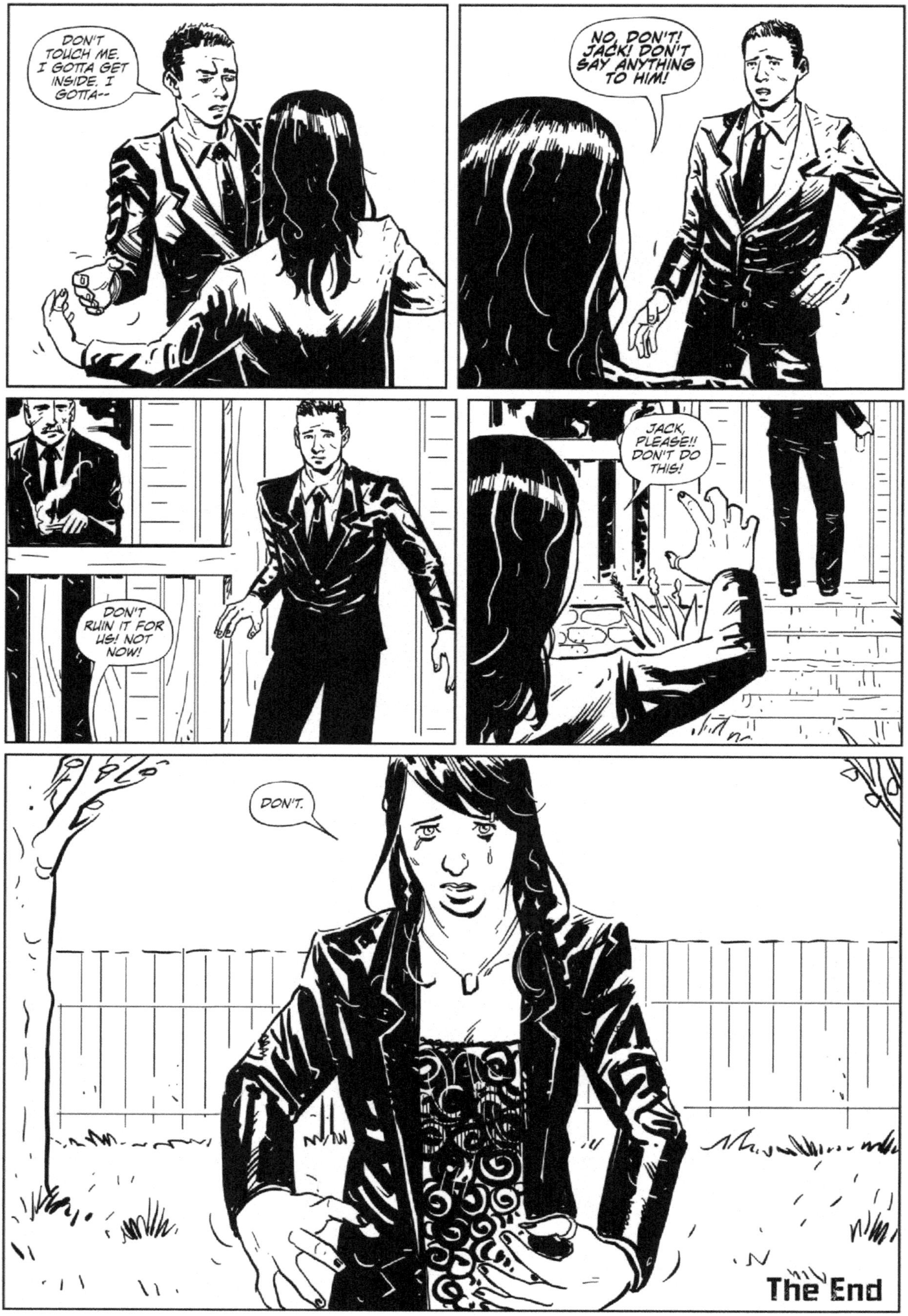
DON'T TOUCH ME. I GOTTA GET INSIDE. I GOTTA--
NO, DON'T! JACK! DON'T SAY ANYTHING TO HIM!
DON'T RUIN IT FOR US! NOT NOW!
JACK, PLEASE!! DON'T DO THIS!
DON'T.
The End

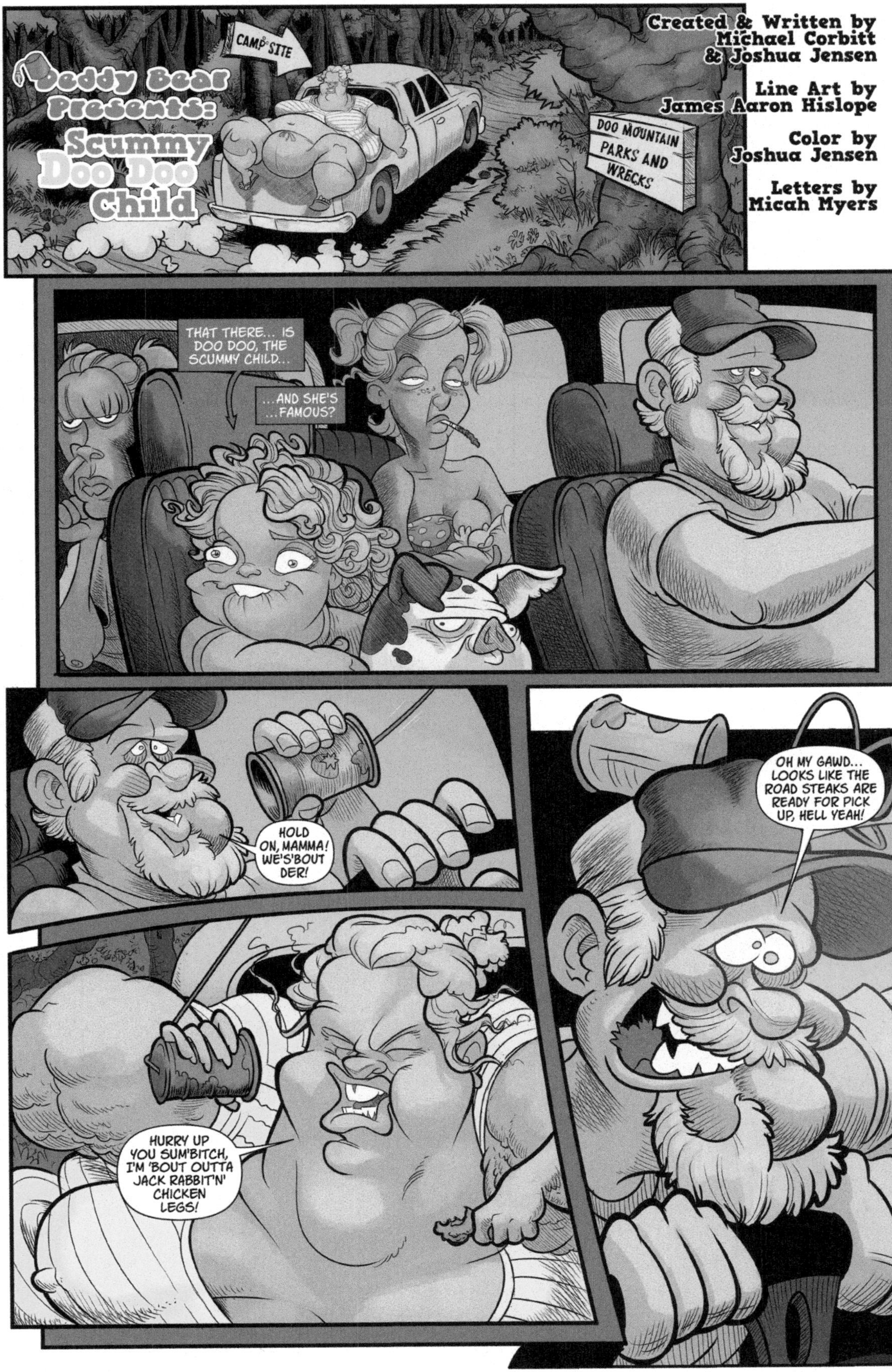
Teddy Bear Presents:
Scummy Doo Doo Child
Created & Written by Michael Corbitt & Joshua Jensen
Line Art by James Aaron Hislope
Color by Joshua Jensen
Letters by Micah Myers
CAMP SITE
DOO MOUNTAIN PARKS AND WRECKS
THAT THERE... IS DOO DOO, THE SCUMMY CHILD...
...AND SHE'S ...FAMOUS?
HOLD ON, MAMMA! WE'S'BOUT DER!
HURRY UP YOU SUM'BITCH, I'M 'BOUT OUTTA JACK RABBIT'N' CHICKEN LEGS!
OH MY GAWD... LOOKS LIKE THE ROAD STEAKS ARE READY FOR PICK UP, HELL YEAH!

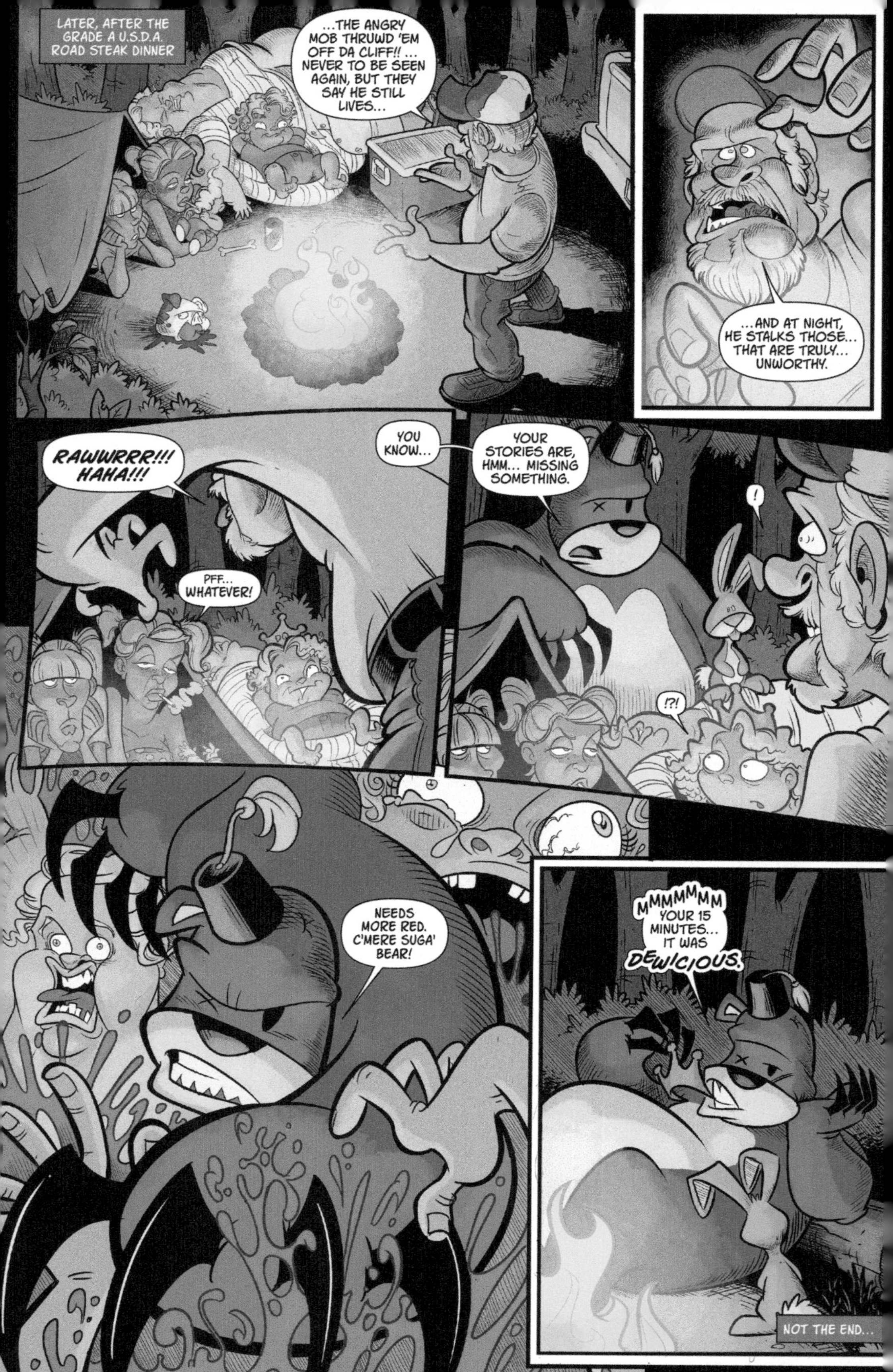
LATER, AFTER THE GRADE A U.S.D.A. ROAD STEAK DINNER
...THE ANGRY MOB THRUWD 'EM OFF DA CLIFF!! ... NEVER TO BE SEEN AGAIN, BUT THEY SAY HE STILL LIVES...
...AND AT NIGHT, HE STALKS THOSE... THAT ARE TRULY... UNWORTHY.
RAWWRRR!!! HAHA!!!
PFF... WHATEVER!
YOU KNOW...
YOUR STORIES ARE, HMM... MISSING SOMETHING.
!
!?!
NEEDS MORE RED. C'MERE SUGA' BEAR!
MMMMMMM YOUR 15 MINUTES... IT WAS DEWICIOUS.
NOT THE END...

I lie to try to hide from eyes that see everything.

A knowing past that passes before the abandoned dreams of youth.

Held down by what will never be held again, I grasp at vapor memories of a damned reality.

Drifting apart and away from everyone and everything that meant something, shadows hiding what can never be.

I am still unworthy.

There is no more light.

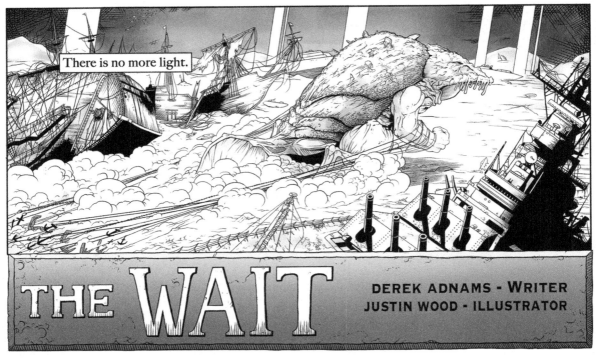

THE WAIT

DEREK ADNAMS - WRITER
JUSTIN WOOD - ILLUSTRATOR

Deliveries

words: Mike Isenberg & Oliver Mertz
pictures: Jeff McComsey

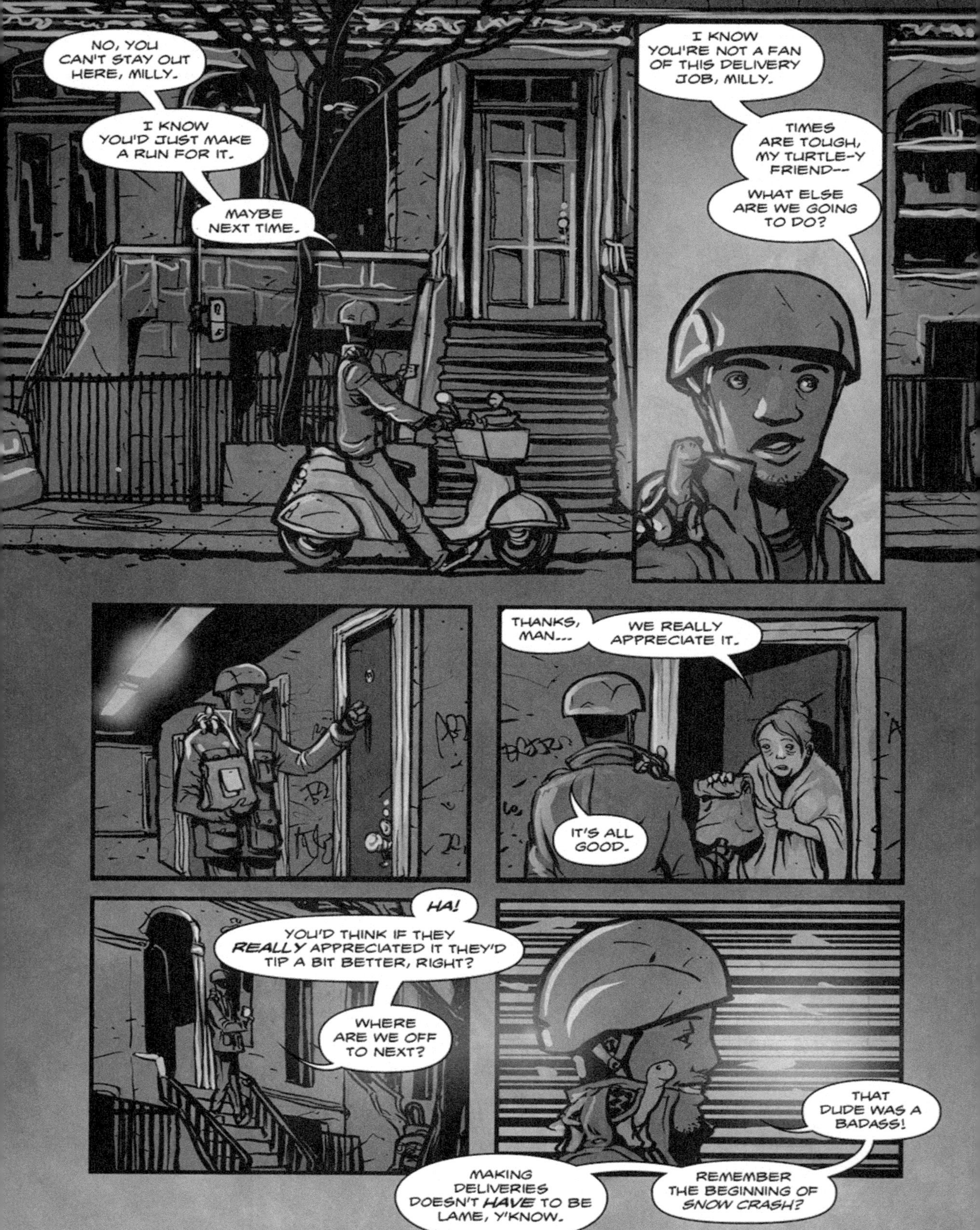
NO, YOU CAN'T STAY OUT HERE, MILLY.
I KNOW YOU'D JUST MAKE A RUN FOR IT.
MAYBE NEXT TIME.
I KNOW YOU'RE NOT A FAN OF THIS DELIVERY JOB, MILLY.
TIMES ARE TOUGH, MY TURTLE-Y FRIEND--
WHAT ELSE ARE WE GOING TO DO?
THANKS, MAN...
WE REALLY APPRECIATE IT.
IT'S ALL GOOD.
HA!
YOU'D THINK IF THEY REALLY APPRECIATED IT THEY'D TIP A BIT BETTER, RIGHT?
WHERE ARE WE OFF TO NEXT?
THAT DUDE WAS A BADASS!
REMEMBER THE BEGINNING OF SNOW CRASH?
MAKING DELIVERIES DOESN'T HAVE TO BE LAME, Y'KNOW.

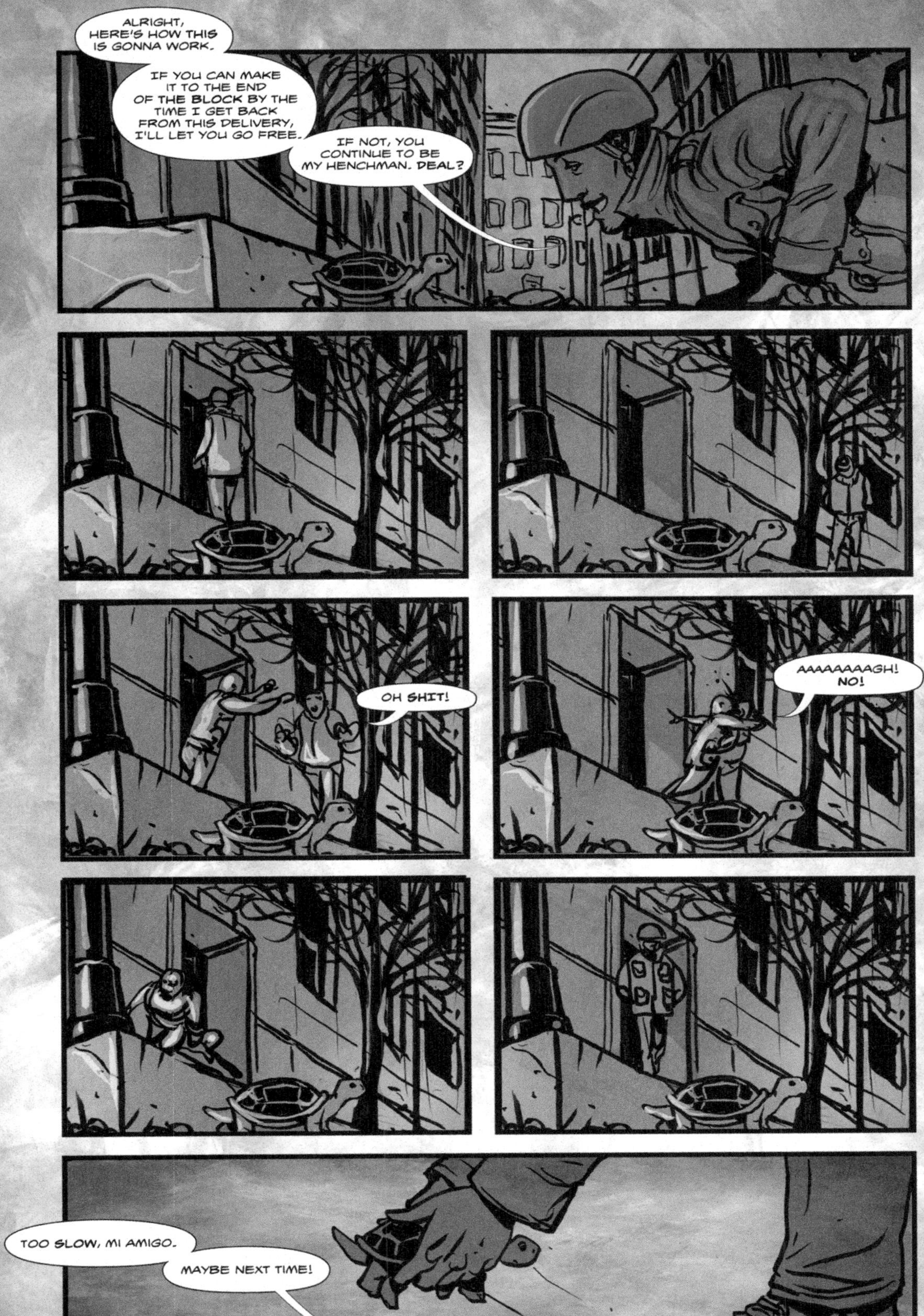

ALRIGHT, HERE'S HOW THIS IS GONNA WORK.
IF YOU CAN MAKE IT TO THE END OF THE **BLOCK** BY THE TIME I GET BACK FROM THIS DELIVERY, I'LL LET YOU GO FREE.
IF NOT, YOU CONTINUE TO BE MY HENCHMAN. **DEAL?**
OH **SHIT!**
AAAAAAAAGH! NO!
TOO **SLOW,** MI AMIGO.
MAYBE NEXT TIME!

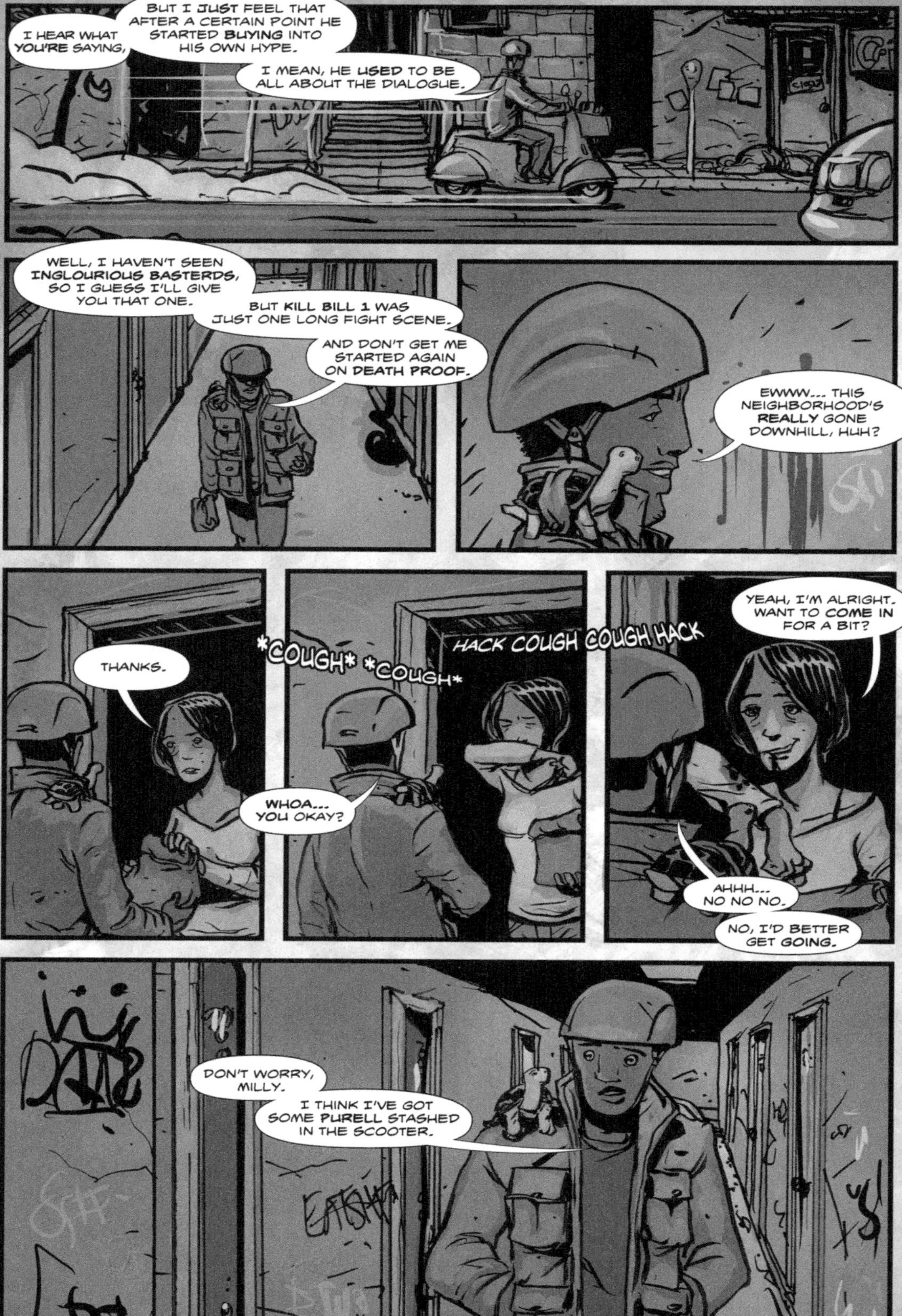

I HEAR WHAT YOU'RE SAYING,
BUT I JUST FEEL THAT AFTER A CERTAIN POINT HE STARTED BUYING INTO HIS OWN HYPE.
I MEAN, HE USED TO BE ALL ABOUT THE DIALOGUE.
WELL, I HAVEN'T SEEN INGLOURIOUS BASTERDS, SO I GUESS I'LL GIVE YOU THAT ONE.
BUT KILL BILL 1 WAS JUST ONE LONG FIGHT SCENE.
AND DON'T GET ME STARTED AGAIN ON DEATH PROOF.
EWWW... THIS NEIGHBORHOOD'S REALLY GONE DOWNHILL, HUH?
THANKS.
COUGH *COUGH*
HACK COUGH COUGH HACK
WHOA... YOU OKAY?
YEAH, I'M ALRIGHT. WANT TO COME IN FOR A BIT?
AHHH... NO NO NO.
NO, I'D BETTER GET GOING.
DON'T WORRY, MILLY.
I THINK I'VE GOT SOME PURELL STASHED IN THE SCOOTER.

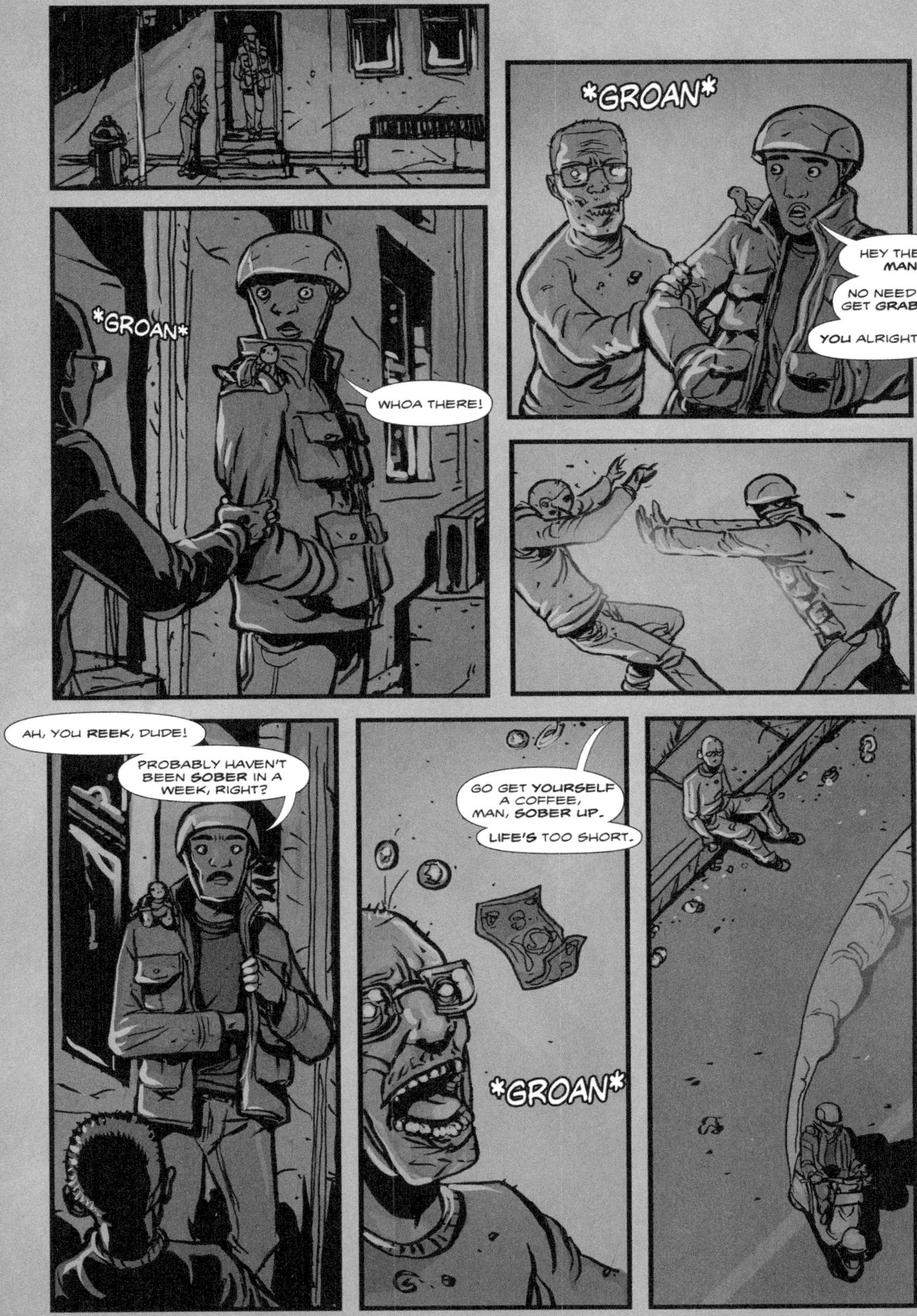
GROAN
HEY THERE, MAN.
NO NEED TO GET GRABBY!
YOU ALRIGHT?
GROAN
WHOA THERE!
AH, YOU REEK, DUDE!
PROBABLY HAVEN'T BEEN SOBER IN A WEEK, RIGHT?
GO GET YOURSELF A COFFEE, MAN, SOBER UP.
LIFE'S TOO SHORT.
GROAN

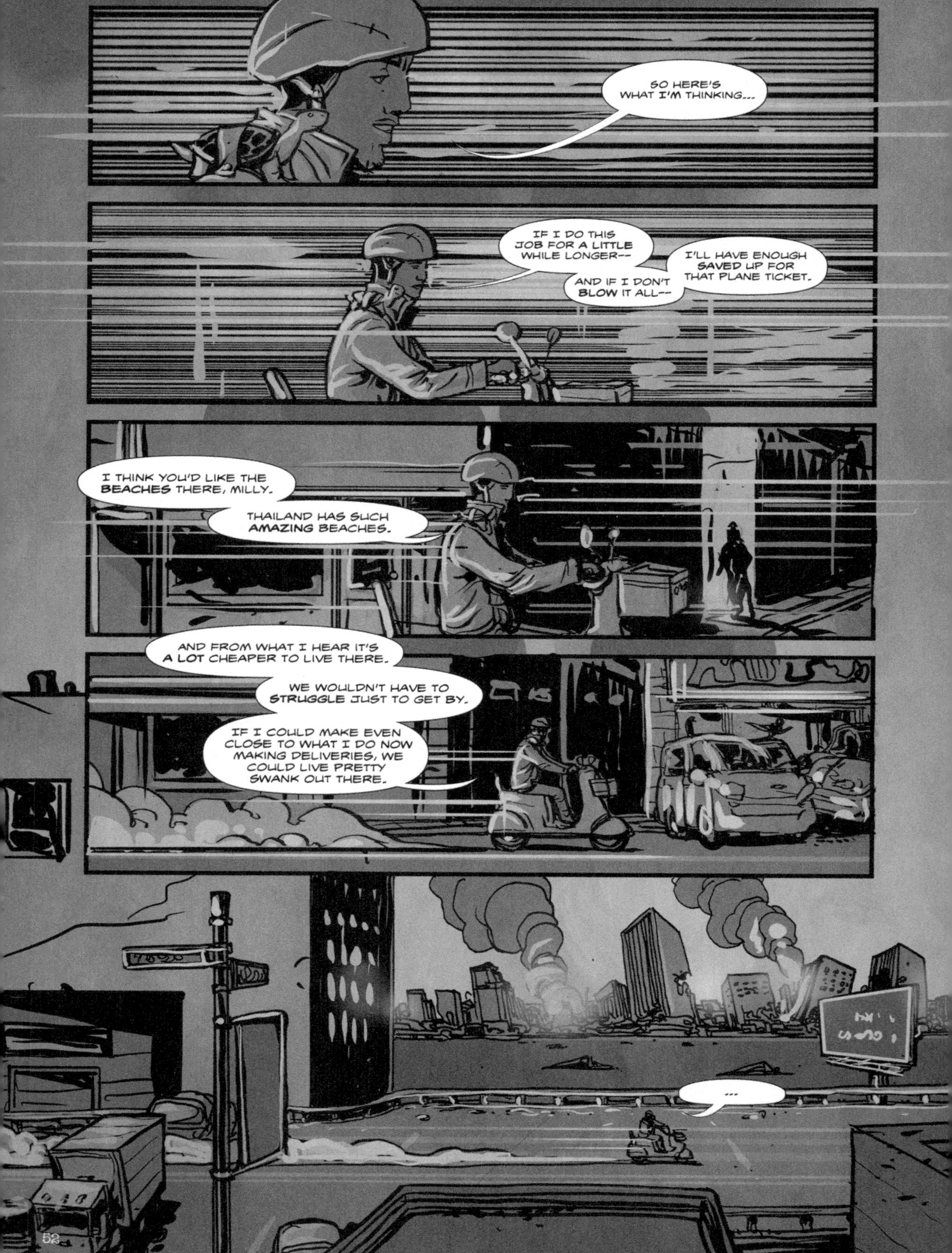
SO HERE'S WHAT I'M THINKING...
IF I DO THIS JOB FOR A LITTLE WHILE LONGER--
AND IF I DON'T BLOW IT ALL--
I'LL HAVE ENOUGH SAVED UP FOR THAT PLANE TICKET.
I THINK YOU'D LIKE THE BEACHES THERE, MILLY.
THAILAND HAS SUCH AMAZING BEACHES.
AND FROM WHAT I HEAR IT'S A LOT CHEAPER TO LIVE THERE.
WE WOULDN'T HAVE TO STRUGGLE JUST TO GET BY.
IF I COULD MAKE EVEN CLOSE TO WHAT I DO NOW MAKING DELIVERIES, WE COULD LIVE PRETTY SWANK OUT THERE.
...

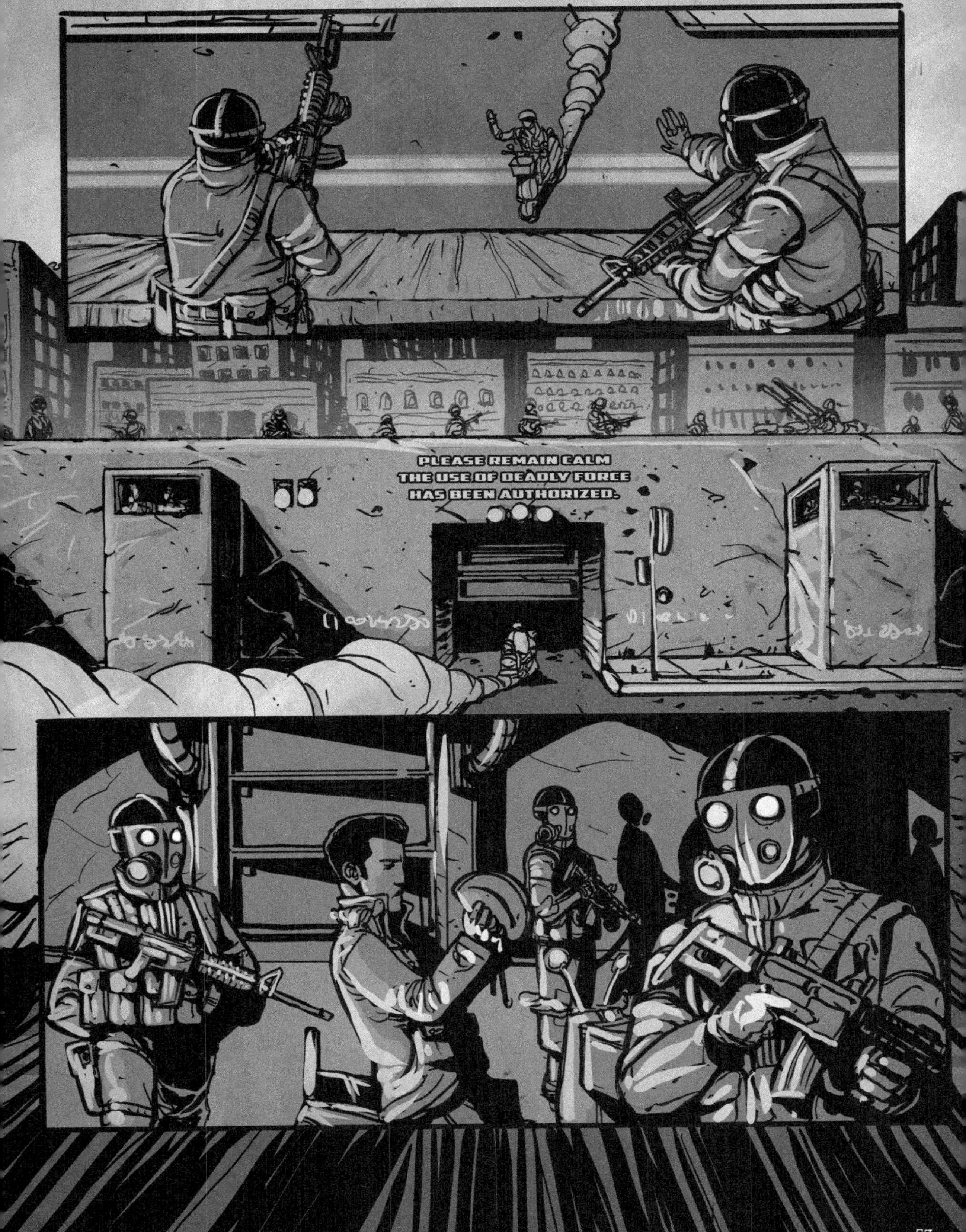
PLEASE REMAIN CALM
THE USE OF DEADLY FORCE
HAS BEEN AUTHORIZED.

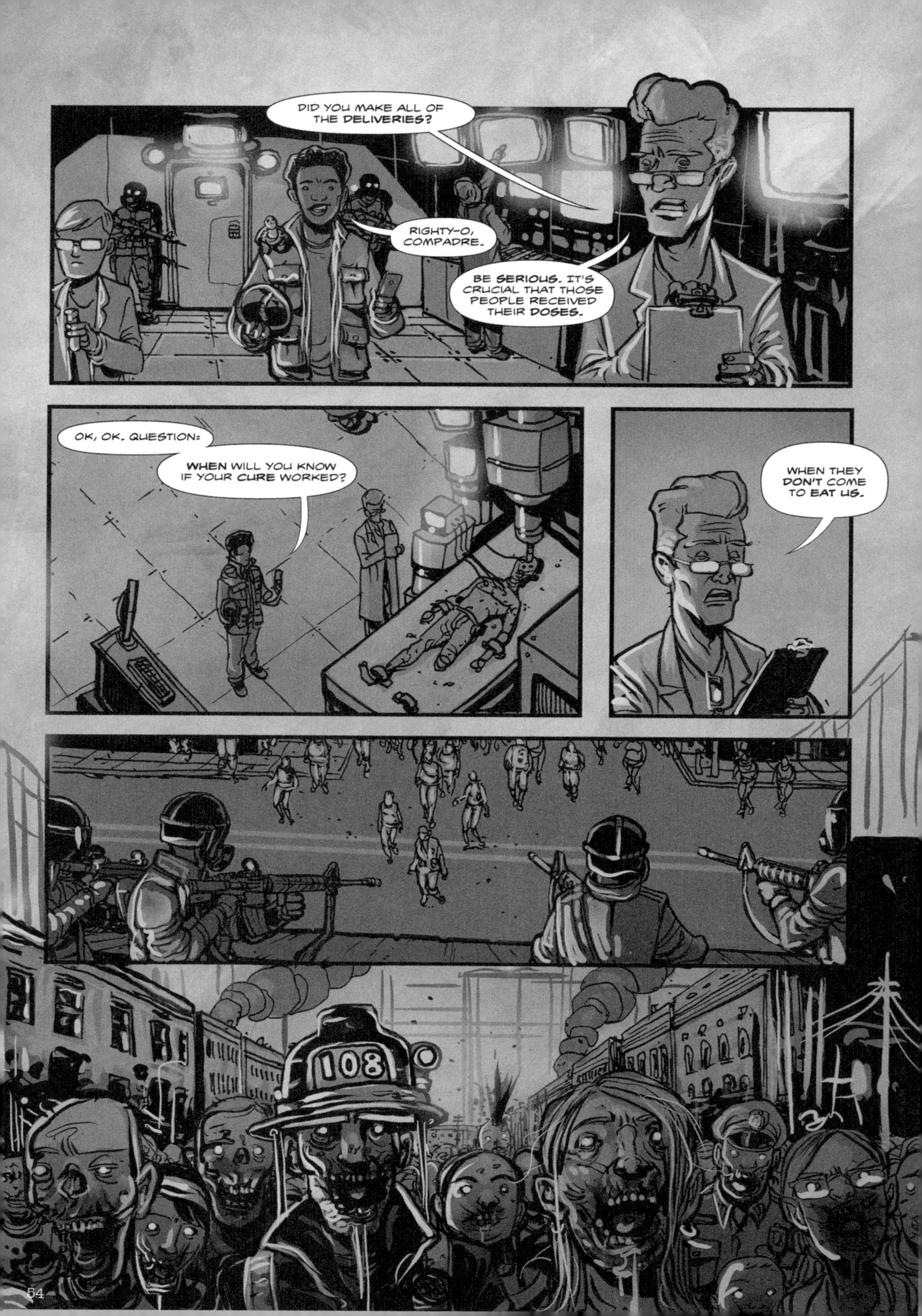
DID YOU MAKE ALL OF THE DELIVERIES?
RIGHTY-O, COMPADRE.
BE SERIOUS. IT'S CRUCIAL THAT THOSE PEOPLE RECEIVED THEIR DOSES.
OK, OK. QUESTION:
WHEN WILL YOU KNOW IF YOUR CURE WORKED?
WHEN THEY DON'T COME TO EAT US.
108

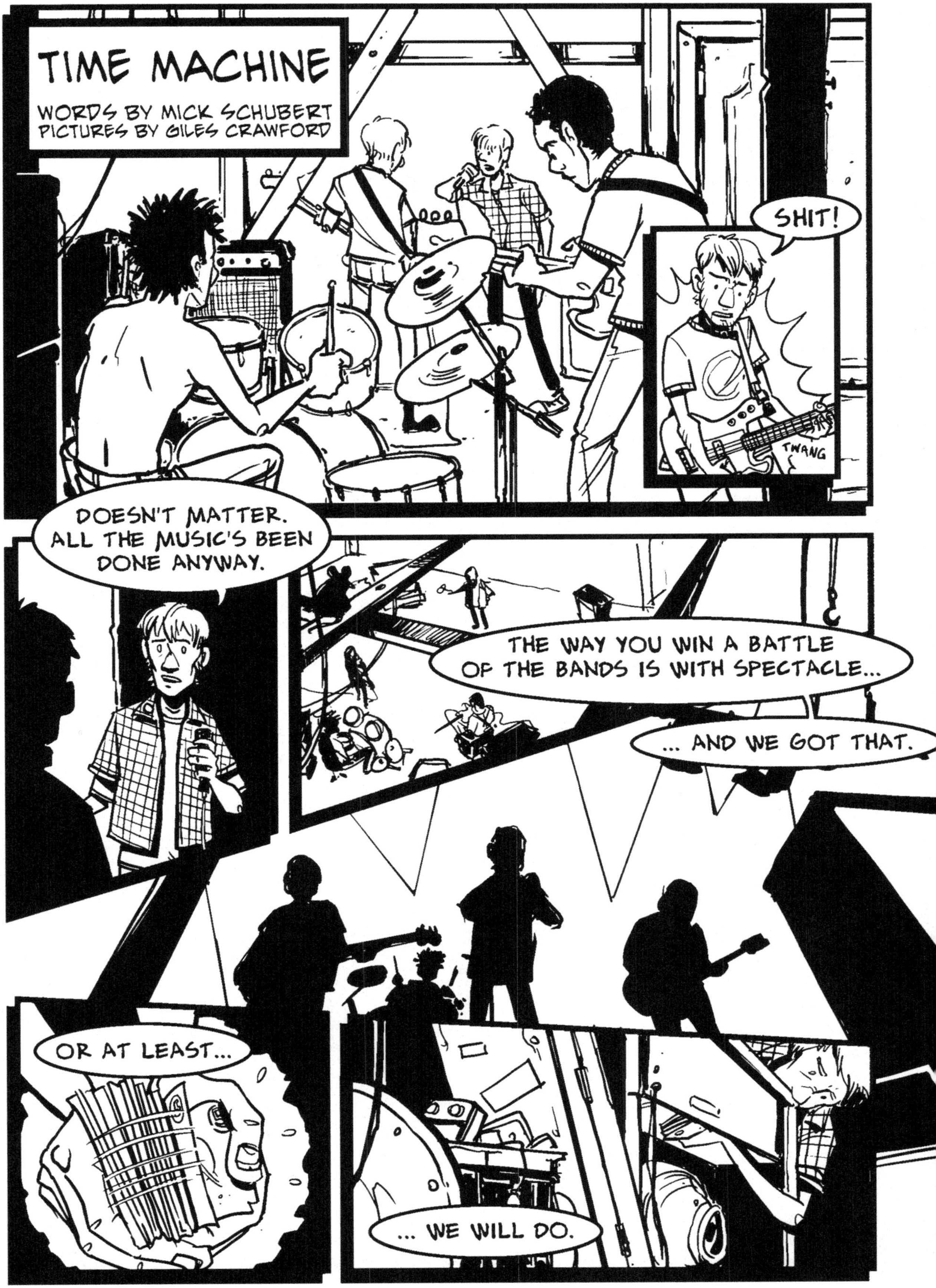
TIME MACHINE
WORDS BY MICK SCHUBERT
PICTURES BY GILES CRAWFORD
SHIT!
TWANG
DOESN'T MATTER. ALL THE MUSIC'S BEEN DONE ANYWAY.
THE WAY YOU WIN A BATTLE OF THE BANDS IS WITH SPECTACLE...
... AND WE GOT THAT.
OR AT LEAST...
... WE WILL DO.

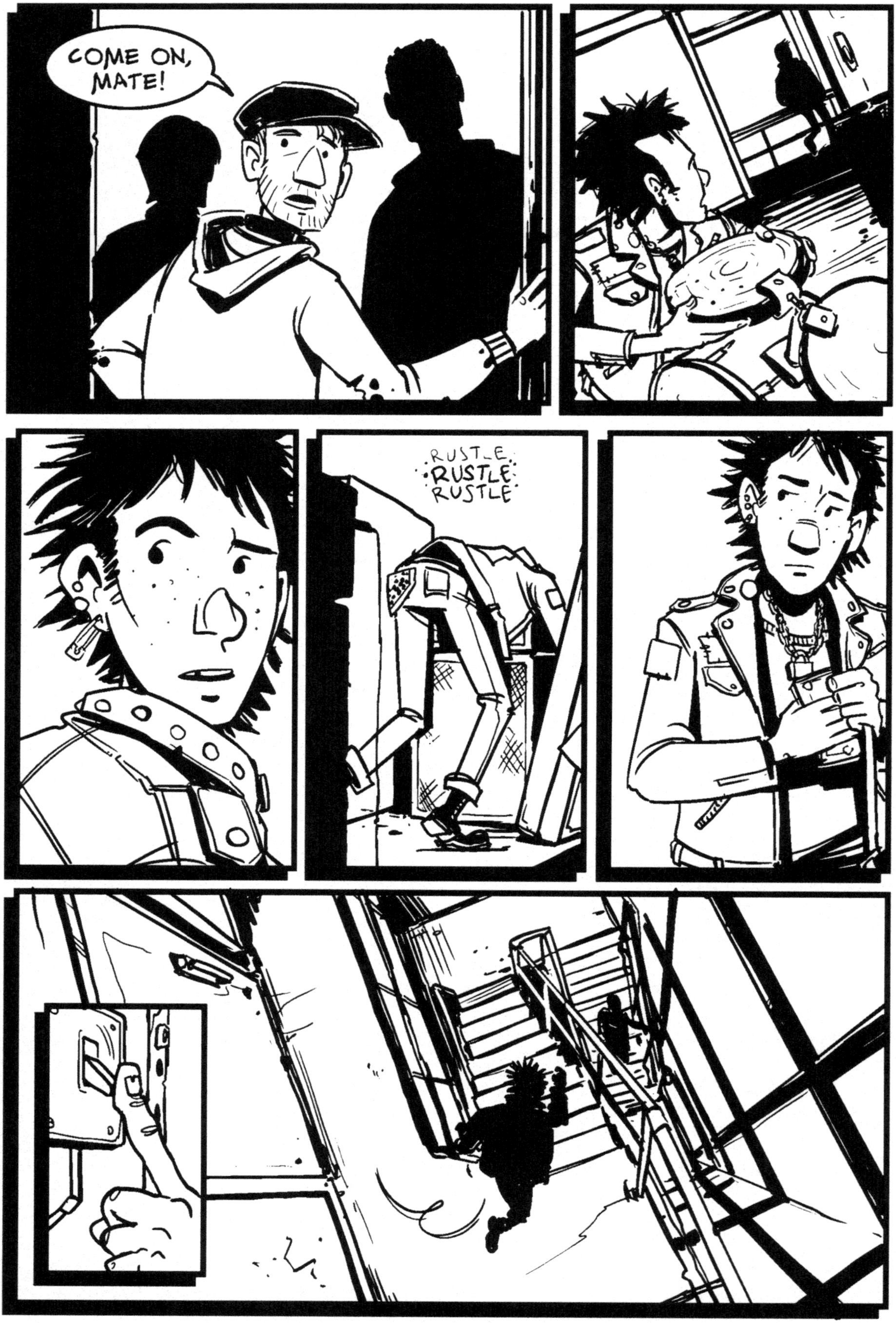
COME ON, MATE!
RUSTLE
RUSTLE
RUSTLE

NEXT DAY...

WHAT'S GOIN' ON?

THIS BLOODY IDIOT

BLEW OUR WHOLE BUDGET ON FUCKING COCAINE!

NOW HOW'RE WE GOIN' TO WIN THE BATTLE OF THE BANDS?

GUYS.

I CAN'T BELIEVE THIS HAPPENED AGAIN HE MIGHT'VE ... LAST SH... ...TH US BLOODY IDIOT ... ...RUMM... ...ONG WITH YO... ... YOU WERE N... ...TO BE WATCHING HIM I ... NOT 'IT WAS ...OUR ...RA... WHY DO

GUYS.

WHAT ARE WE CALLED?

'TIME MACHINE

WELL?

GIVE ME A HAND.

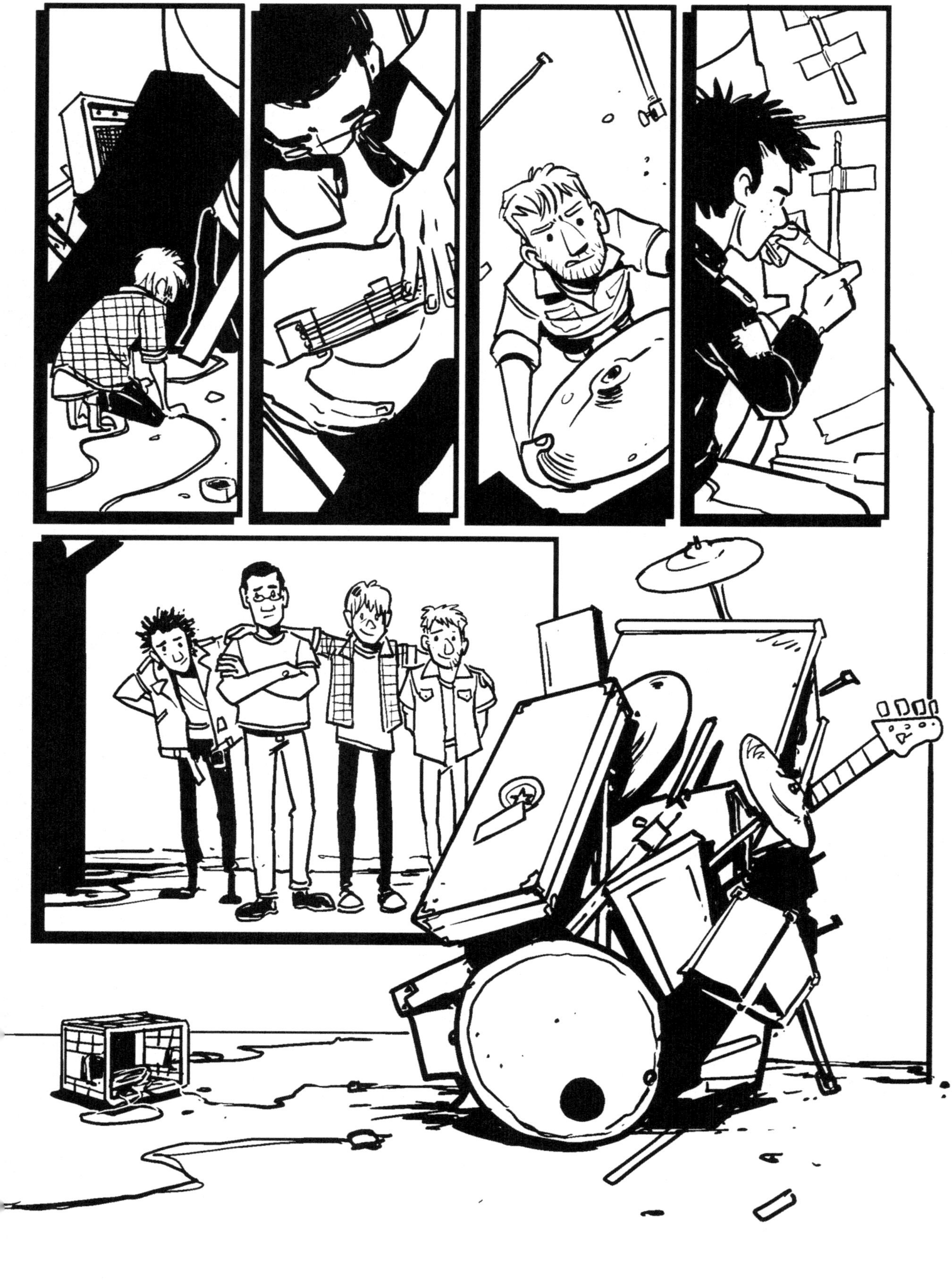

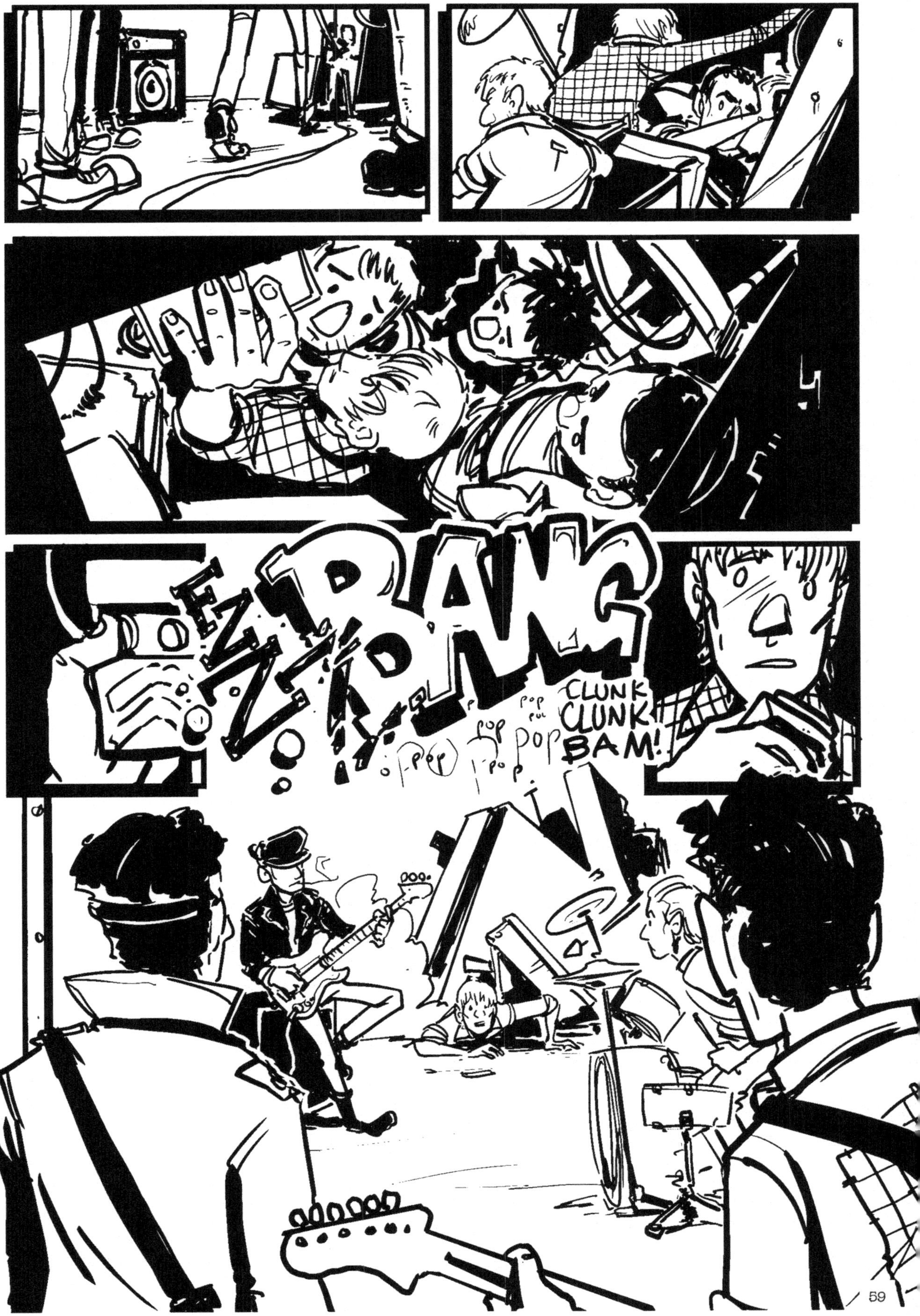
pop
pop
pop
CLUNK
CLUNK
BAM!

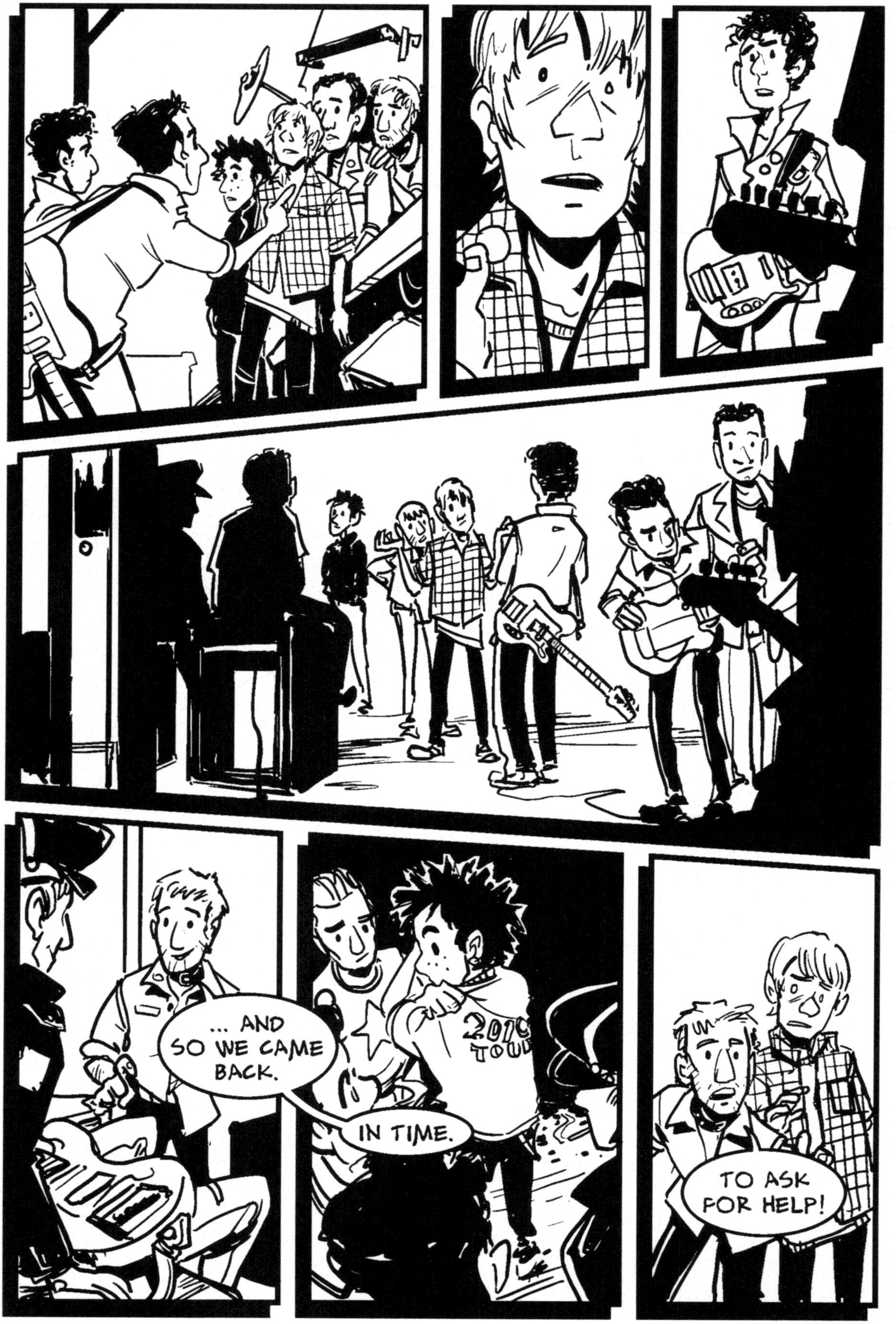
... AND SO WE CAME BACK.
IN TIME.
TO ASK FOR HELP!

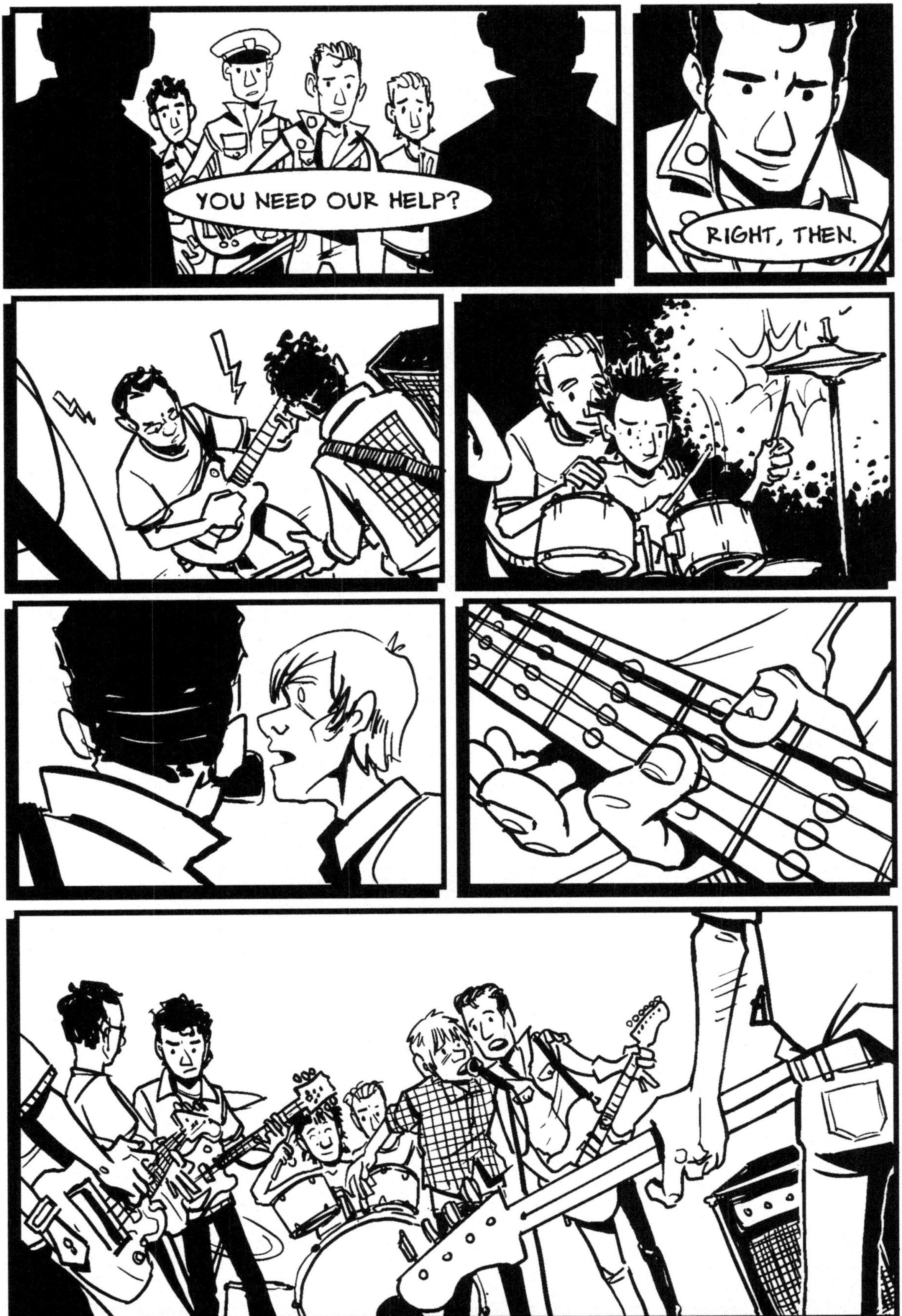
YOU NEED OUR HELP?
RIGHT, THEN.

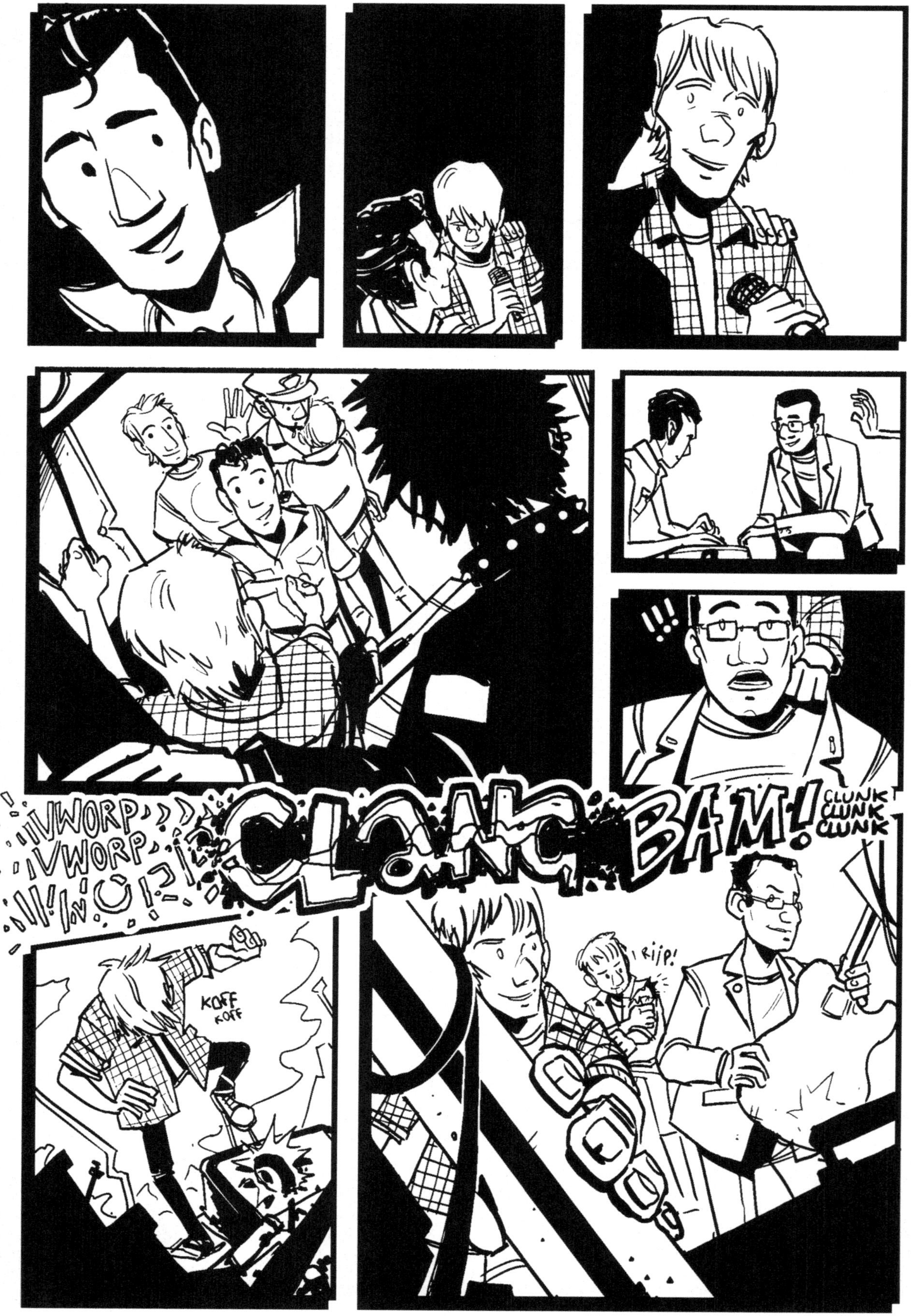
!!!
¡VWORP
¡VWORP
CLANG
BAM!
CLUNK
CLUNK
CLUNK
KOFF
KOFF
¡RIJP!

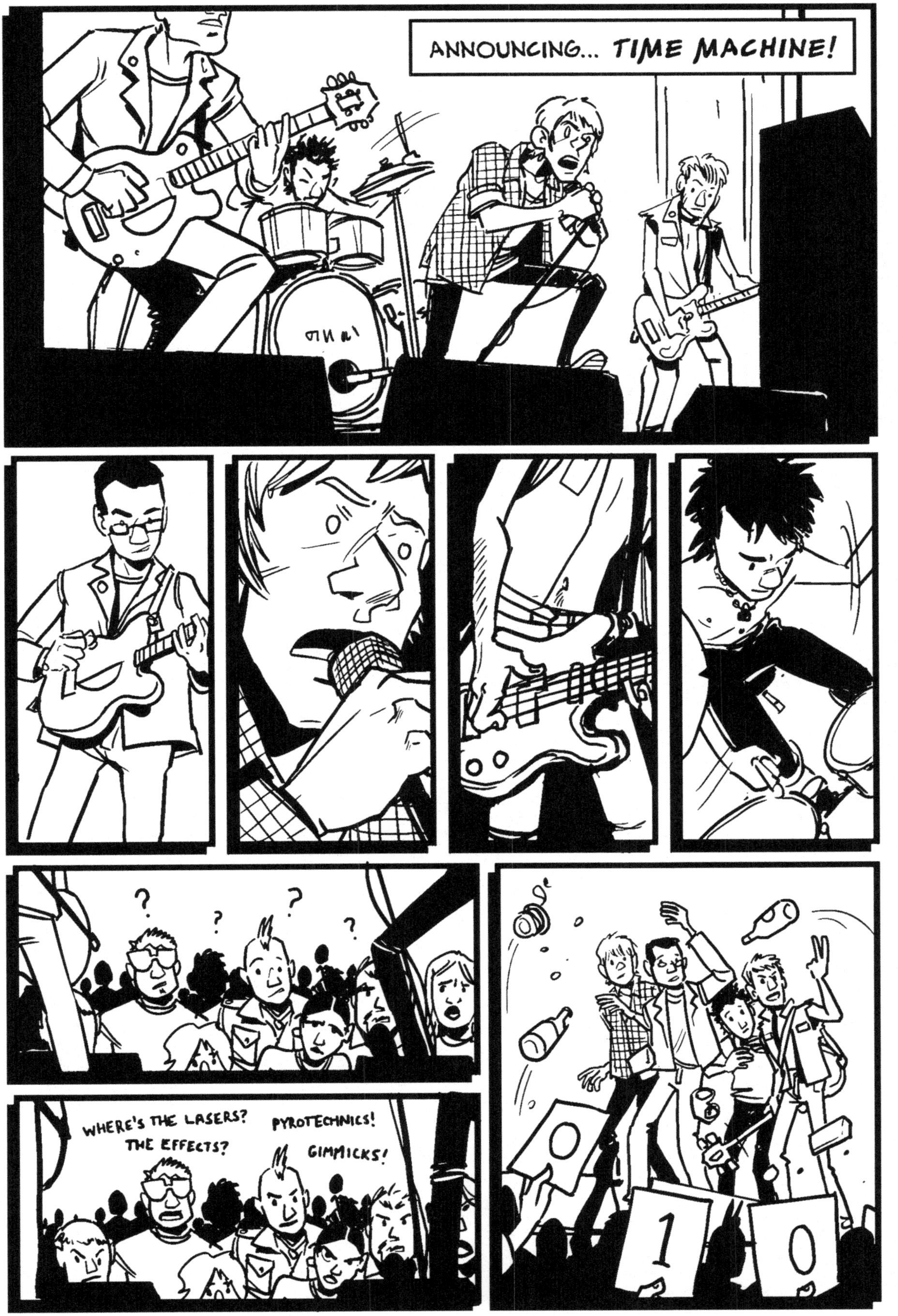
ANNOUNCING... TIME MACHINE!
?
?
?
?
WHERE'S THE LASERS?
THE EFFECTS?
PYROTECHNICS!
GIMMICKS!
0
1
0

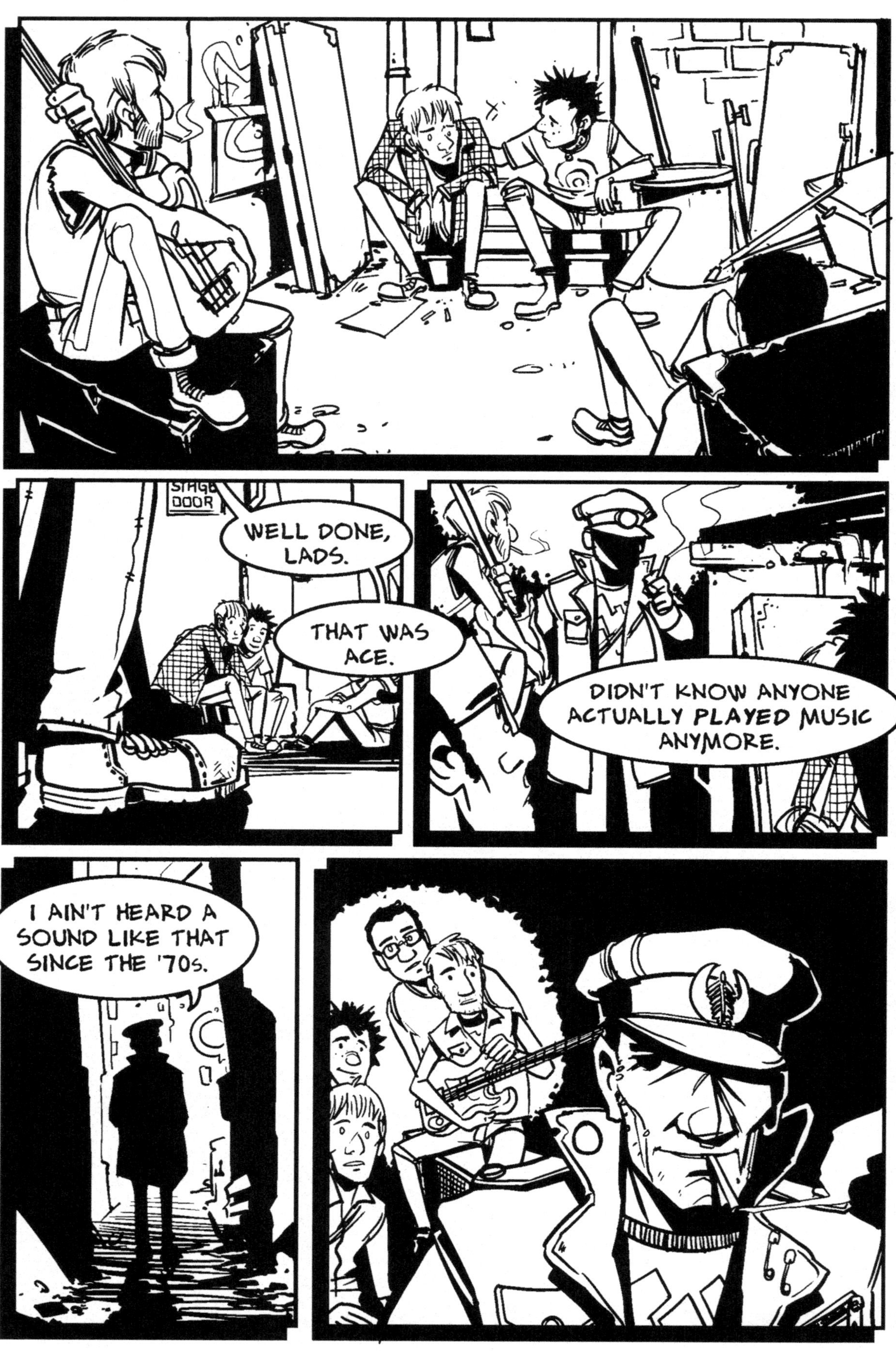
STAGE DOOR
WELL DONE, LADS.
THAT WAS ACE.
DIDN'T KNOW ANYONE ACTUALLY PLAYED MUSIC ANYMORE.
I AIN'T HEARD A SOUND LIKE THAT SINCE THE '70s.

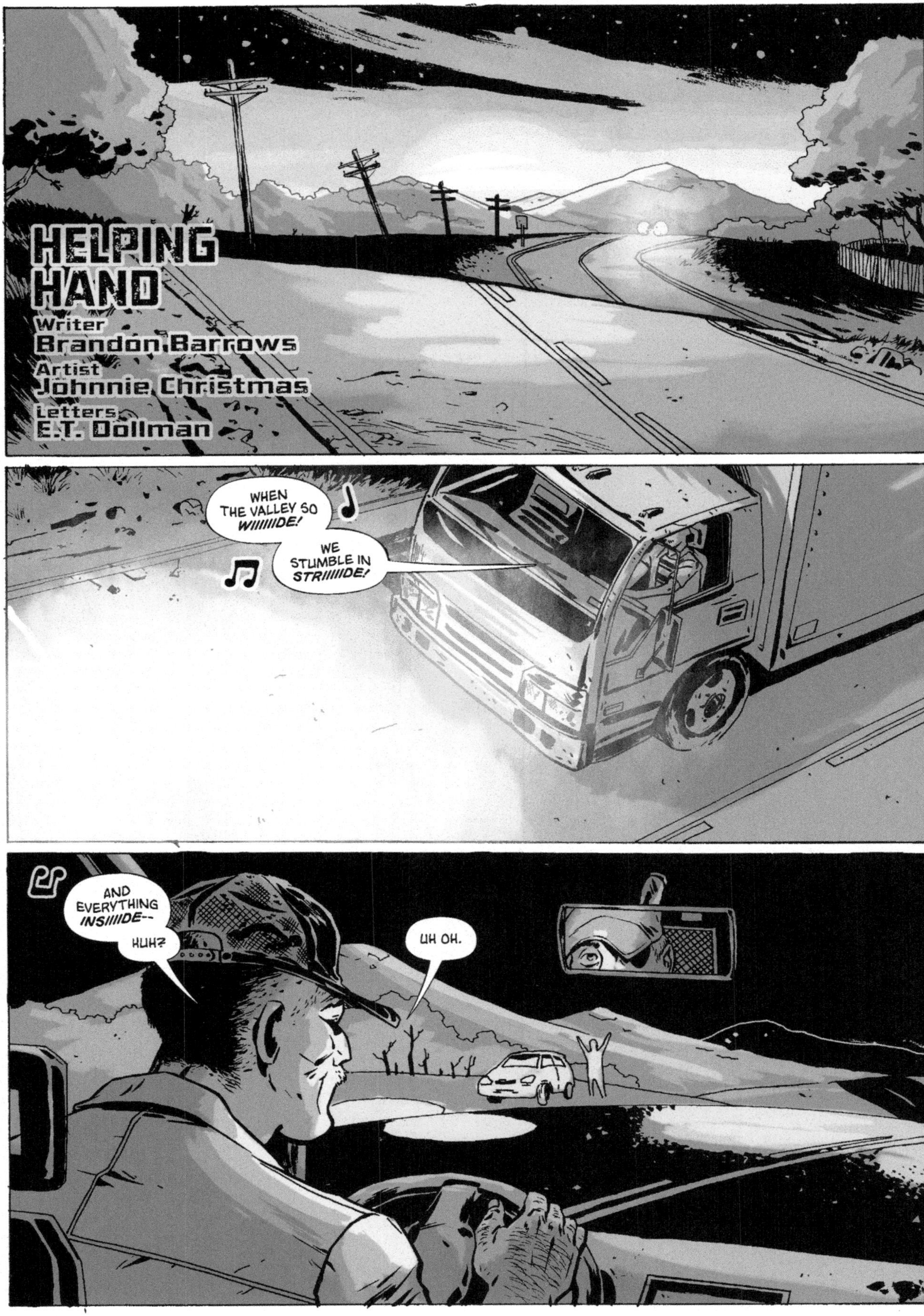
HELPING HAND
Writer
Brandon Barrows
Artist
Johnnie Christmas
Letters
E.T. Dollman
WHEN THE VALLEY SO WIIIIIDE!
WE STUMBLE IN STRIIIIIDE!
AND EVERYTHING INSIIIDE--
HUH?
UH OH.

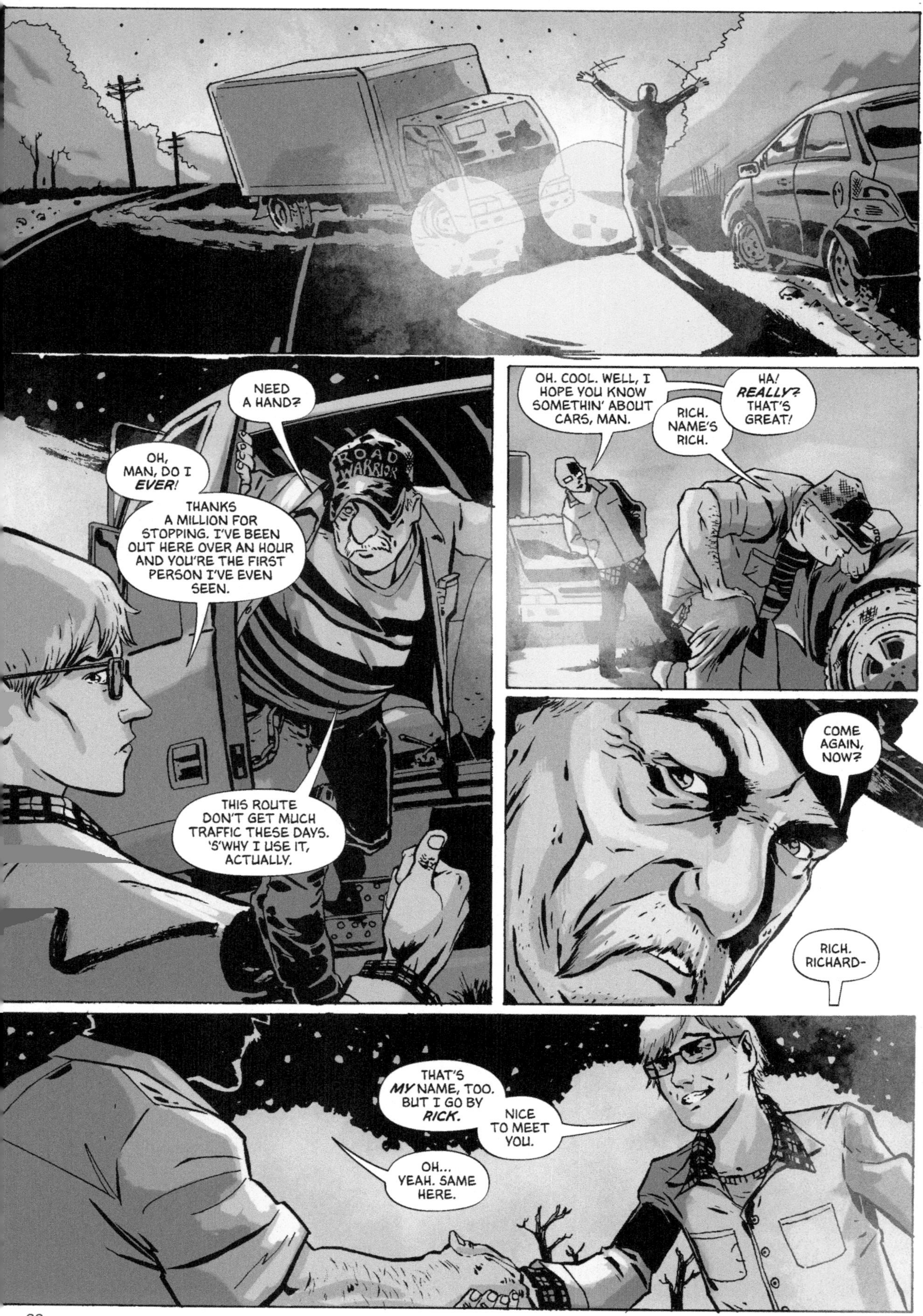
NEED A HAND?
OH, MAN, DO I *EVER*!
THANKS A MILLION FOR STOPPING. I'VE BEEN OUT HERE OVER AN HOUR AND YOU'RE THE FIRST PERSON I'VE EVEN SEEN.
THIS ROUTE DON'T GET MUCH TRAFFIC THESE DAYS. 'S'WHY I USE IT, ACTUALLY.
OH. COOL. WELL, I HOPE YOU KNOW SOMETHIN' ABOUT CARS, MAN.
RICH. NAME'S RICH.
HA! *REALLY?* THAT'S GREAT!
COME AGAIN, NOW?
RICH. RICHARD-
THAT'S *MY* NAME, TOO. BUT I GO BY *RICK*.
NICE TO MEET YOU.
OH... YEAH. SAME HERE.

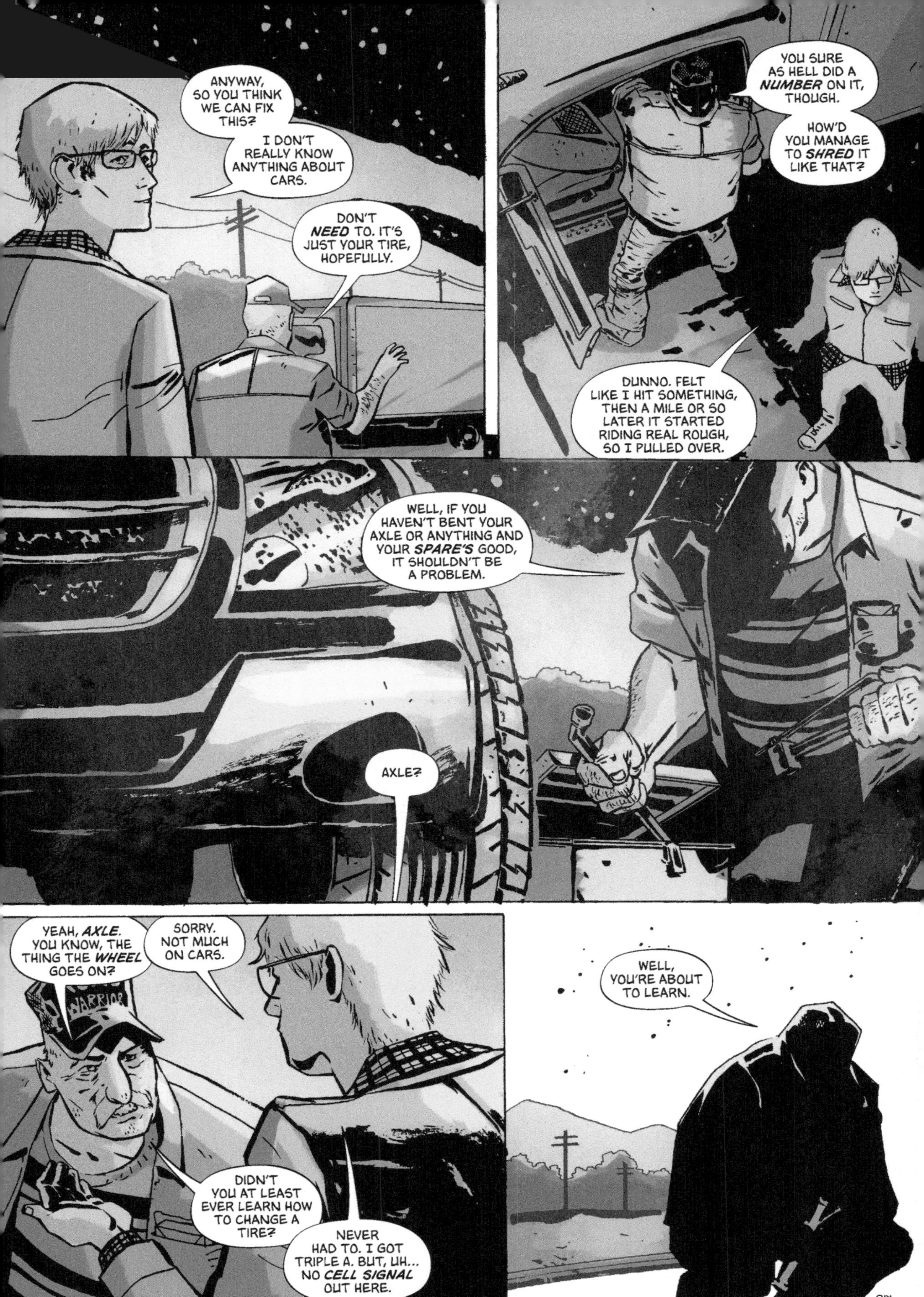
ANYWAY, SO YOU THINK WE CAN FIX THIS?
I DON'T REALLY KNOW ANYTHING ABOUT CARS.
DON'T *NEED* TO. IT'S JUST YOUR TIRE, HOPEFULLY.
YOU SURE AS HELL DID A *NUMBER* ON IT, THOUGH.
HOW'D YOU MANAGE TO *SHRED* IT LIKE THAT?
DUNNO. FELT LIKE I HIT SOMETHING, THEN A MILE OR SO LATER IT STARTED RIDING REAL ROUGH, SO I PULLED OVER.
WELL, IF YOU HAVEN'T BENT YOUR AXLE OR ANYTHING AND YOUR *SPARE'S* GOOD, IT SHOULDN'T BE A PROBLEM.
AXLE?
YEAH, *AXLE*. YOU KNOW, THE THING THE *WHEEL* GOES ON?
SORRY. NOT MUCH ON CARS.
WARRIOR
DIDN'T YOU AT LEAST EVER LEARN HOW TO CHANGE A TIRE?
NEVER HAD TO. I GOT TRIPLE A. BUT, UH... NO *CELL SIGNAL* OUT HERE.
WELL, YOU'RE ABOUT TO LEARN.

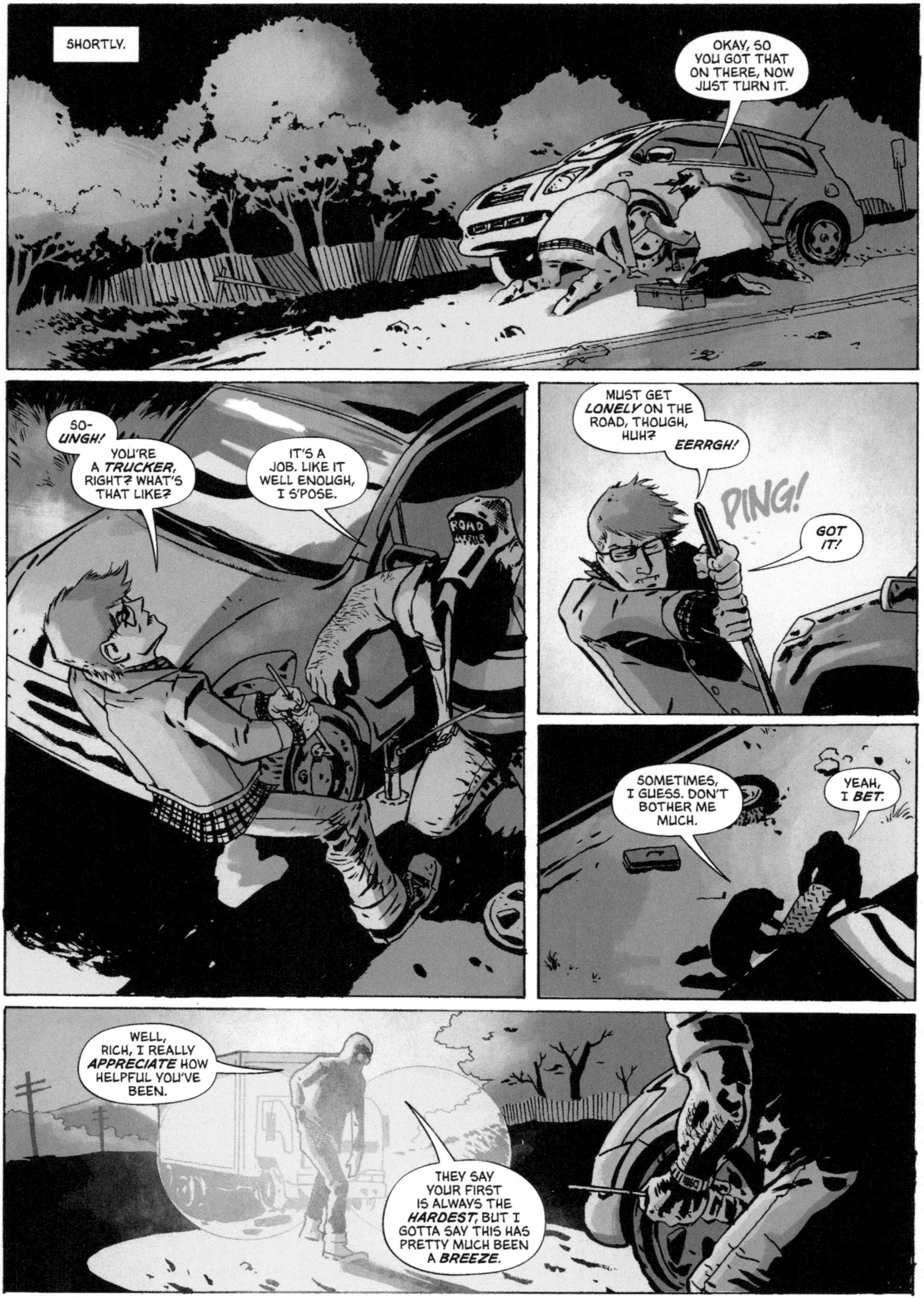
SHORTLY.
OKAY, SO YOU GOT THAT ON THERE, NOW JUST TURN IT.
SO- UNGH!
YOU'RE A TRUCKER, RIGHT? WHAT'S THAT LIKE?
IT'S A JOB. LIKE IT WELL ENOUGH, I S'POSE.
ROAD
MUST GET LONELY ON THE ROAD, THOUGH, HUH?
EERRGH!
PING!
GOT IT!
SOMETIMES, I GUESS. DON'T BOTHER ME MUCH.
YEAH, I BET.
WELL, RICH, I REALLY APPRECIATE HOW HELPFUL YOU'VE BEEN.
THEY SAY YOUR FIRST IS ALWAYS THE HARDEST, BUT I GOTTA SAY THIS HAS PRETTY MUCH BEEN A BREEZE.

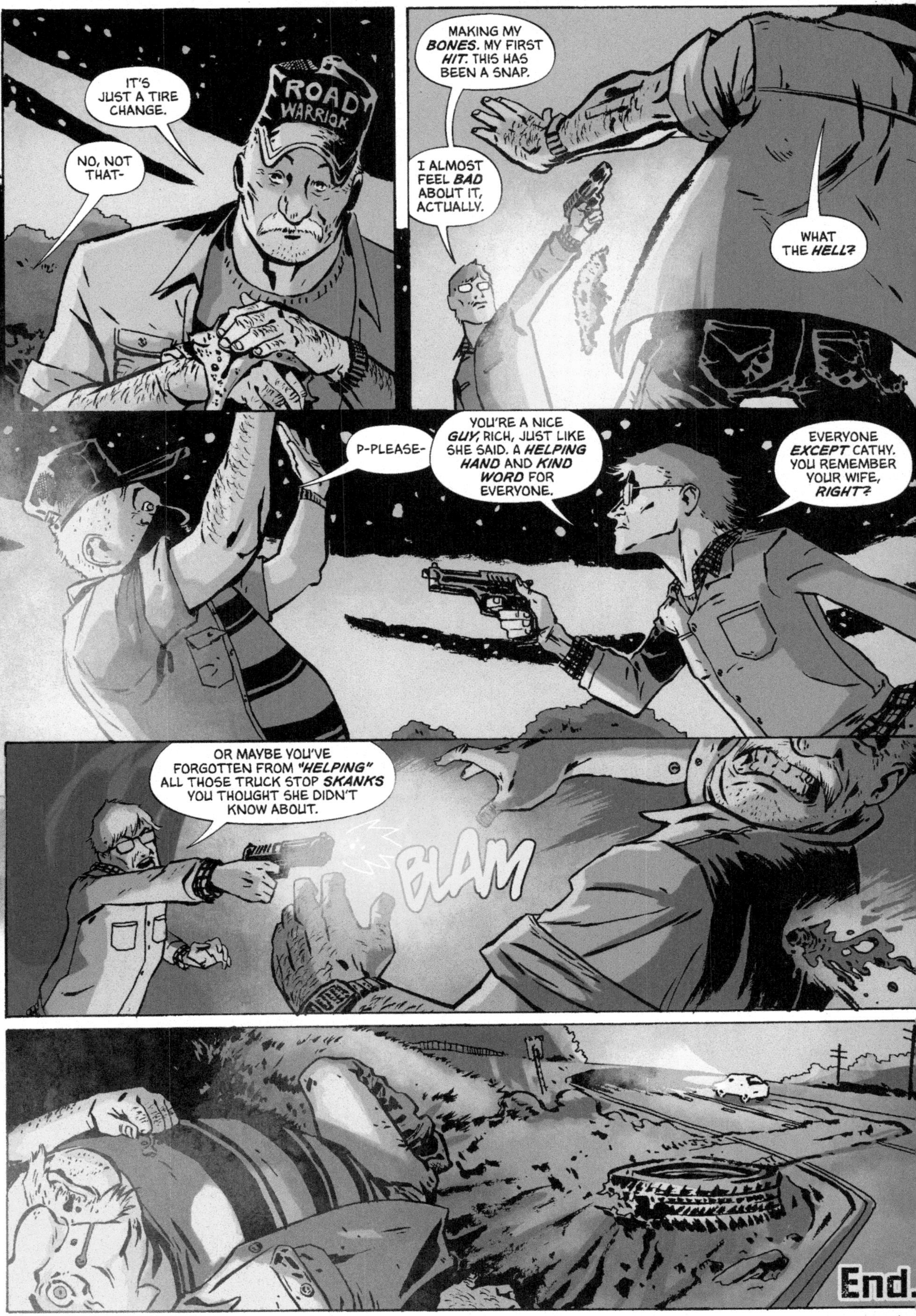
IT'S JUST A TIRE CHANGE.
NO, NOT THAT-
ROAD WARRIOR
MAKING MY BONES. MY FIRST HIT. THIS HAS BEEN A SNAP.
I ALMOST FEEL BAD ABOUT IT, ACTUALLY.
WHAT THE HELL?
P-PLEASE-
YOU'RE A NICE GUY, RICH, JUST LIKE SHE SAID. A HELPING HAND AND KIND WORD FOR EVERYONE.
EVERYONE EXCEPT CATHY. YOU REMEMBER YOUR WIFE, RIGHT?
OR MAYBE YOU'VE FORGOTTEN FROM "HELPING" ALL THOSE TRUCK STOP SKANKS YOU THOUGHT SHE DIDN'T KNOW ABOUT.
BLAM
End.

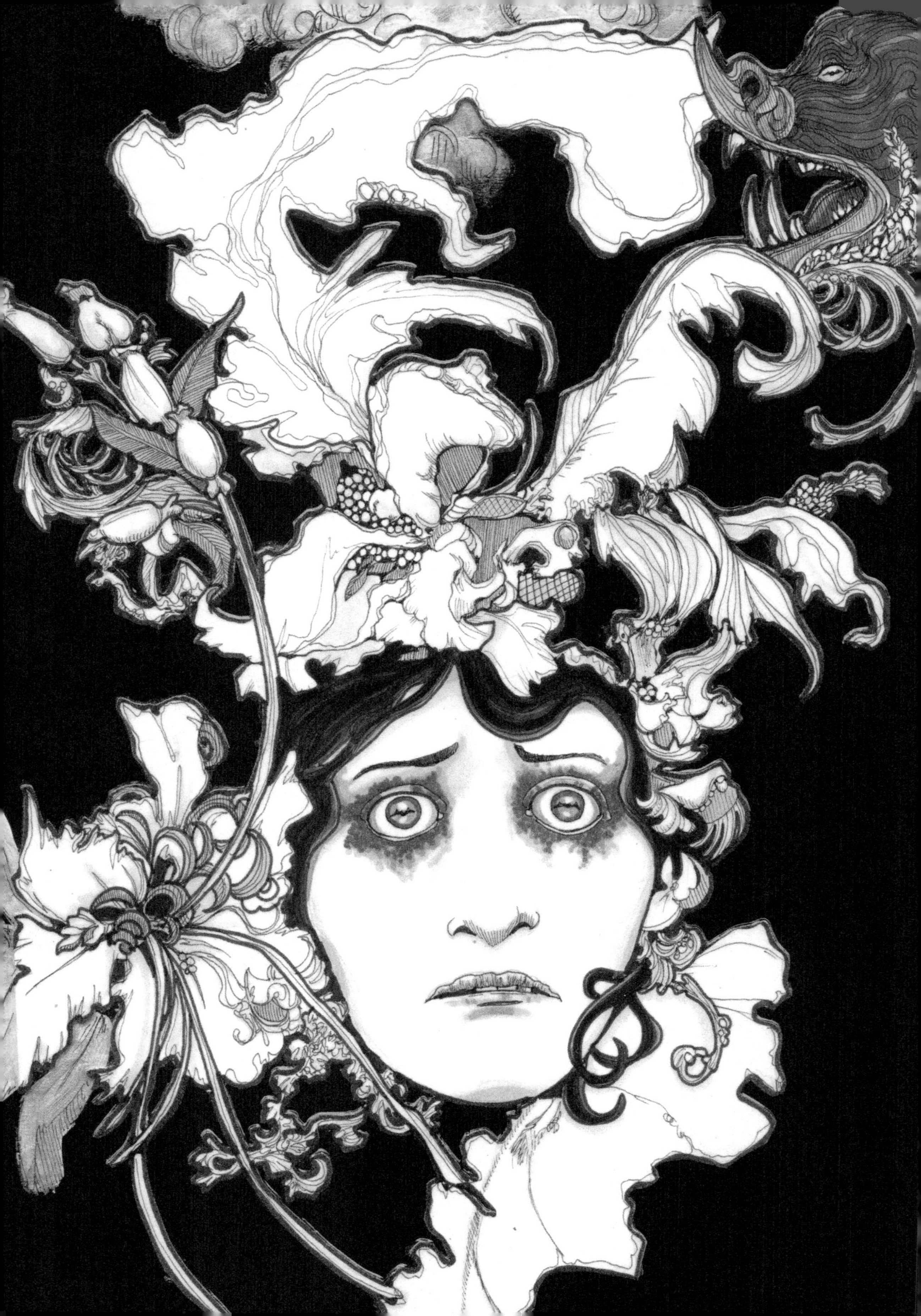

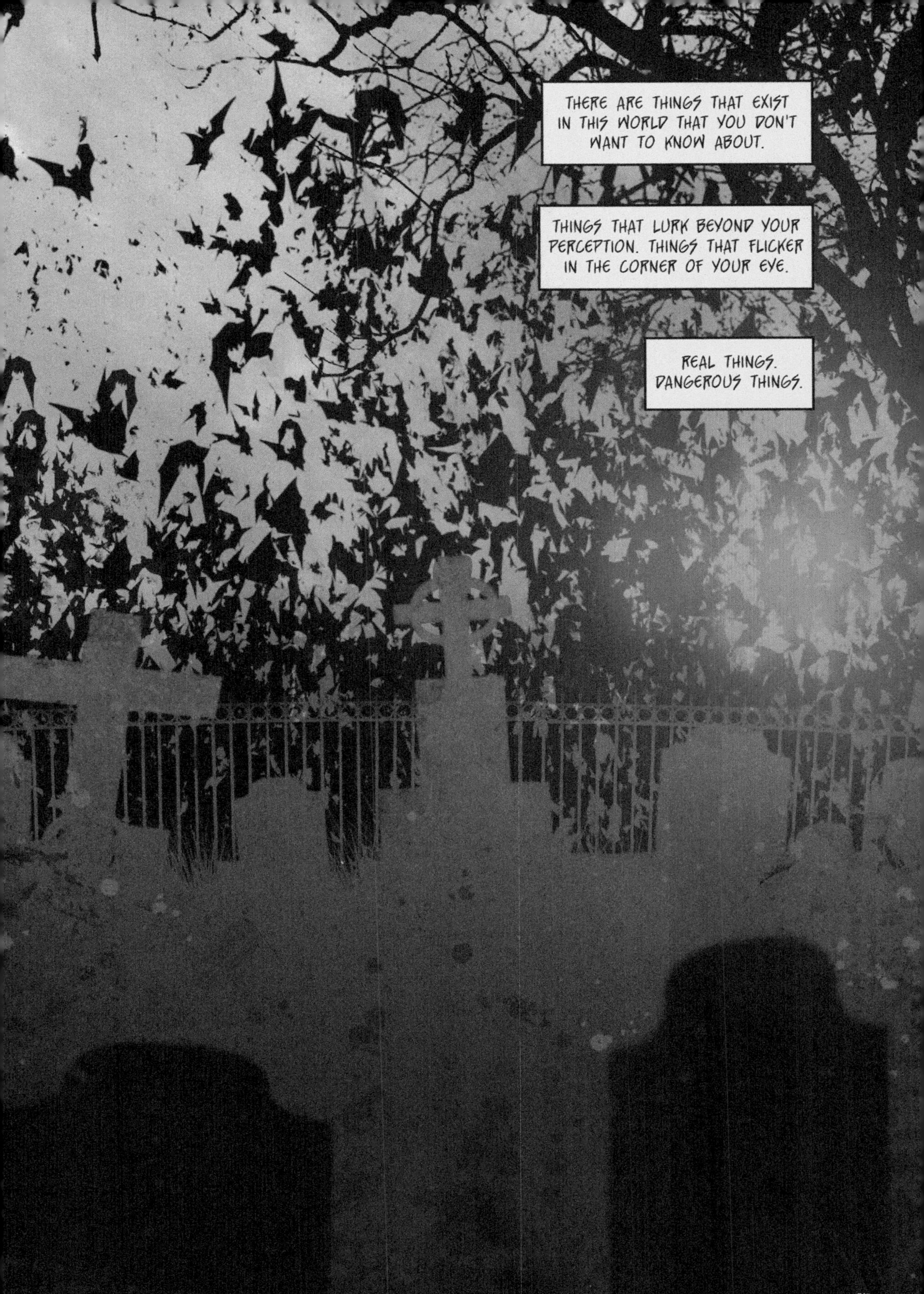

THERE ARE THINGS THAT EXIST IN THIS WORLD THAT YOU DON'T WANT TO KNOW ABOUT.
THINGS THAT LURK BEYOND YOUR PERCEPTION. THINGS THAT FLICKER IN THE CORNER OF YOUR EYE.
REAL THINGS. DANGEROUS THINGS.

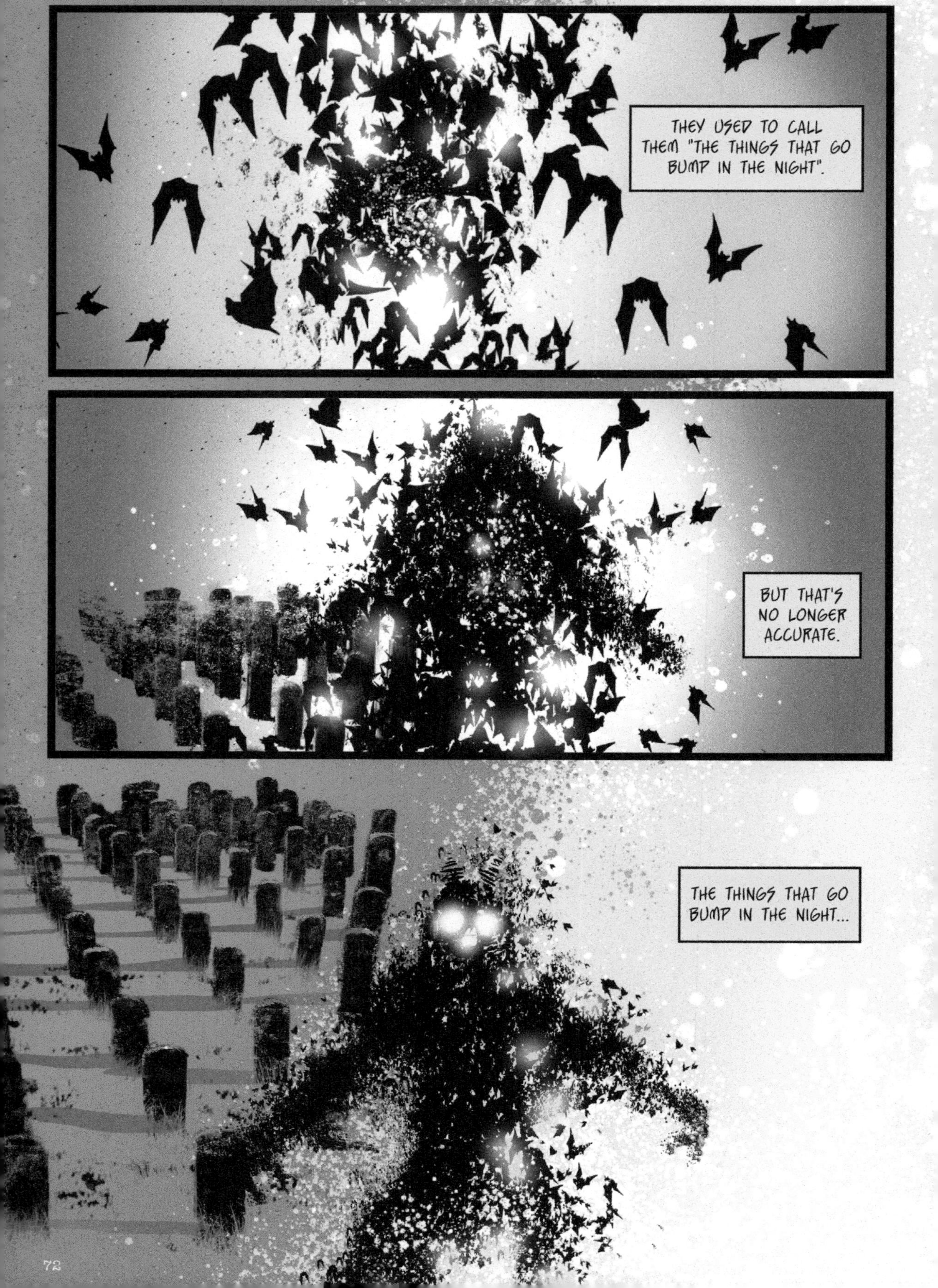
THEY USED TO CALL THEM "THE THINGS THAT GO BUMP IN THE NIGHT".
BUT THAT'S NO LONGER ACCURATE.
THE THINGS THAT GO BUMP IN THE NIGHT...

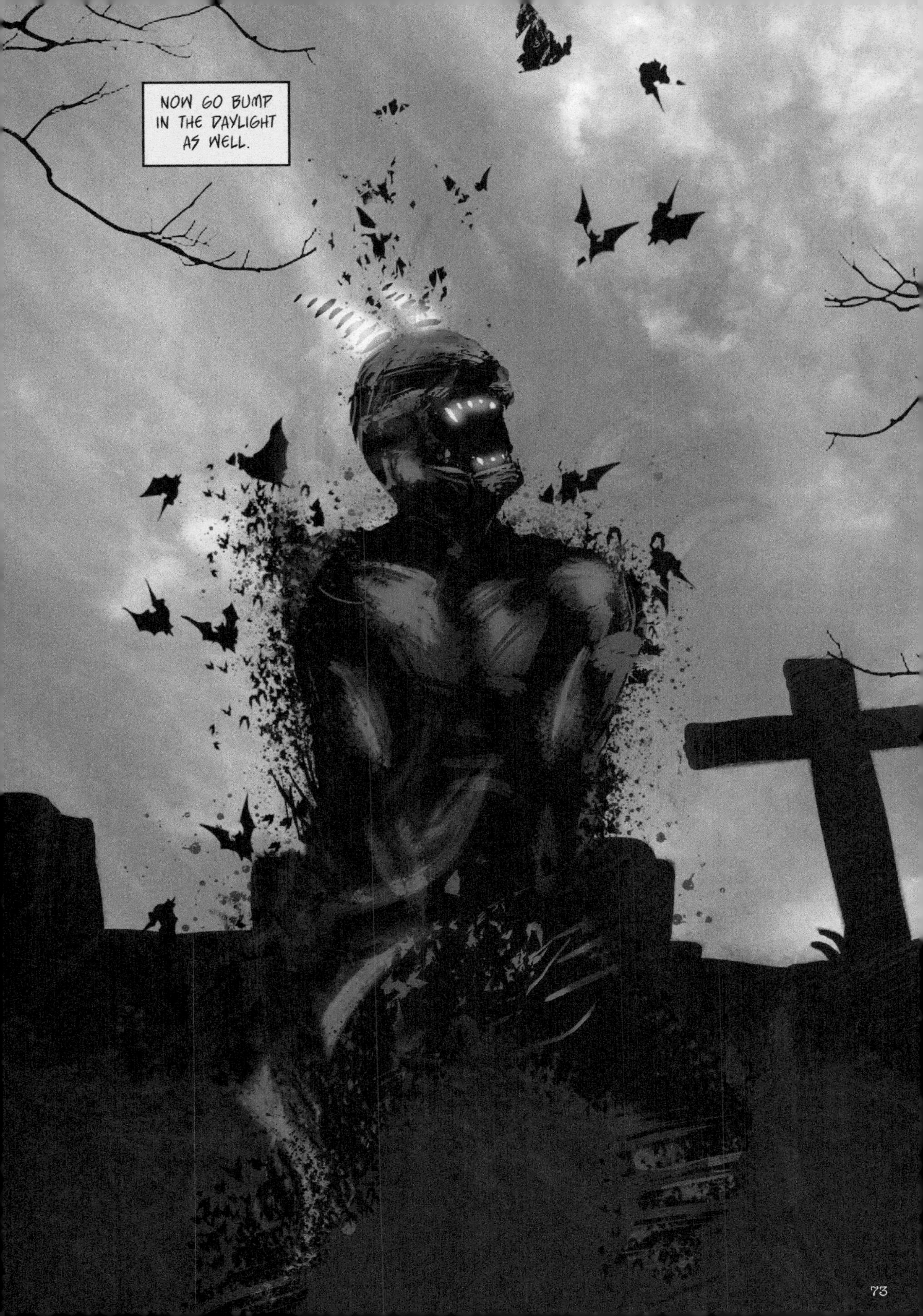
NOW GO BUMP IN THE DAYLIGHT AS WELL.

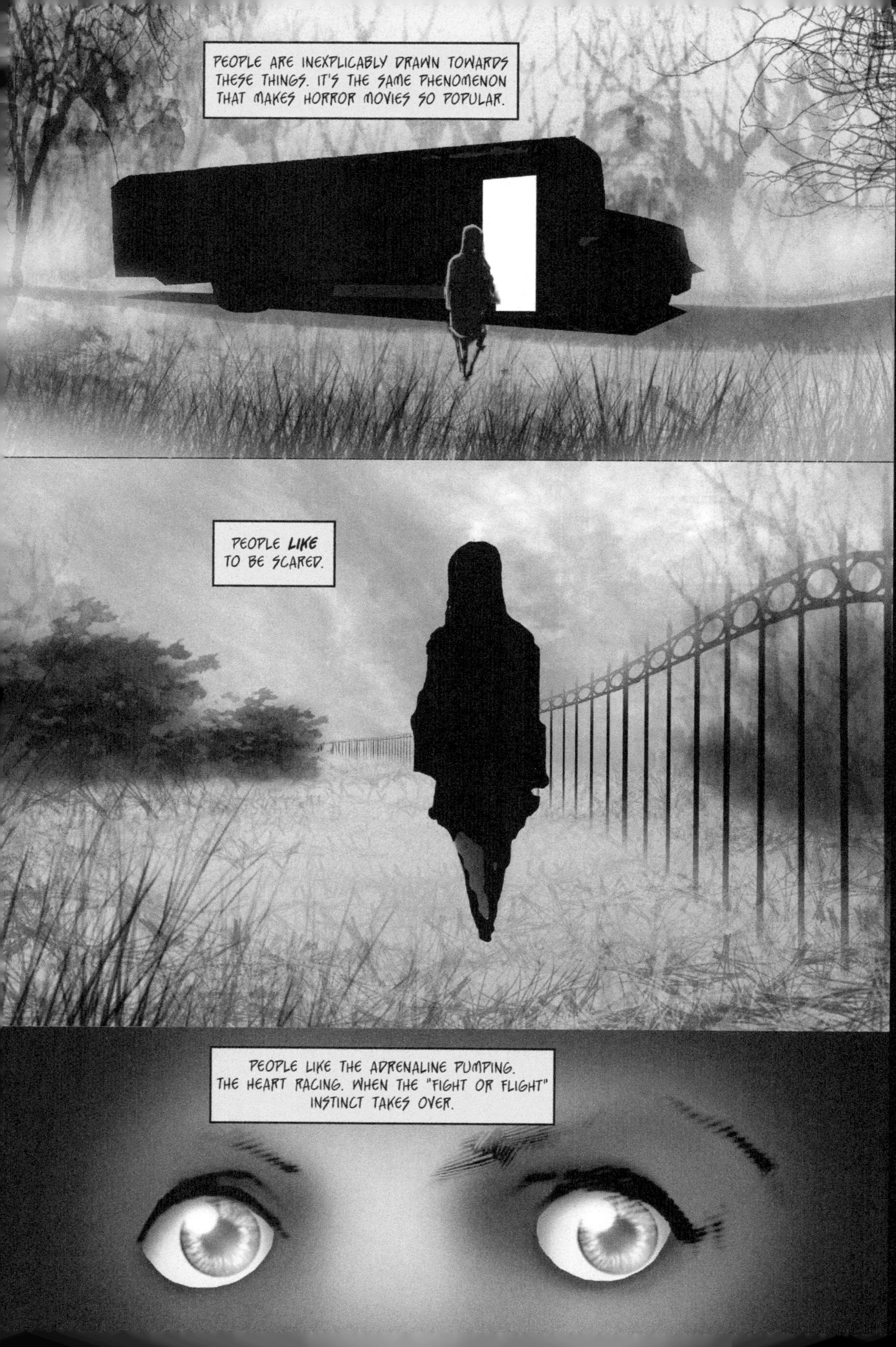
PEOPLE ARE INEXPLICABLY DRAWN TOWARDS THESE THINGS. IT'S THE SAME PHENOMENON THAT MAKES HORROR MOVIES SO POPULAR.
PEOPLE **LIKE** TO BE SCARED.
PEOPLE LIKE THE ADRENALINE PUMPING. THE HEART RACING. WHEN THE "FIGHT OR FLIGHT" INSTINCT TAKES OVER.

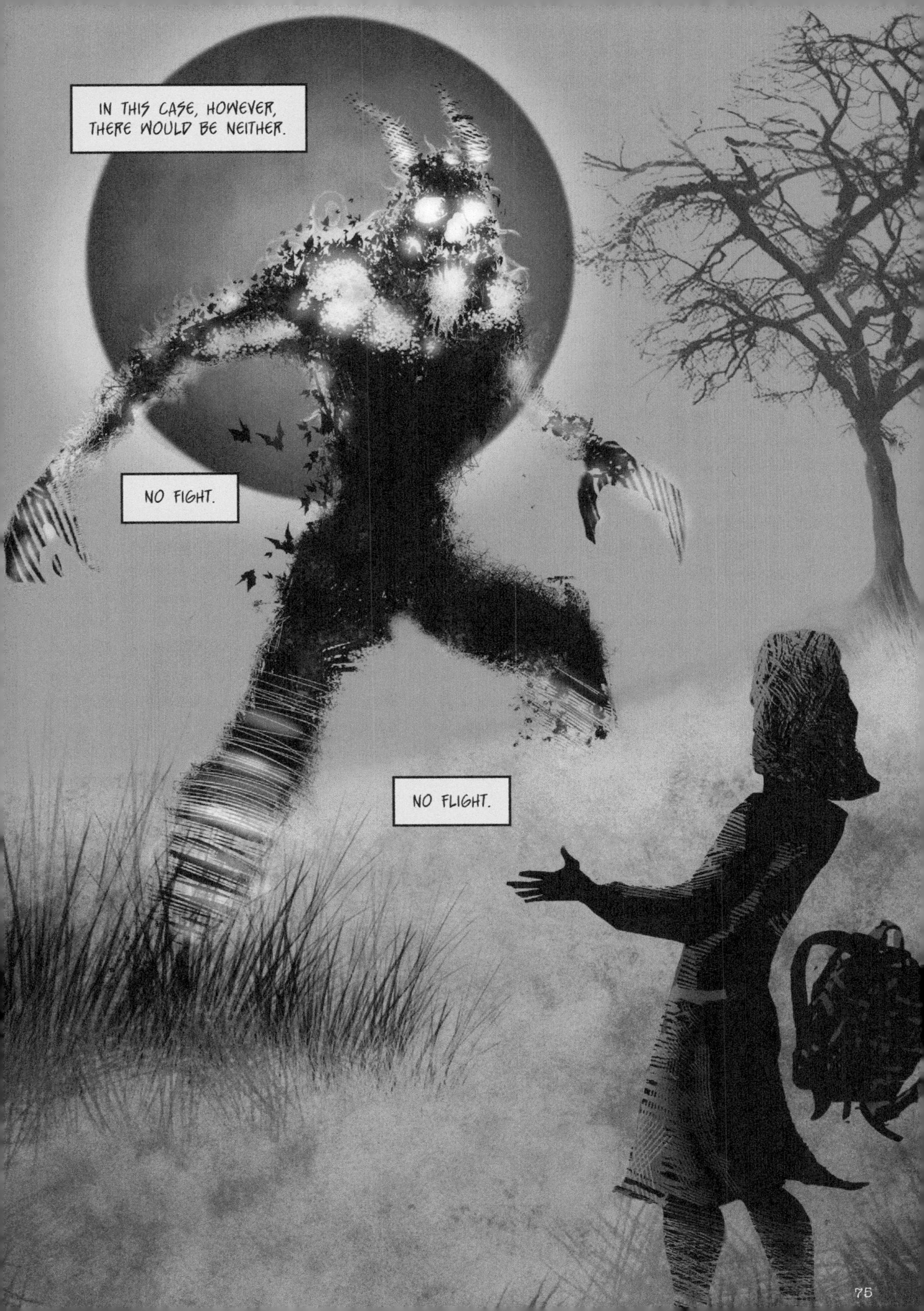
IN THIS CASE, HOWEVER, THERE WOULD BE NEITHER.
NO FIGHT.
NO FLIGHT.

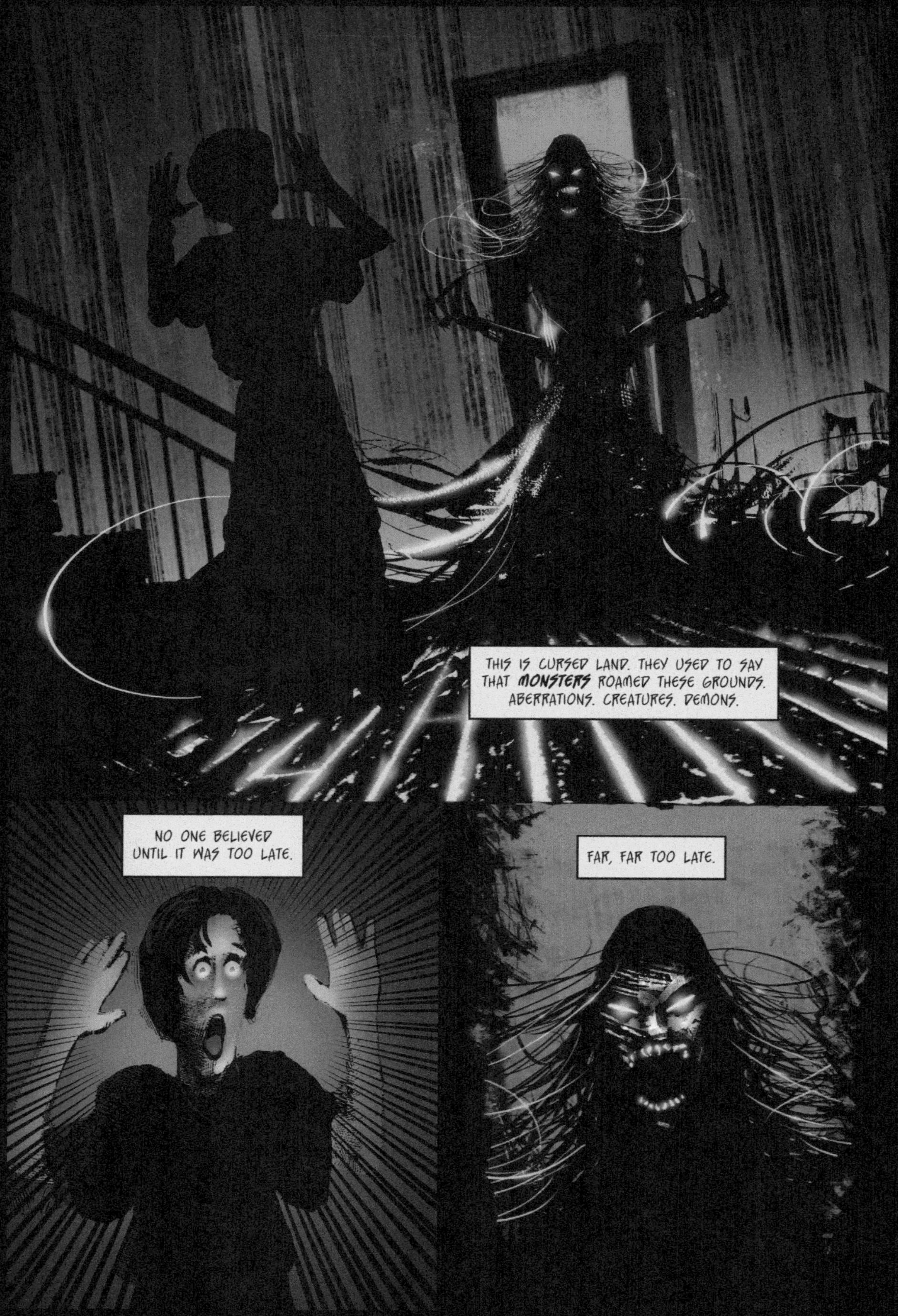
THIS IS CURSED LAND. THEY USED TO SAY THAT MONSTERS ROAMED THESE GROUNDS. ABERRATIONS. CREATURES. DEMONS.
NO ONE BELIEVED UNTIL IT WAS TOO LATE.
FAR, FAR TOO LATE.

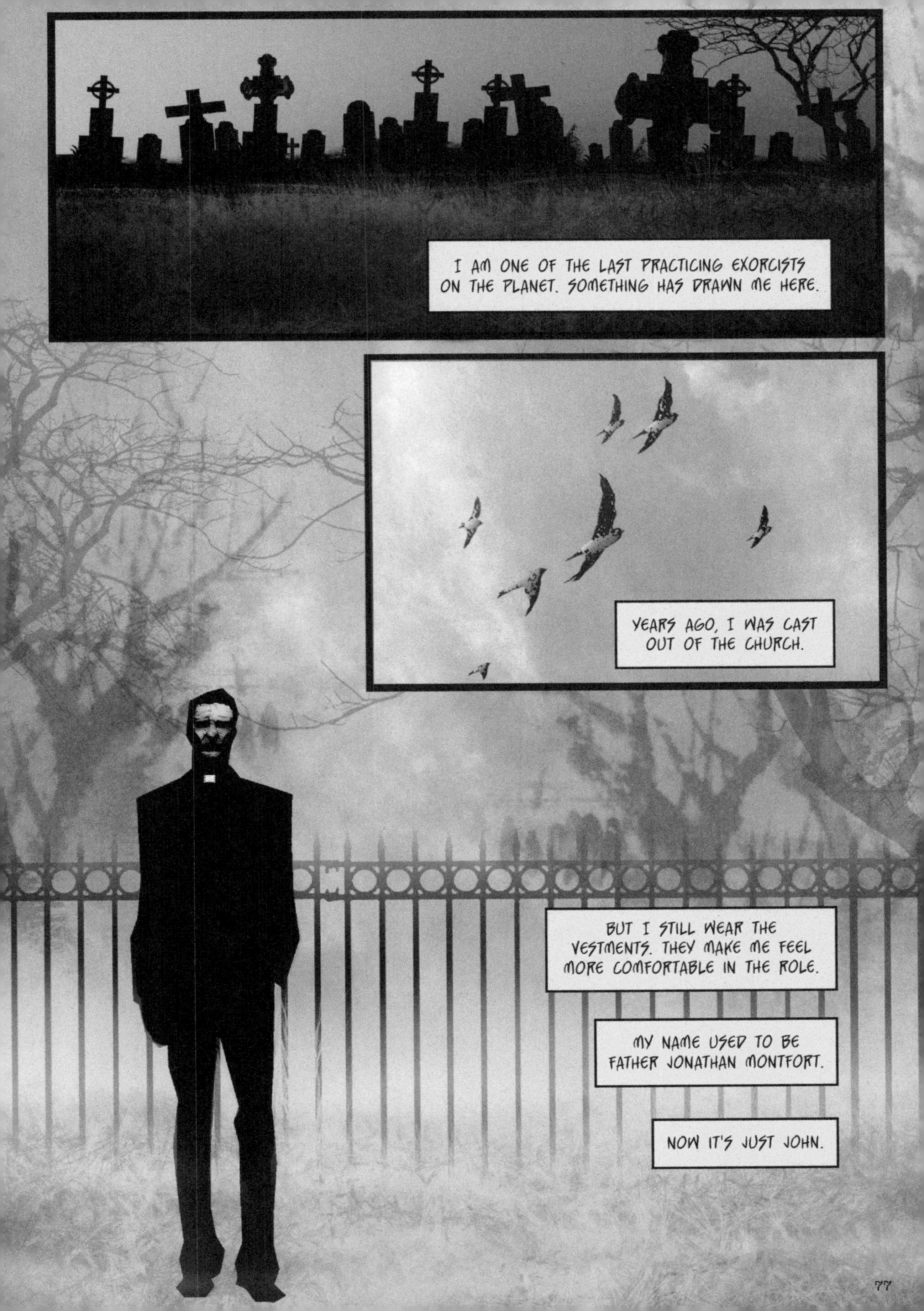
I AM ONE OF THE LAST PRACTICING EXORCISTS ON THE PLANET. SOMETHING HAS DRAWN ME HERE.
YEARS AGO, I WAS CAST OUT OF THE CHURCH.
BUT I STILL WEAR THE VESTMENTS. THEY MAKE ME FEEL MORE COMFORTABLE IN THE ROLE.
MY NAME USED TO BE FATHER JONATHAN MONTFORT.
NOW IT'S JUST JOHN.

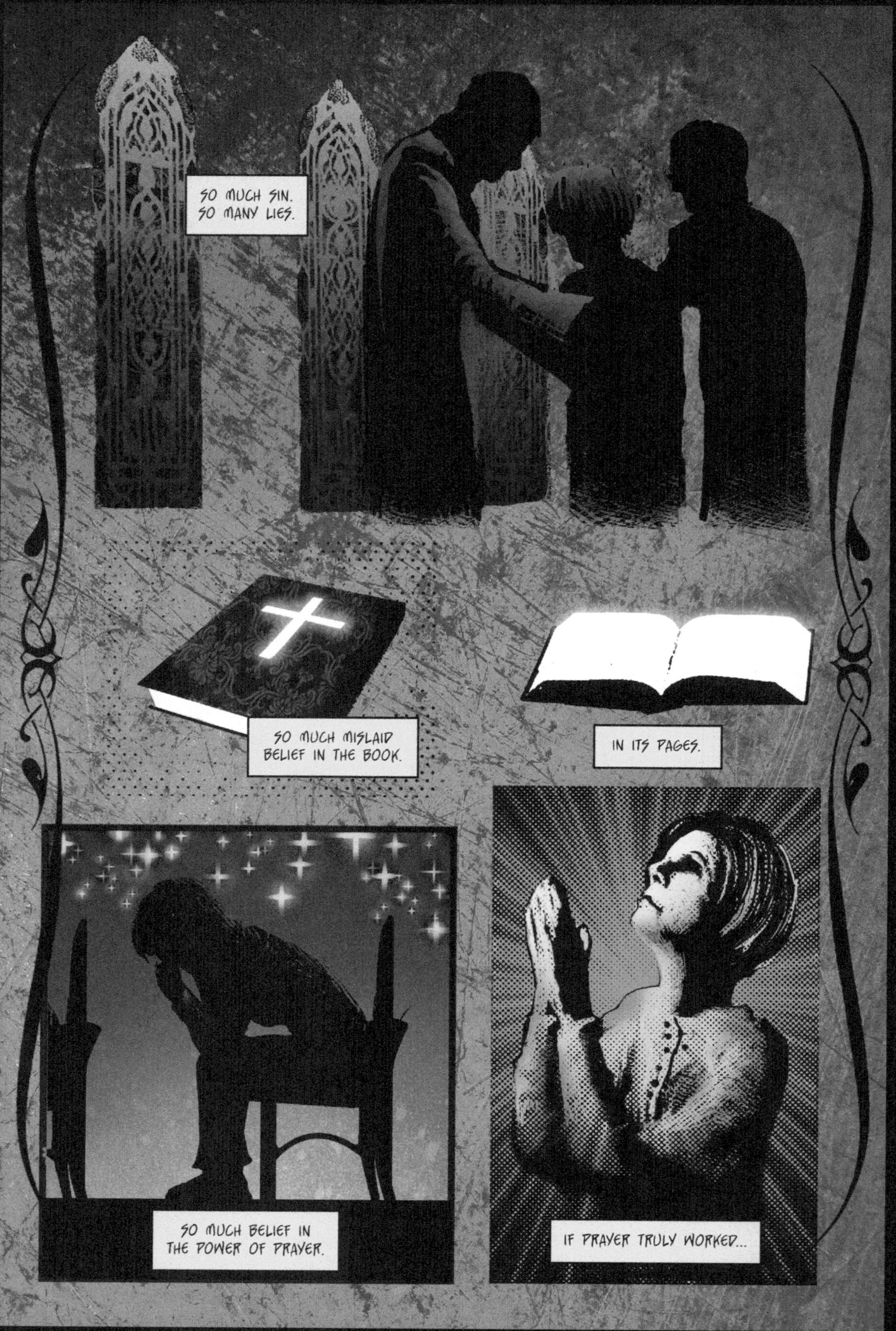
SO MUCH SIN.
SO MANY LIES.
SO MUCH MISLAID BELIEF IN THE BOOK.
IN ITS PAGES.
SO MUCH BELIEF IN THE POWER OF PRAYER.
IF PRAYER TRULY WORKED...

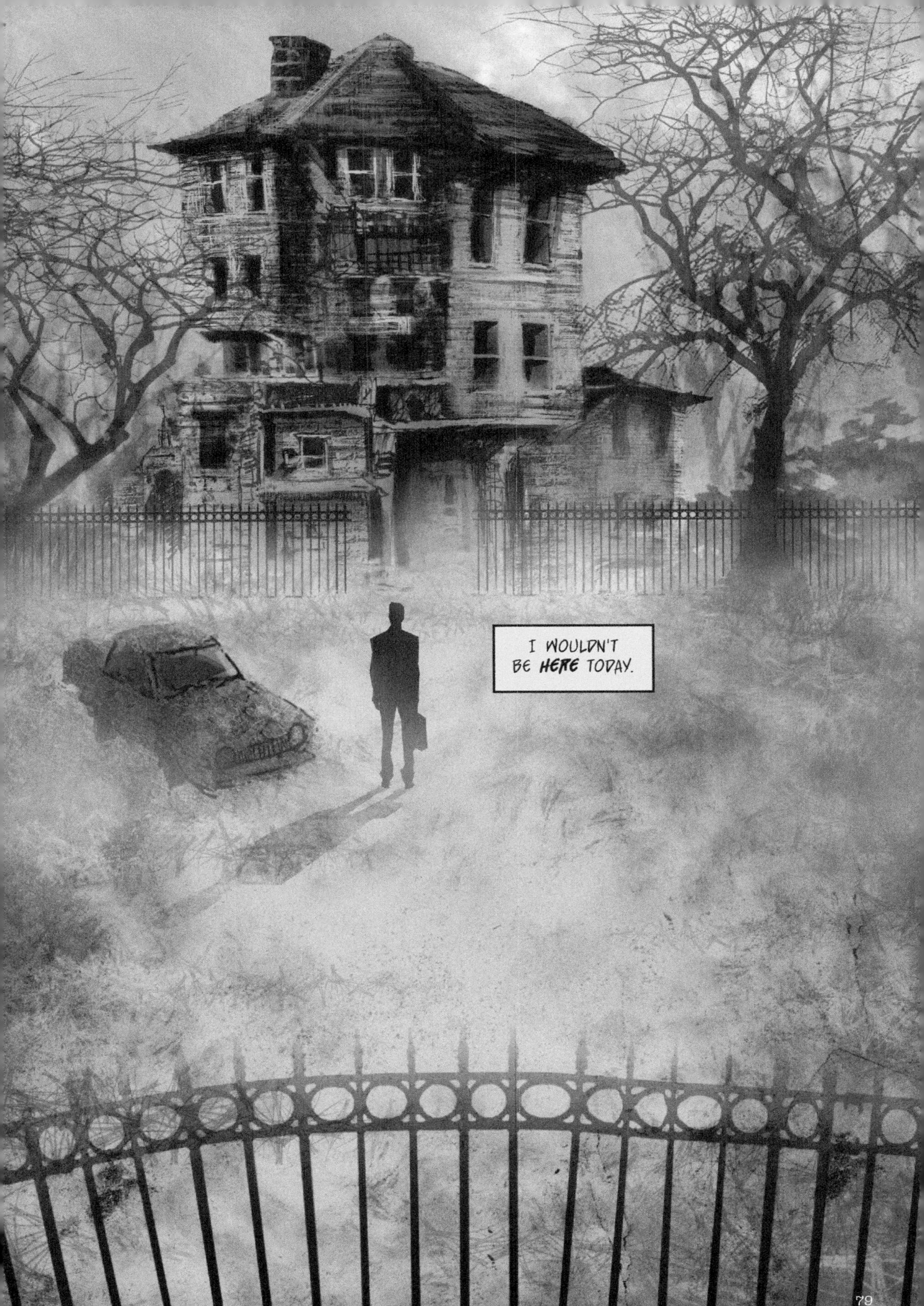
I WOULDN'T BE HERE TODAY.

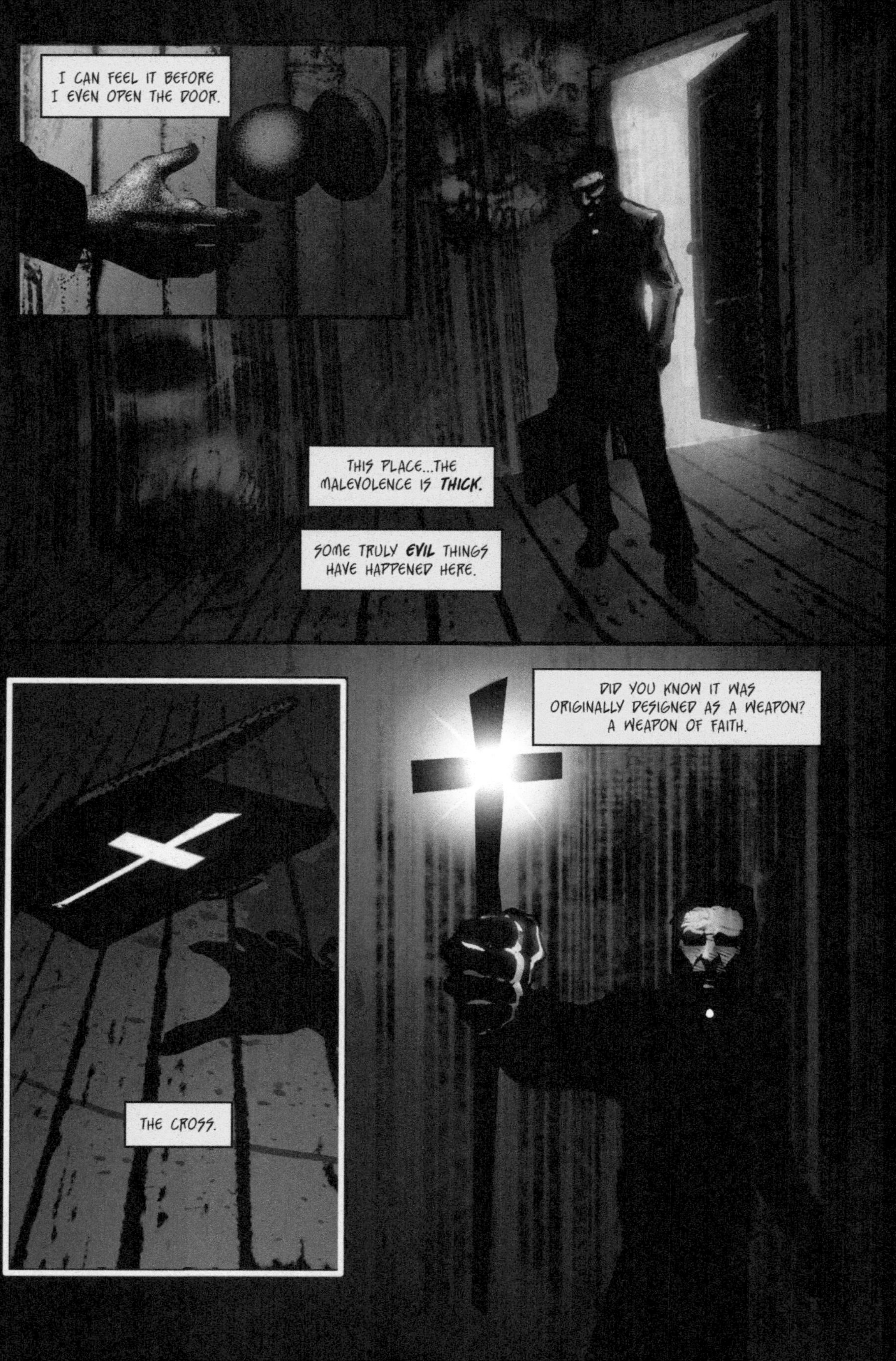
I CAN FEEL IT BEFORE I EVEN OPEN THE DOOR.
THIS PLACE...THE MALEVOLENCE IS THICK.
SOME TRULY EVIL THINGS HAVE HAPPENED HERE.
THE CROSS.
DID YOU KNOW IT WAS ORIGINALLY DESIGNED AS A WEAPON? A WEAPON OF FAITH.

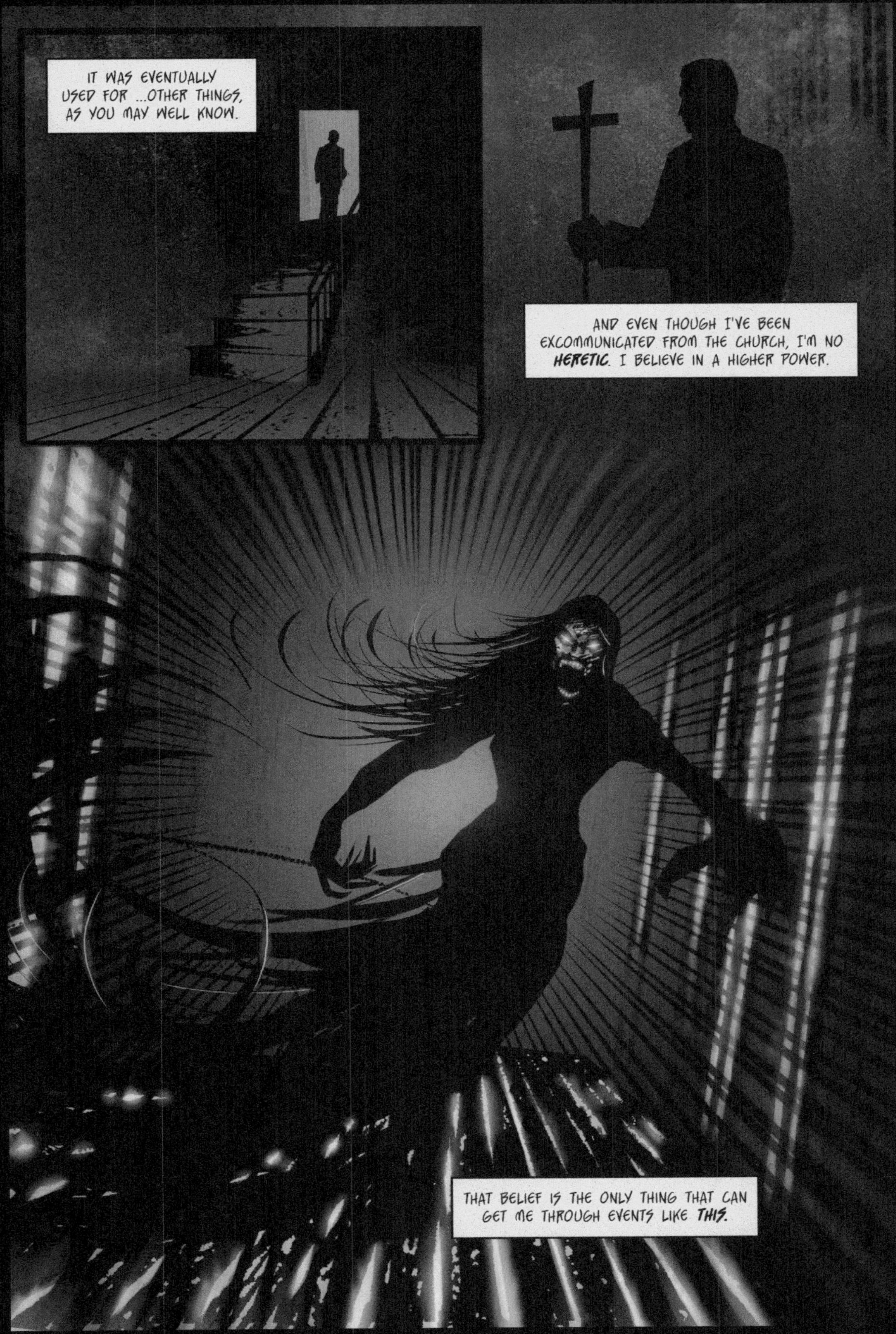
IT WAS EVENTUALLY USED FOR ...OTHER THINGS, AS YOU MAY WELL KNOW.
AND EVEN THOUGH I'VE BEEN EXCOMMUNICATED FROM THE CHURCH, I'M NO **HERETIC**. I BELIEVE IN A HIGHER POWER.
THAT BELIEF IS THE ONLY THING THAT CAN GET ME THROUGH EVENTS LIKE **THIS**.

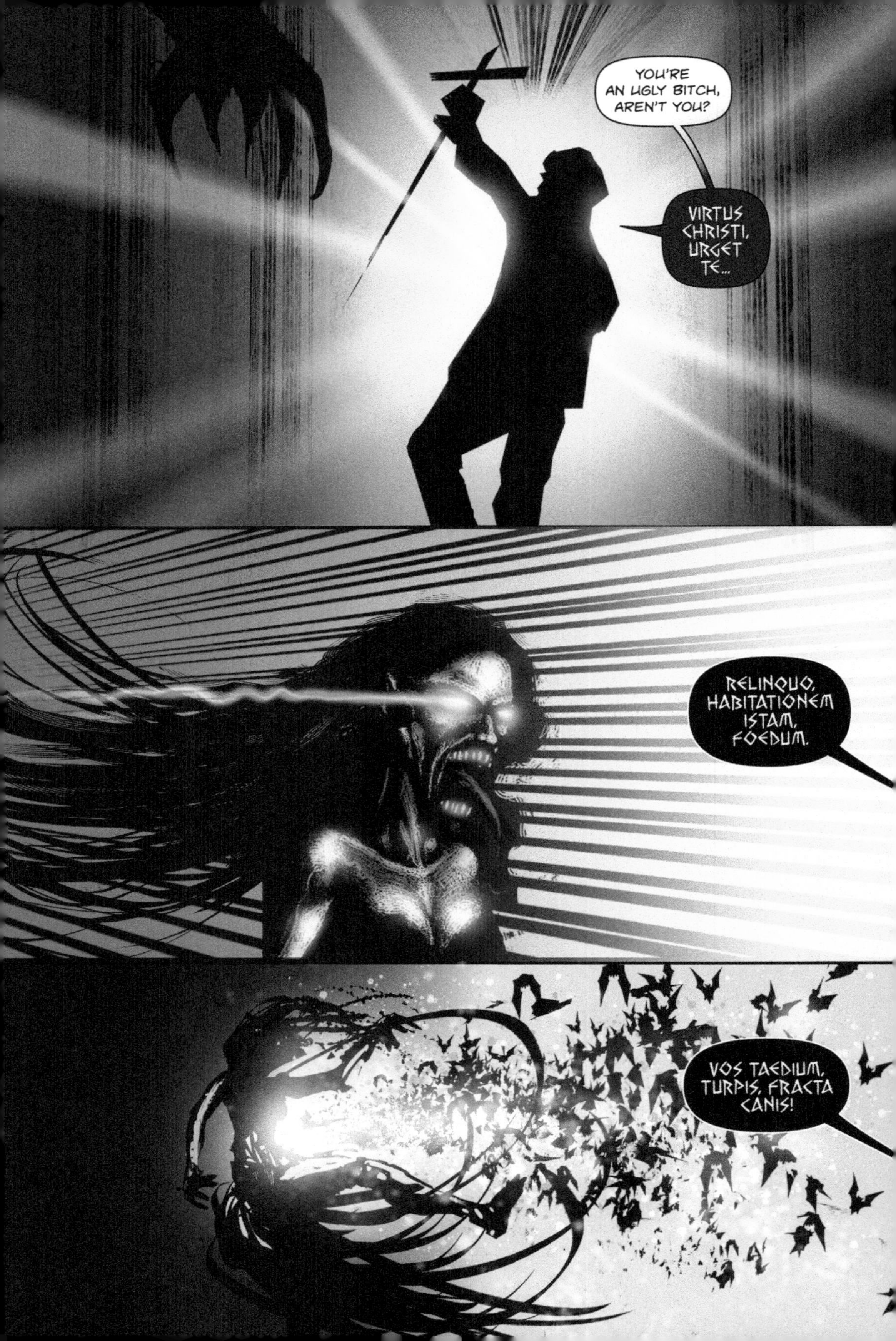
YOU'RE AN UGLY BITCH, AREN'T YOU?
VIRTUS CHRISTI, URGET TE...
RELINQUO, HABITATIONEM ISTAM, FOEDUM.
VOS TAEDIUM, TURPIS, FRACTA CANIS!

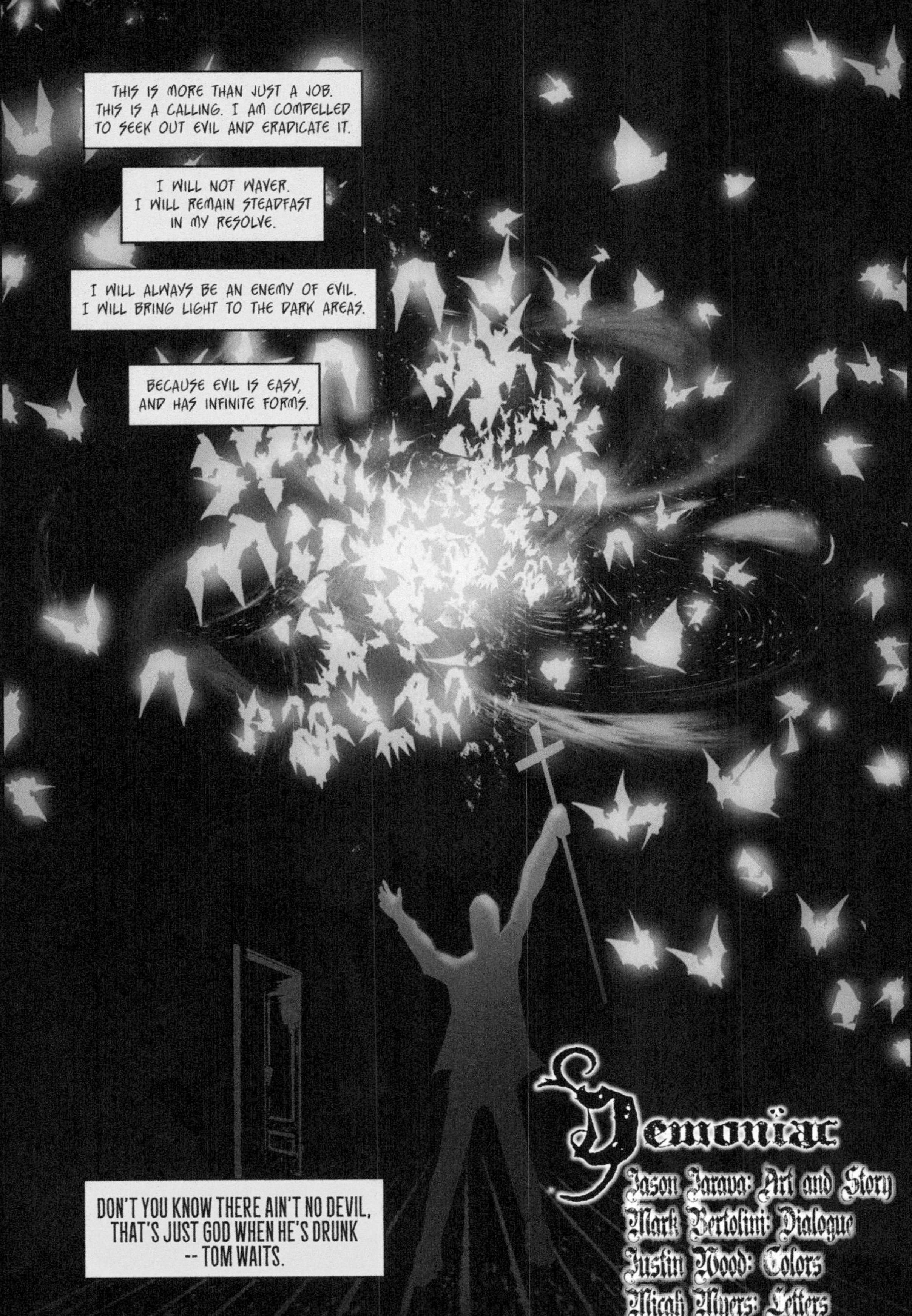
THIS IS MORE THAN JUST A JOB. THIS IS A CALLING. I AM COMPELLED TO SEEK OUT EVIL AND ERADICATE IT.
I WILL NOT WAVER. I WILL REMAIN STEADFAST IN MY RESOLVE.
I WILL ALWAYS BE AN ENEMY OF EVIL. I WILL BRING LIGHT TO THE DARK AREAS.
BECAUSE EVIL IS EASY, AND HAS INFINITE FORMS.
DON'T YOU KNOW THERE AIN'T NO DEVIL, THAT'S JUST GOD WHEN HE'S DRUNK -- TOM WAITS.
Demoniac
Jason Jarava: Art and Story
Mark Bertolini: Dialogue
Justin Wood: Colors
Micah Myers: Letters

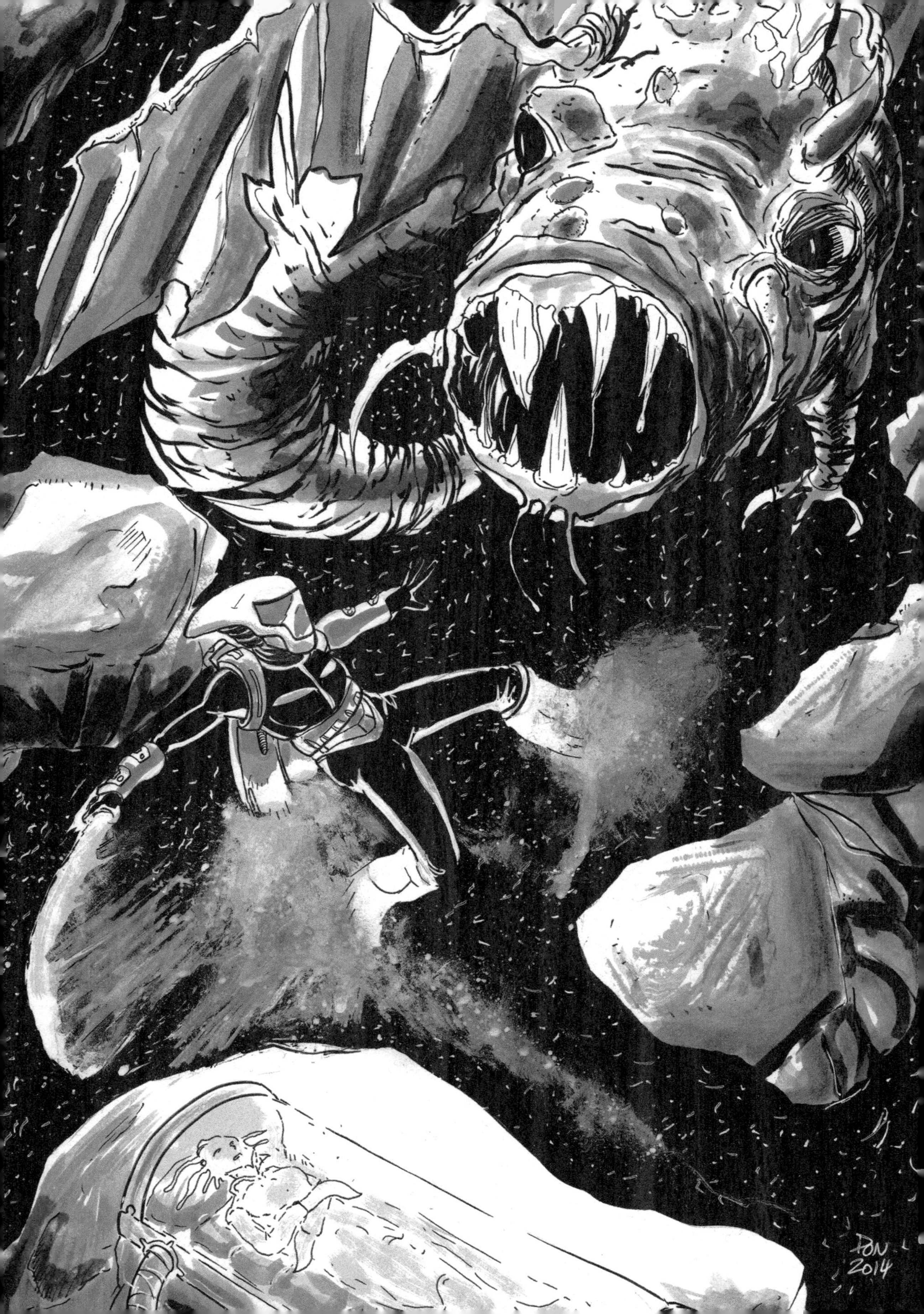
DON
2014

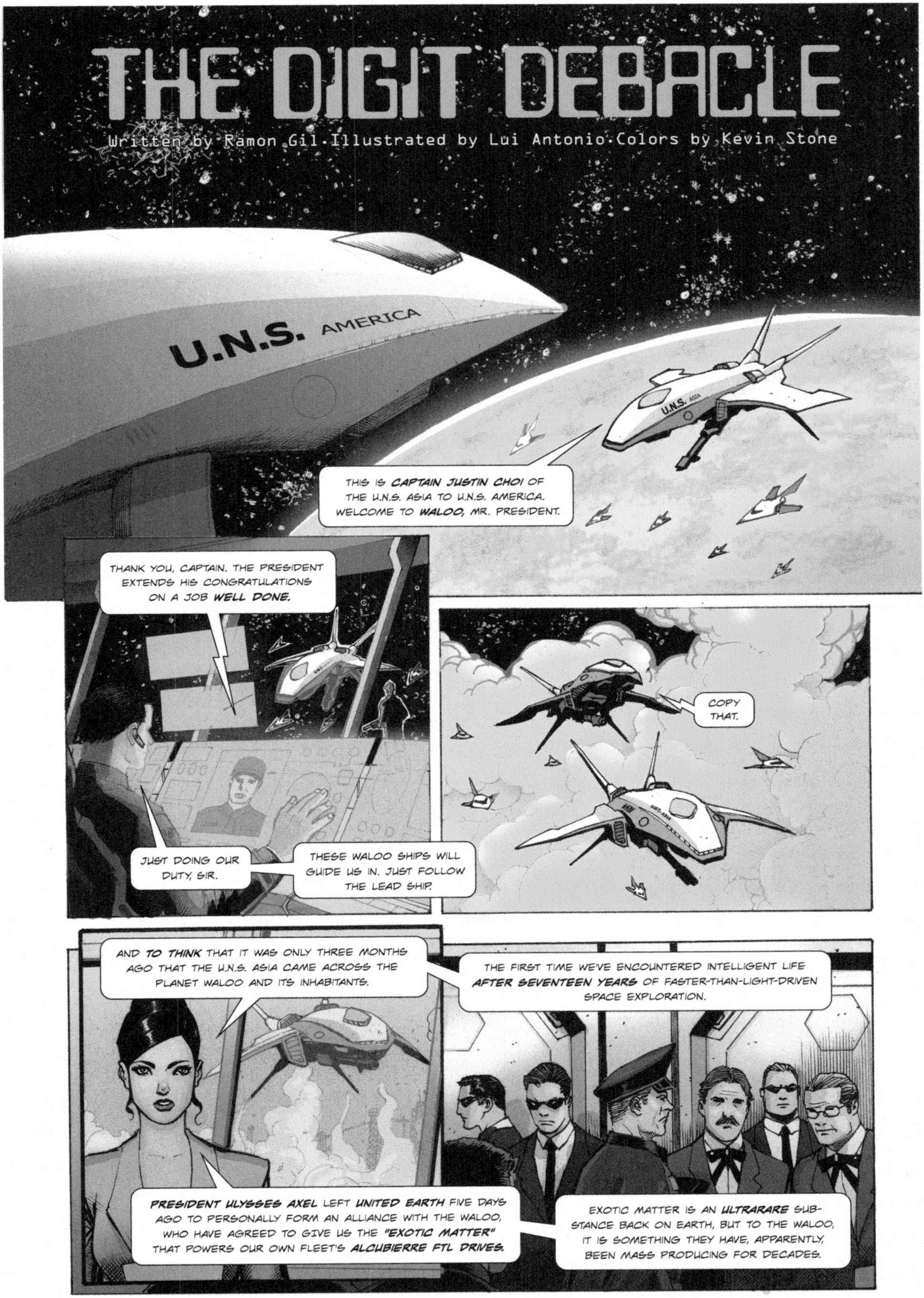
THE DIGIT DEBACLE
Written by Ramon Gil · Illustrated by Lui Antonio · Colors by Kevin Stone
U.N.S. AMERICA
U.N.S. ASIA
THIS IS CAPTAIN JUSTIN CHOI OF THE U.N.S. ASIA TO U.N.S. AMERICA. WELCOME TO WALOO, MR. PRESIDENT.
THANK YOU, CAPTAIN. THE PRESIDENT EXTENDS HIS CONGRATULATIONS ON A JOB WELL DONE.
JUST DOING OUR DUTY, SIR.
THESE WALOO SHIPS WILL GUIDE US IN. JUST FOLLOW THE LEAD SHIP.
COPY THAT.
AND TO THINK THAT IT WAS ONLY THREE MONTHS AGO THAT THE U.N.S. ASIA CAME ACROSS THE PLANET WALOO AND ITS INHABITANTS.
THE FIRST TIME WE'VE ENCOUNTERED INTELLIGENT LIFE AFTER SEVENTEEN YEARS OF FASTER-THAN-LIGHT-DRIVEN SPACE EXPLORATION.
PRESIDENT ULYSSES AXEL LEFT UNITED EARTH FIVE DAYS AGO TO PERSONALLY FORM AN ALLIANCE WITH THE WALOO, WHO HAVE AGREED TO GIVE US THE "EXOTIC MATTER" THAT POWERS OUR OWN FLEET'S ALCUBIERRE FTL DRIVES.
EXOTIC MATTER IS AN ULTRARARE SUBSTANCE BACK ON EARTH, BUT TO THE WALOO, IT IS SOMETHING THEY HAVE, APPARENTLY, BEEN MASS PRODUCING FOR DECADES.

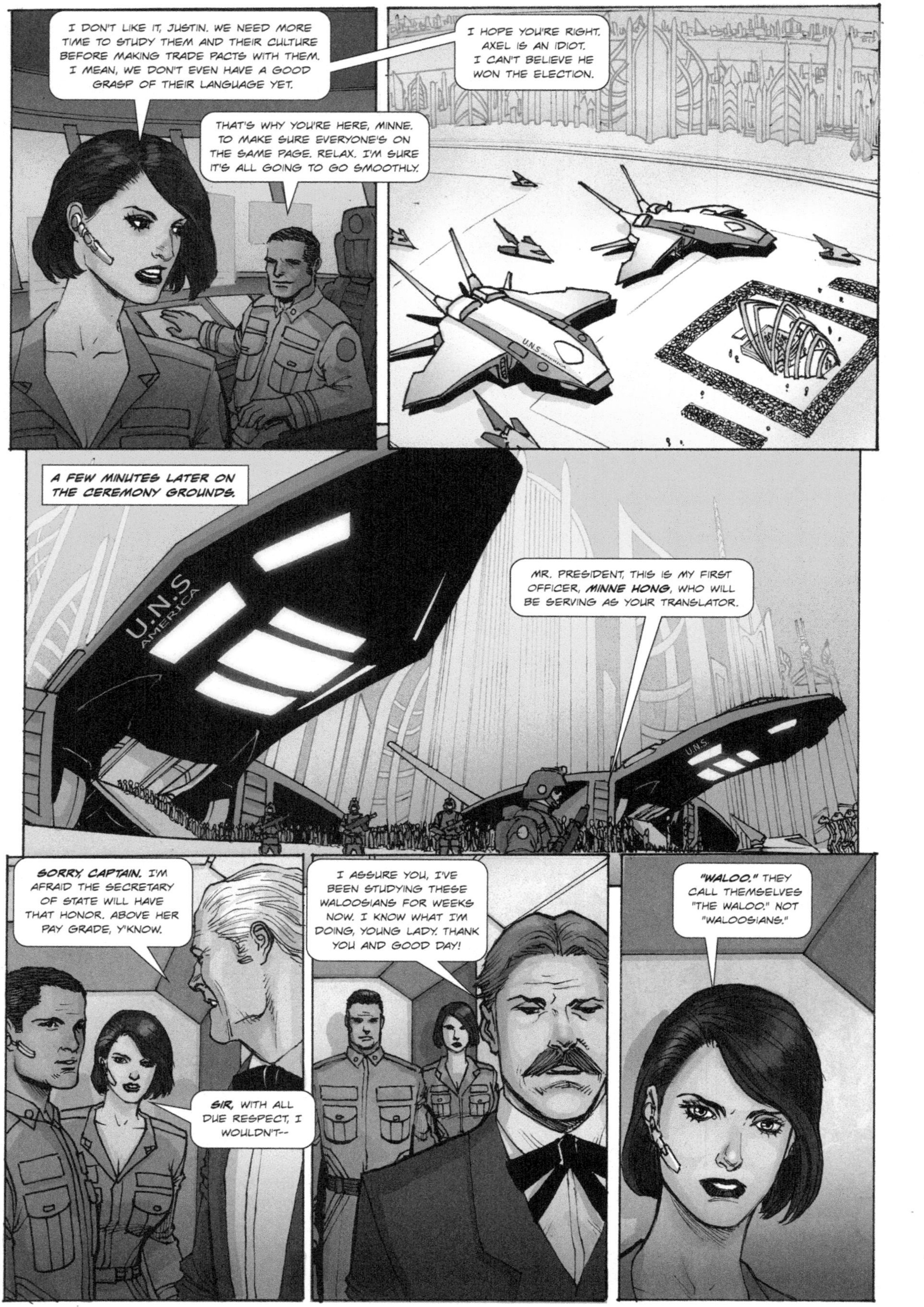
I DON'T LIKE IT, JUSTIN. WE NEED MORE TIME TO STUDY THEM AND THEIR CULTURE BEFORE MAKING TRADE PACTS WITH THEM. I MEAN, WE DON'T EVEN HAVE A GOOD GRASP OF THEIR LANGUAGE YET.
THAT'S WHY YOU'RE HERE, MINNE. TO MAKE SURE EVERYONE'S ON THE SAME PAGE. RELAX. I'M SURE IT'S ALL GOING TO GO SMOOTHLY.
I HOPE YOU'RE RIGHT. AXEL IS AN IDIOT. I CAN'T BELIEVE HE WON THE ELECTION.
U.N.S AMERICA
A FEW MINUTES LATER ON THE CEREMONY GROUNDS.
U.N.S AMERICA
MR. PRESIDENT, THIS IS MY FIRST OFFICER, MINNE HONG, WHO WILL BE SERVING AS YOUR TRANSLATOR.
U.N.S.
SORRY, CAPTAIN. I'M AFRAID THE SECRETARY OF STATE WILL HAVE THAT HONOR. ABOVE HER PAY GRADE, Y'KNOW.
SIR, WITH ALL DUE RESPECT, I WOULDN'T--
I ASSURE YOU, I'VE BEEN STUDYING THESE WALOOSIANS FOR WEEKS NOW. I KNOW WHAT I'M DOING, YOUNG LADY. THANK YOU AND GOOD DAY!
"WALOO." THEY CALL THEMSELVES "THE WALOO." NOT "WALOOSIANS."

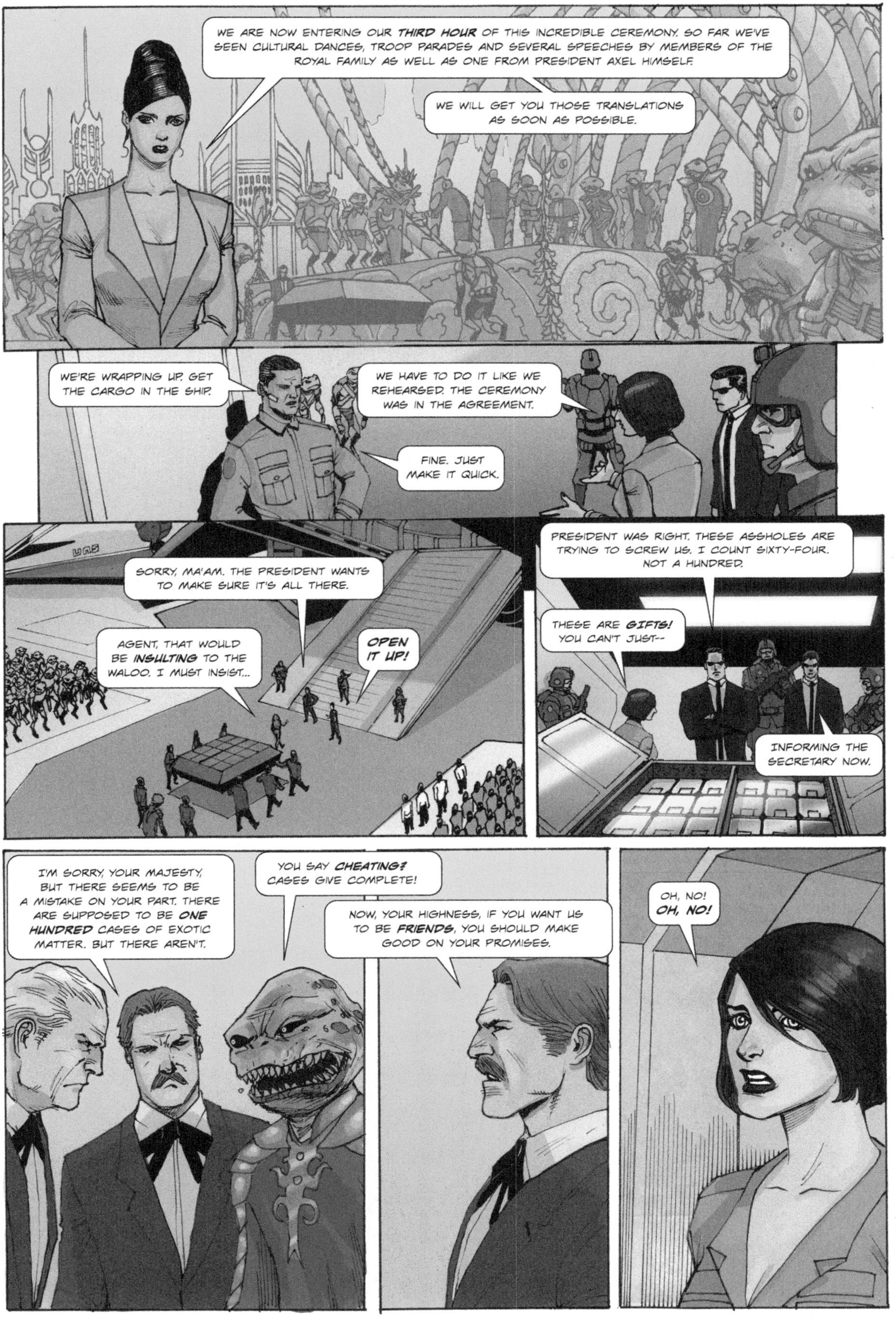

WE ARE NOW ENTERING OUR **THIRD HOUR** OF THIS INCREDIBLE CEREMONY. SO FAR WE'VE SEEN CULTURAL DANCES, TROOP PARADES AND SEVERAL SPEECHES BY MEMBERS OF THE ROYAL FAMILY AS WELL AS ONE FROM PRESIDENT AXEL HIMSELF.
WE WILL GET YOU THOSE TRANSLATIONS AS SOON AS POSSIBLE.
WE'RE WRAPPING UP. GET THE CARGO IN THE SHIP.
WE HAVE TO DO IT LIKE WE REHEARSED. THE CEREMONY WAS IN THE AGREEMENT.
FINE. JUST MAKE IT QUICK.
SORRY, MA'AM. THE PRESIDENT WANTS TO MAKE SURE IT'S ALL THERE.
AGENT, THAT WOULD BE **INSULTING** TO THE WALOO. I MUST INSIST...
OPEN IT UP!
PRESIDENT WAS RIGHT. THESE ASSHOLES ARE TRYING TO SCREW US. I COUNT SIXTY-FOUR. NOT A HUNDRED.
THESE ARE **GIFTS!** YOU CAN'T JUST--
INFORMING THE SECRETARY NOW.
I'M SORRY, YOUR MAJESTY, BUT THERE SEEMS TO BE A MISTAKE ON YOUR PART. THERE ARE SUPPOSED TO BE **ONE HUNDRED** CASES OF EXOTIC MATTER. BUT THERE AREN'T.
YOU SAY **CHEATING?** CASES GIVE COMPLETE!
NOW, YOUR HIGHNESS, IF YOU WANT US TO BE **FRIENDS**, YOU SHOULD MAKE GOOD ON YOUR PROMISES.
OH, NO! **OH, NO!**

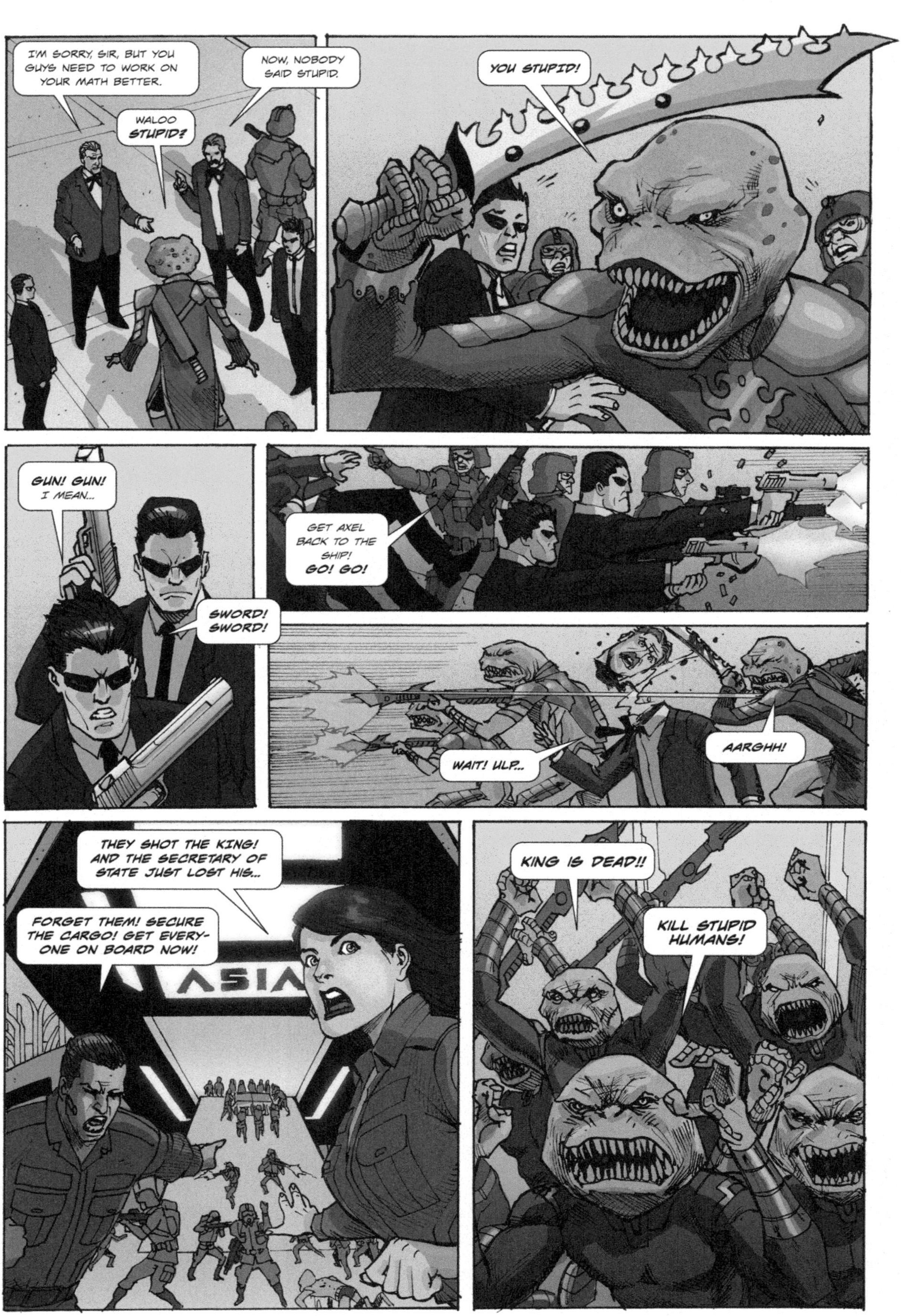

I'M SORRY, SIR, BUT YOU GUYS NEED TO WORK ON YOUR MATH BETTER.
WALOO STUPID?
NOW, NOBODY SAID STUPID.
YOU STUPID!
GUN! GUN! I MEAN...
SWORD! SWORD!
GET AXEL BACK TO THE SHIP! GO! GO!
WAIT! ULP...
AARGHH!
THEY SHOT THE KING! AND THE SECRETARY OF STATE JUST LOST HIS...
FORGET THEM! SECURE THE CARGO! GET EVERY-ONE ON BOARD NOW!
ASIA
KING IS DEAD!!
KILL STUPID HUMANS!

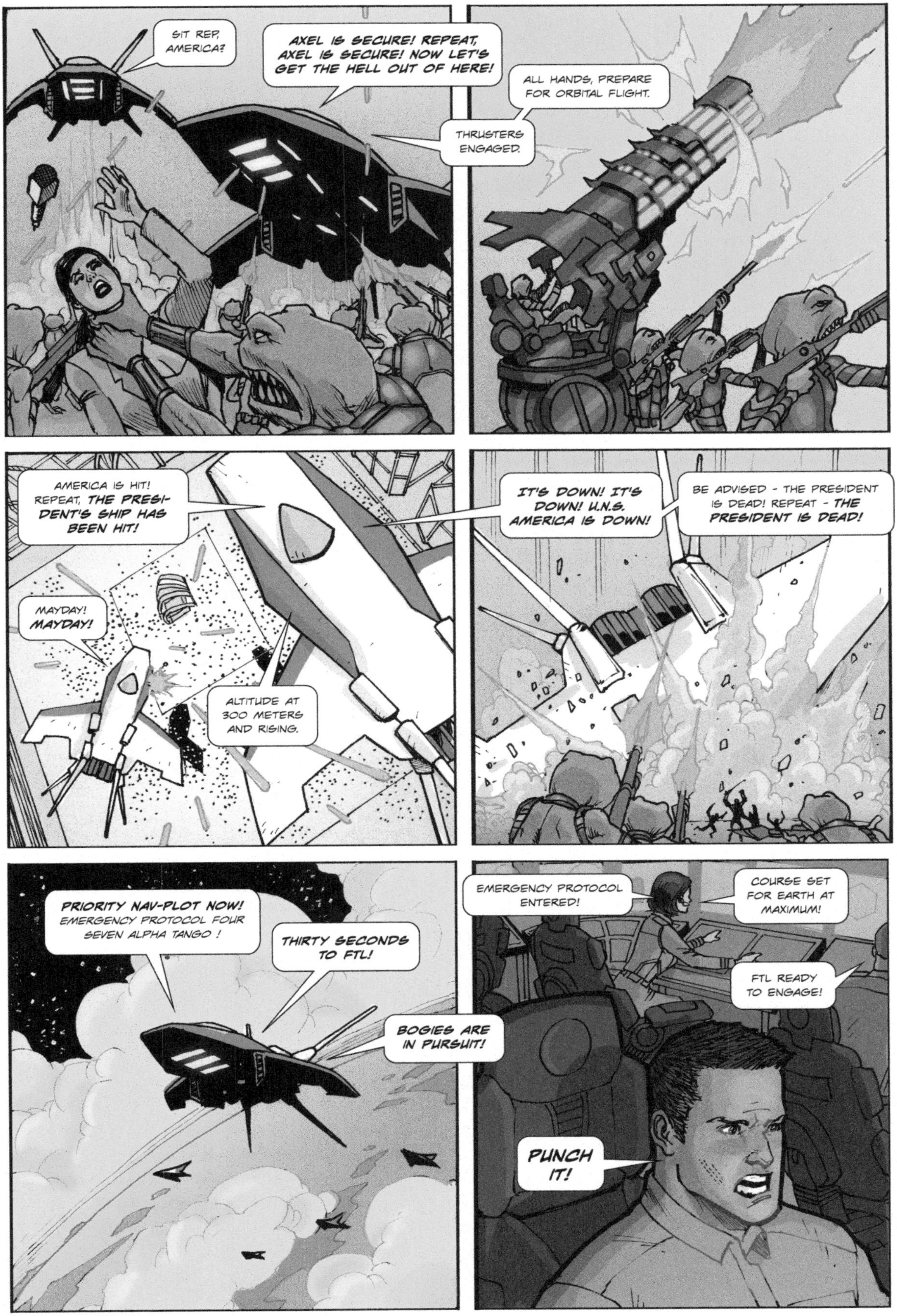
SIT REP, AMERICA?
AXEL IS SECURE! REPEAT, AXEL IS SECURE! NOW LET'S GET THE HELL OUT OF HERE!
THRUSTERS ENGAGED.
ALL HANDS, PREPARE FOR ORBITAL FLIGHT.
AMERICA IS HIT! REPEAT, THE PRESIDENT'S SHIP HAS BEEN HIT!
MAYDAY! MAYDAY!
ALTITUDE AT 300 METERS AND RISING.
IT'S DOWN! IT'S DOWN! U.N.S. AMERICA IS DOWN!
BE ADVISED - THE PRESIDENT IS DEAD! REPEAT - THE PRESIDENT IS DEAD!
PRIORITY NAV-PLOT NOW! EMERGENCY PROTOCOL FOUR SEVEN ALPHA TANGO !
THIRTY SECONDS TO FTL!
BOGIES ARE IN PURSUIT!
EMERGENCY PROTOCOL ENTERED!
COURSE SET FOR EARTH AT MAXIMUM!
FTL READY TO ENGAGE!
PUNCH IT!

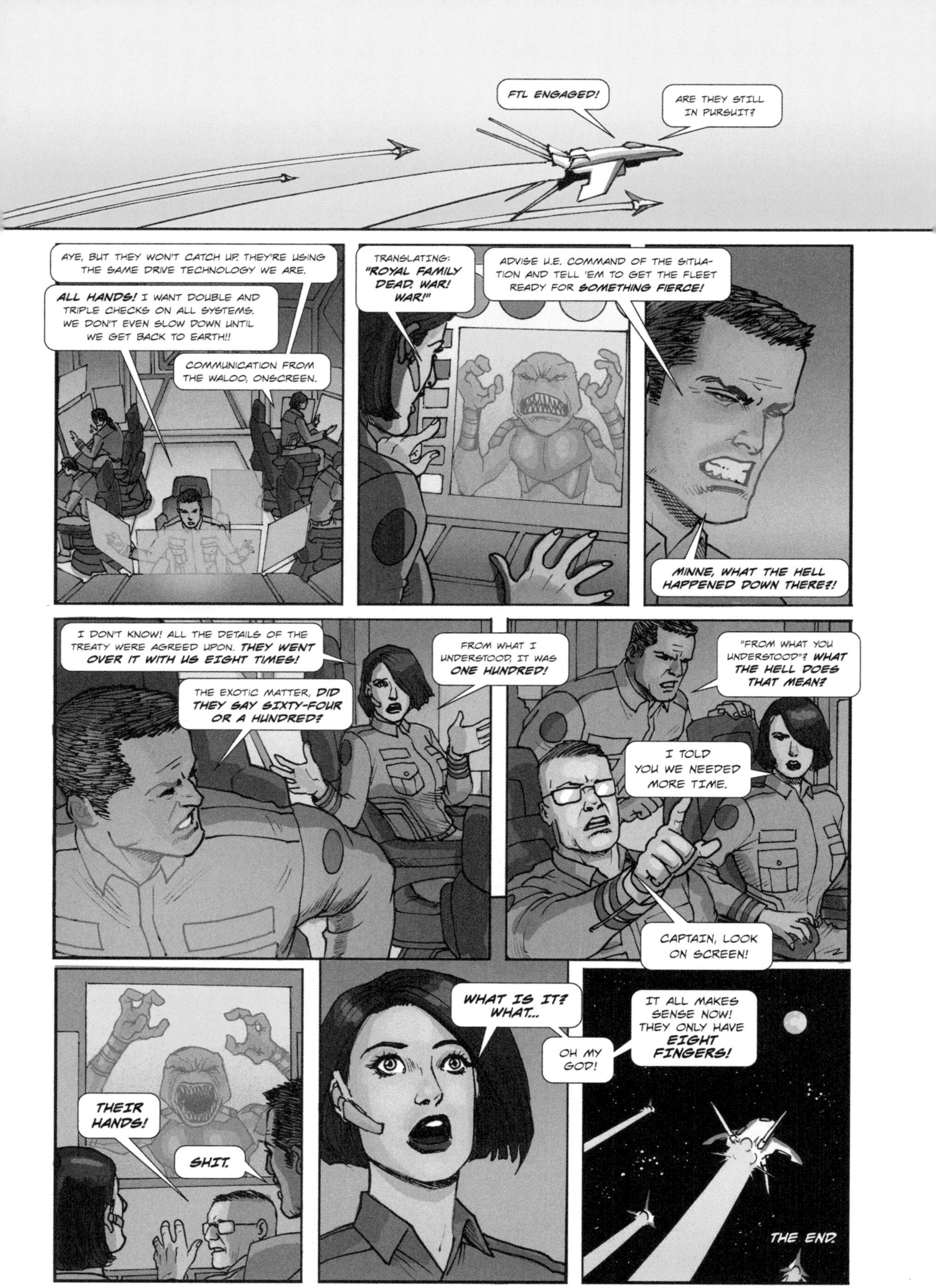
FTL ENGAGED!
ARE THEY STILL IN PURSUIT?
AYE, BUT THEY WON'T CATCH UP. THEY'RE USING THE SAME DRIVE TECHNOLOGY WE ARE.
ALL HANDS! I WANT DOUBLE AND TRIPLE CHECKS ON ALL SYSTEMS. WE DON'T EVEN SLOW DOWN UNTIL WE GET BACK TO EARTH!!
COMMUNICATION FROM THE WALOO, ONSCREEN.
TRANSLATING: "ROYAL FAMILY DEAD. WAR! WAR!"
ADVISE U.E. COMMAND OF THE SITUATION AND TELL 'EM TO GET THE FLEET READY FOR SOMETHING FIERCE!
MINNE, WHAT THE HELL HAPPENED DOWN THERE?!
I DON'T KNOW! ALL THE DETAILS OF THE TREATY WERE AGREED UPON. THEY WENT OVER IT WITH US EIGHT TIMES!
THE EXOTIC MATTER, DID THEY SAY SIXTY-FOUR OR A HUNDRED?
FROM WHAT I UNDERSTOOD, IT WAS ONE HUNDRED!
"FROM WHAT YOU UNDERSTOOD"? WHAT THE HELL DOES THAT MEAN?
I TOLD YOU WE NEEDED MORE TIME.
CAPTAIN, LOOK ON SCREEN!
THEIR HANDS!
SHIT.
WHAT IS IT? WHAT...
OH MY GOD!
IT ALL MAKES SENSE NOW! THEY ONLY HAVE EIGHT FINGERS!
THE END.

THERE

STORY HANSEL MORENO
ART CLAIRE CONNELLY

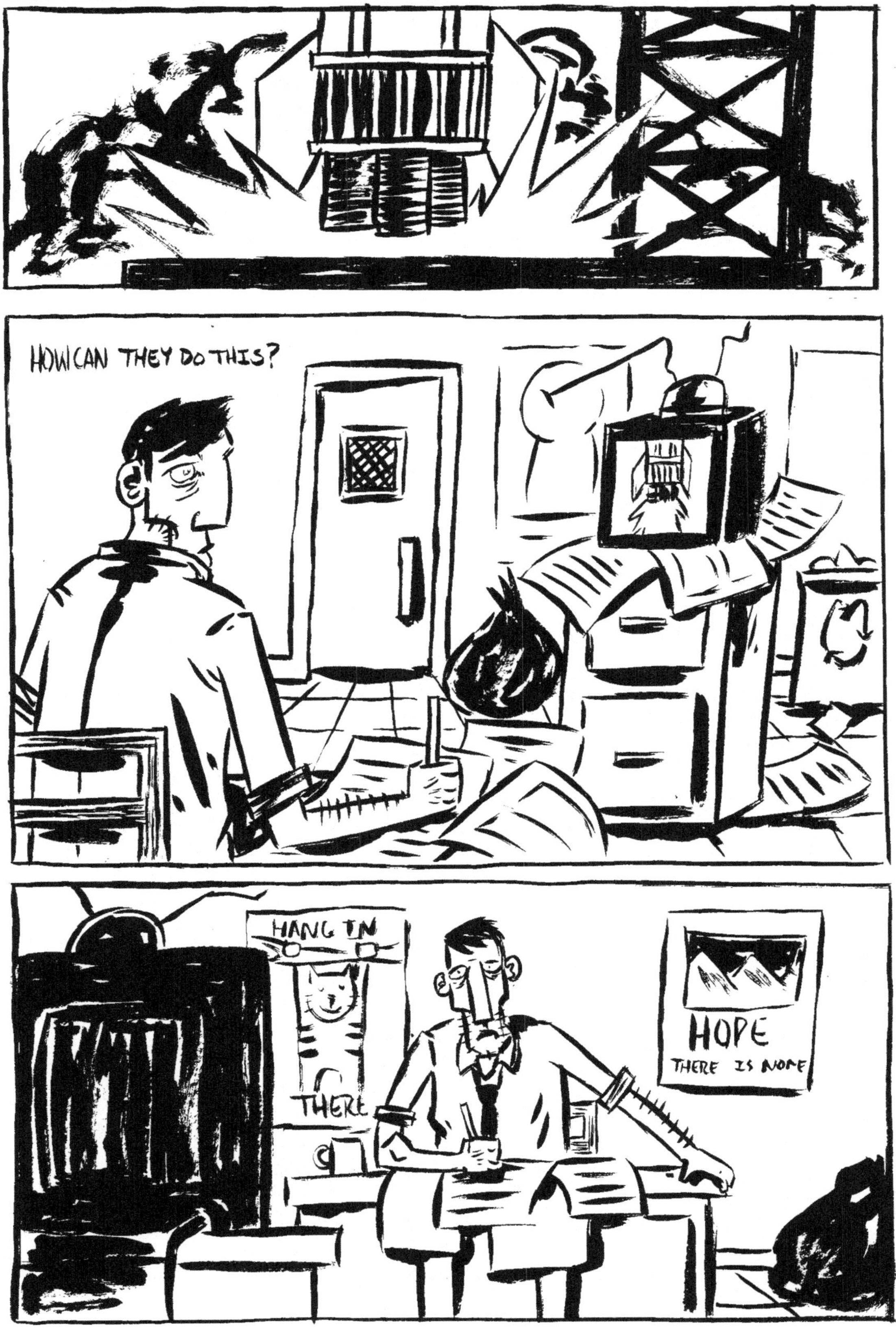
HOW CAN THEY DO THIS?
HANG IN
THERE
HOPE
THERE IS NONE

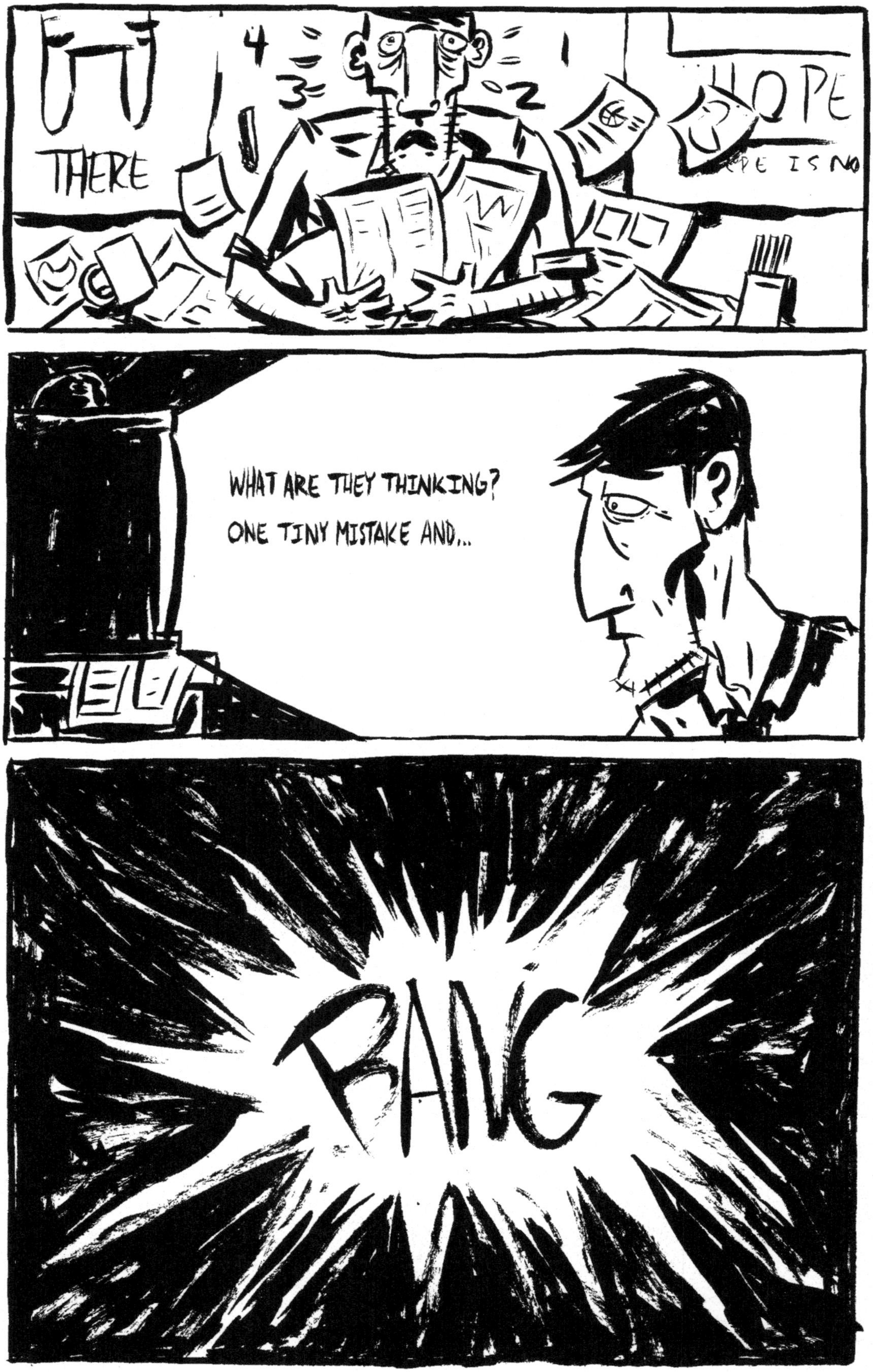
THERE
HOPE
WHAT ARE THEY THINKING?
ONE TINY MISTAKE AND...
BANG

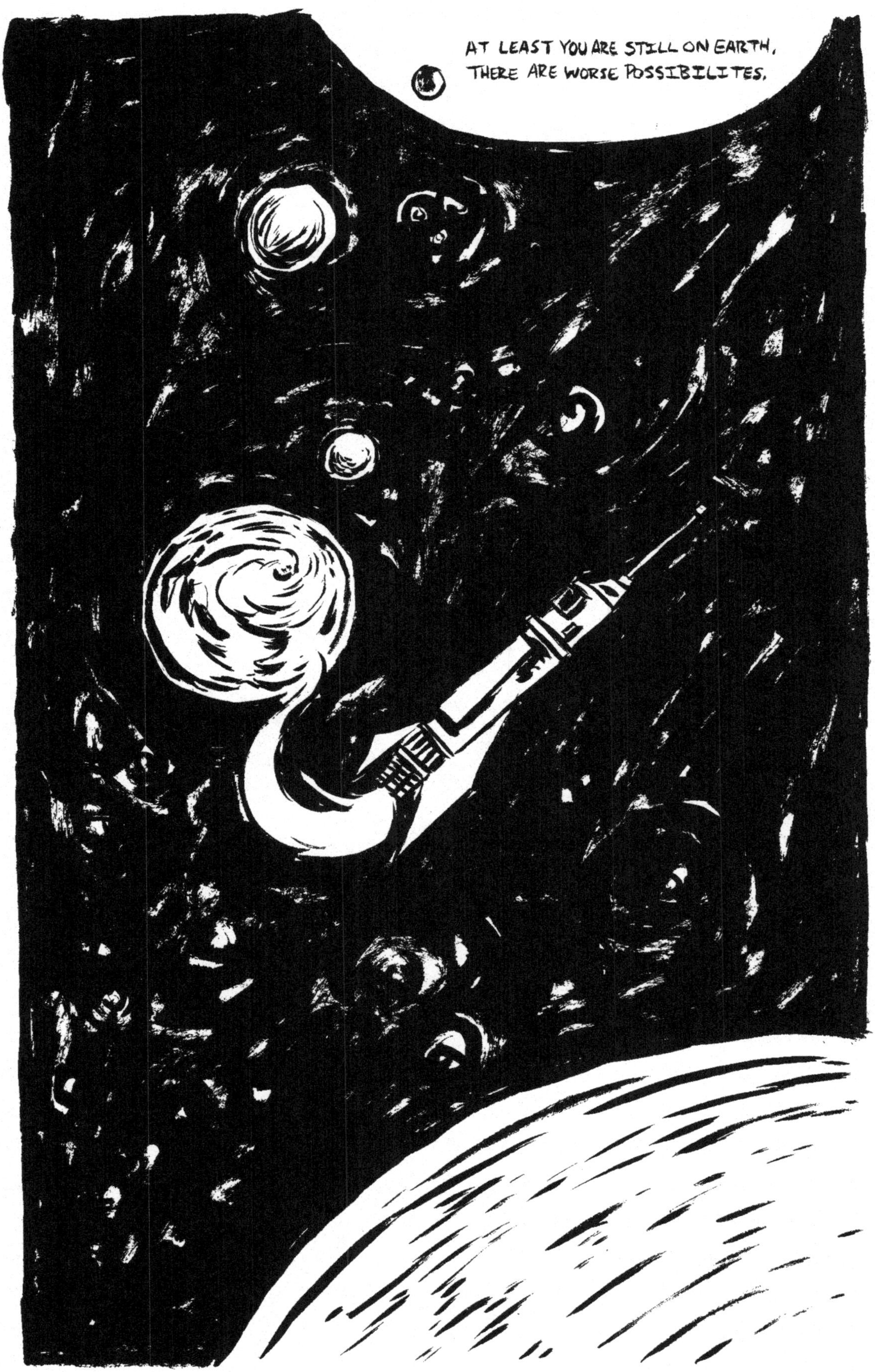
AT LEAST YOU ARE STILL ON EARTH.
THERE ARE WORSE POSSIBILITES.

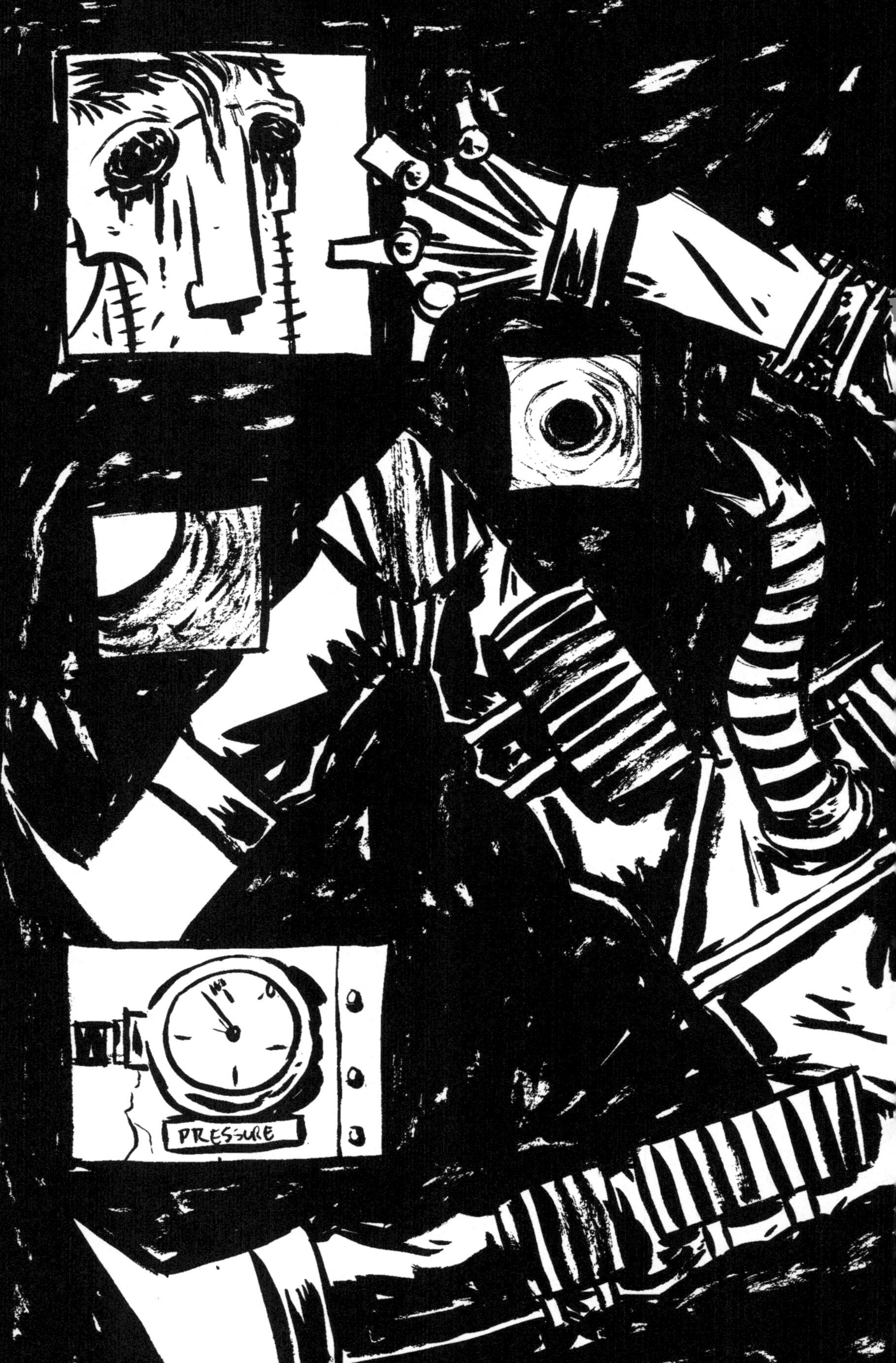
PRESSURE

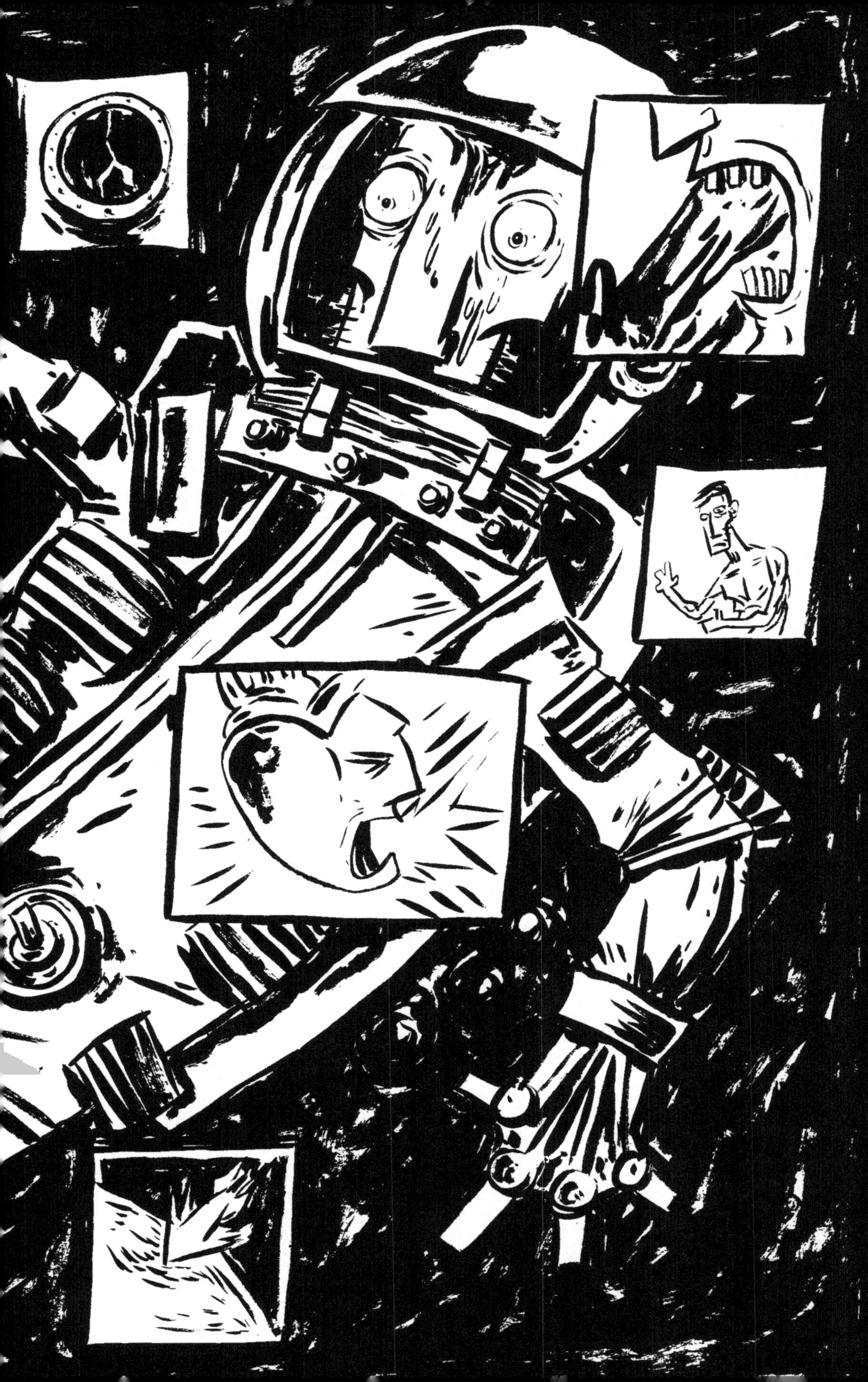

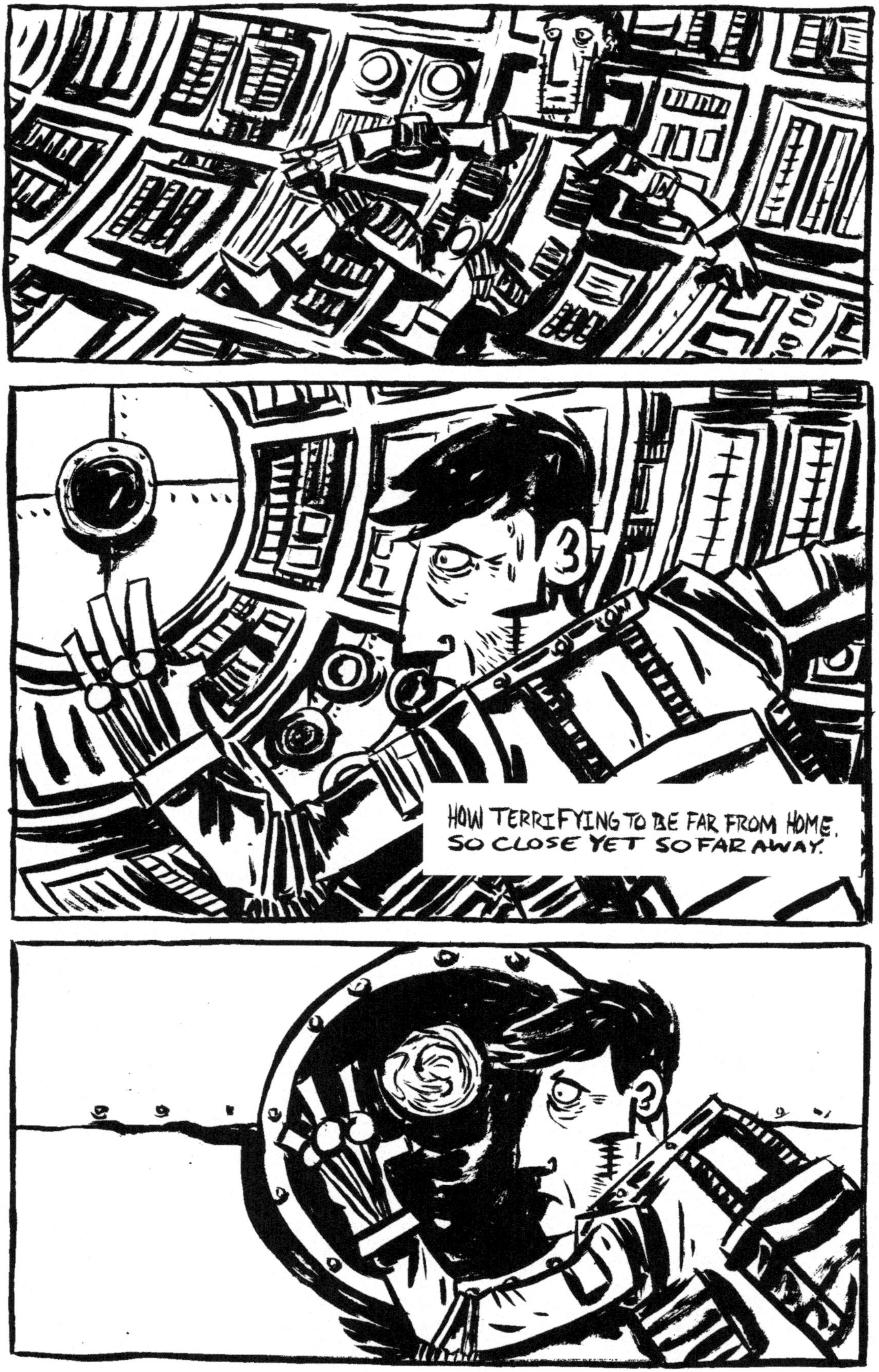
HOW TERRIFYING TO BE FAR FROM HOME.
SO CLOSE YET SO FAR AWAY.

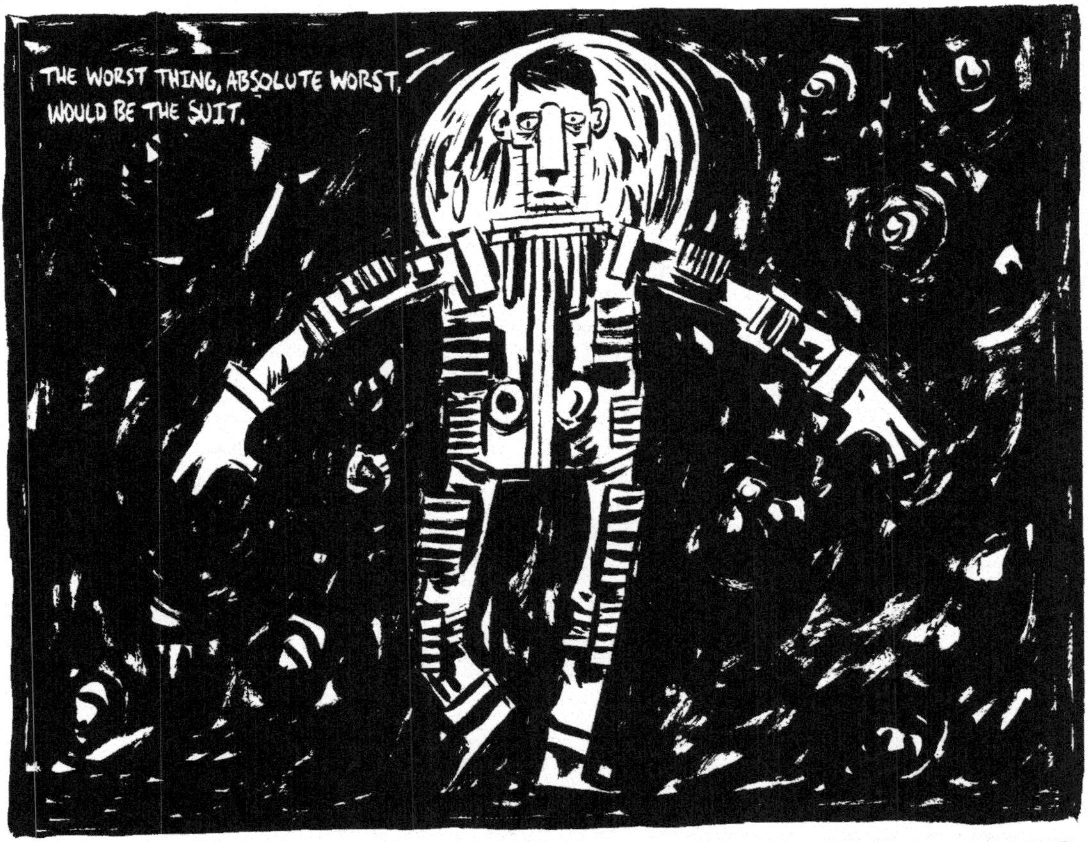
THE WORST THING, ABSOLUTE WORST, WOULD BE THE SUIT.

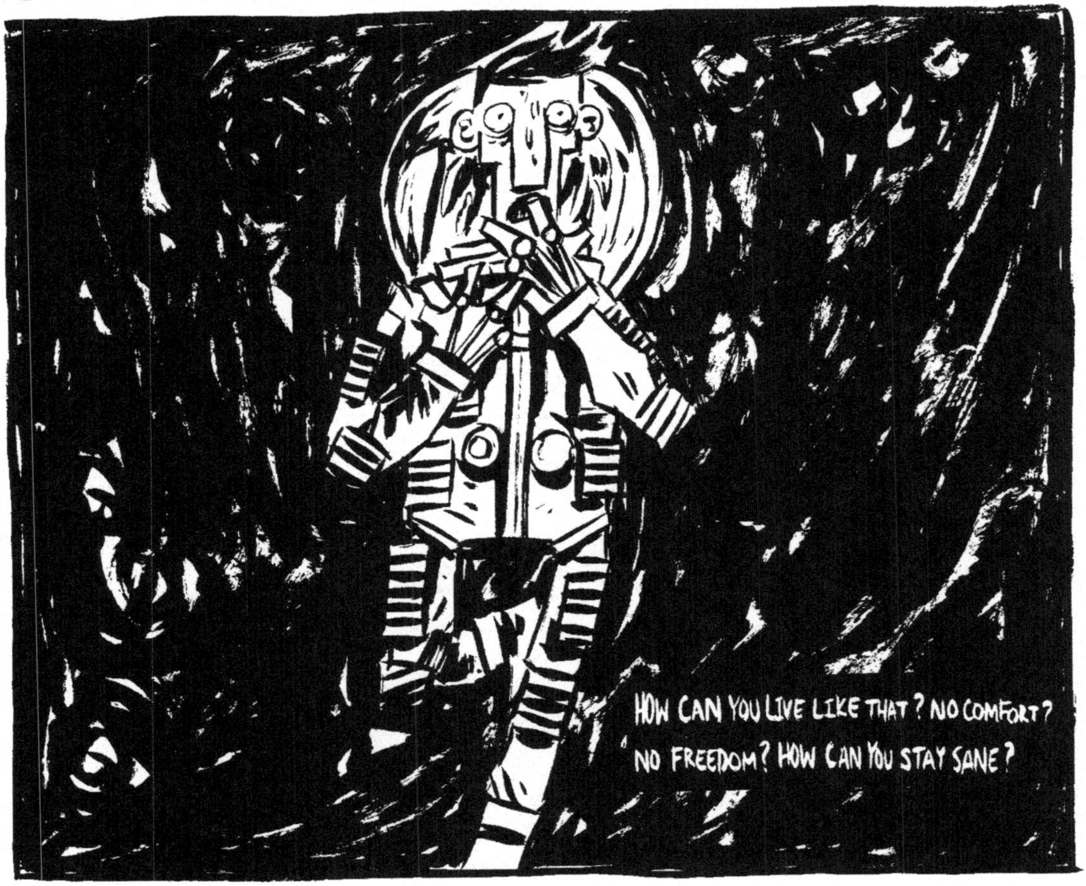
HOW CAN YOU LIVE LIKE THAT? NO COMFORT? NO FREEDOM? HOW CAN YOU STAY SANE?

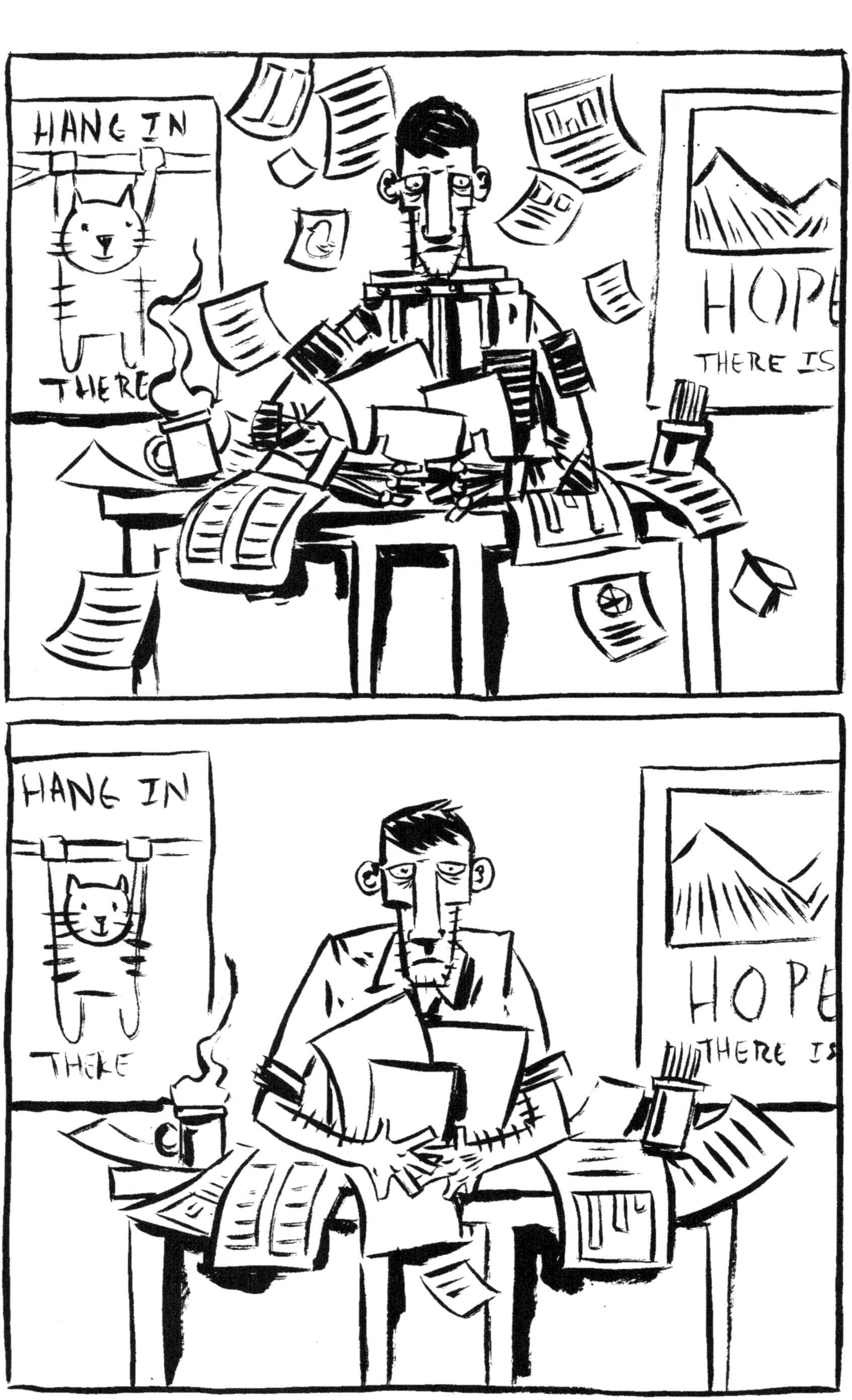
HANG IN
THERE
HOPE
THERE IS
HANG IN
THERE
HOPE
THERE IS

DEREK ADNAMS @DAdnams
The first thing he remembers looking at is AMAZING SPIDER-MAN #188, in 1979. The stories have been locked inside his head for a long time. Now they're escaping.

TOM ALEXANDER @TomEAlexander
Writer with stories appearing in various anthologies. Tom enjoys reading, mixed martial arts, and metalworking. He lives in Arkansas with his wife and son.

FABIO ANGELINI
A graphic designer living in Rome. "Kreator" is his first comics coloring gig.
designhardkore.com

LUI ANTONIO
Artist for WARHAMMER (BOOM! Studios) and RED SONJA (Dark Horse). When he's not drawing comics, Lui works in advertising and drawing sketch cards.
stompboxxx.deviantart.com

JOSEPH BAKER
Provided color art for Devil's Due, Image, Marvel UK, and DC Comics. He enjoys coloring within the lines, and when the need arises, outside of them.
facebook.com/TestSubjectsPhoenix

BRANDON BARROWS @BrandonBarrows
Ghastly Award winning horror comics writer. He's best known for his detective comic series JACK HAMMER (Action Lab). Brandon also writes prose and poetry.
brandonbarrowscomics.com

MARK BERTOLINI @mark_bertolini
Comic book writer of BREAKNECK and SCUM OF THE EARTH (Action Lab). Mark is also a contributor to IMAGINARY DRUGS (IDW). He spends the ~10 months of the Canadian winter holed up in a bunker making comics.

BIG PANTS! ME
Duo co-founded by Joe Simmons & P.B. DeBerry. They write, draw, letter, and have beards that are certified lethal weapons. Joie @pizzaandcomics and Paulie @bigpantsme

DON CARDENAS @DonCardenasArt
Co-creator and artist of PACKS OF THE LOW COUNTRY and artist for GrayHaven Comics and King Bone Press.

FAUSTO CAROTTI
Comic artist and writer, co-creator of DOYLE and other stories, he's now working on the fantasy NERO – ROYAL BLOOD. faustocarotti.com

JOHNNIE CHRISTMAS @j_xmas
Co-creator and artist of SHELTERED (Image). He has illustrated for Valiant Comics, BOOM! Studios, and others. He's an American ex-pat living in Canada. jxmas.com

CLAIRE CONNELLY @CkConnellyDraws
Best known for her offbeat mini comics on ClaireConnellyComics.com, Claire's also the creator of such works as HERE: A SCI-FI EPIC and DOWN WITH THE SHIP. She draws, eats, and sometimes sleeps.

MICHAEL CORBITT
Painter, writer, and father of two boys, he got into comics early in life after his grandmother gave him a stack of X-FACTOR books. He says he owes it all to Dorothy.

GILES CRAWFORD
Comic book artist, animator, and friend to pinnipeds everywhere.
behance,net/redwhiteblack

MARCO "ET DOLLMAN" DELLA VERDE @ETDollman
A comic writer and letterer, he's written for HEAVY METAL magazine and FEMFORCE and lettered comics for AC Comics, IDW, and others.
ETDollman.com

MIKE EXNER III @mikeexner3
Writer for Dark Horse, Digital Webbing, FUBAR Press, and others. He is also the co-founder of Loophole Comics. When he isn't making comics, he can be found toiling away on Tumblr and Twitter.

JIM GIAR
Jim "The Rev" Giar is an artist appearing in the anthologies FUBAR: EMPIRE OF THE RISING DEAD and ONCE UPON A TIME MACHINE. When not making comics, Jim paints murals with the Rust Belt Monster Collective and thwarts alien invasions. chelzostudios.com

RAMON GIL @ramonsgil
Writer of the Scifies comic series and illustrator of LEGENDS OF NASCAR (Vortex). Ramon owns Fresh Concentrate, a design and marketing firm.
ramongil.com

MIKE ISENBERG
Associate Production Coordinator at comiXology and co-writer of FIRST LAW OF MAD SCIENCE. He lives in Harlem with his cats, Tesla and Edison.
firstlawofmadscience.com

JASON JARAVA
An artist living and working in Phoenix, Arizona. Jason enjoys developing personal and collaborative projects dealing with unusual subject matter.
jasonjarava.weebly.com

JE
Hails from a small town in the south of France, where at home he read comic books and in class hid at the back of a small room drawing on tables. He now resides in Florida and still reads comic books, or whatever they're called these days.

JOSHUA JENSEN
Enjoys working with Photoshop and is fascinated with comics. As he says, why not do what you love? joshj81.deviantart.com

JAMES AARON HISLOPE
An artist specializing in cartooning and humorous illustration.
facebook.com/james.hislope

JANET K. LEE @Janet_K_Lee
Eisner Award winning artist for RETURN OF THE DAPPER MEN, co-created with writer Jim McCann. Janet has also illustrated EMMA and NORTHANGER ABBEY for Marvel. As the pre-eminent (and perhaps only!) comic book artist working in decoupage, she often finds herself up to her elbows in glue.

JEFF MCCOMSEY
Editor of the New York Times best-selling anthology series FUBAR.
Jeff primarily spends his time illustrating funny books and anything else that
comes within arm's reach. mccomseycomix.wordpress.com

OLIVER MERTZ
Co-writer of FIRST LAW OF MAD SCIENCE and contributing writer of the New
York Times best-selling anthology series FUBAR. firstlawofmadscience.com

GLENN MØANE
Writer of various sequential stories such as AMERICAN SINNER,
HOMECOMING, and THE GLORY. He claims to be Scandinavia's most obscure
comics writer. glennmoane.blogspot.com

HANSEL MORENO
A comic book writer based out of Texas. When not elbow-deep in gears and other
mechanical equipment, he is chasing down a pizza and thinking up new stories.
egadcomics.tumblr.com

MICAH MYERS @micahmyers
Letterer for ALL HALLOWS EVE, SNARL, and HIGHLANDER 3030. Micah lives
with his wife and is training his two children in the ways of comic book fandom.
micahmyers.daportfolio.com

DAVID NEWBOLD @dnewbold8
Draws comics, hates spiders, and loves hockey.

LAUREN OUSLEY @LaurenOusley
Artist behind GINORMOUS (Stache). When not at the drawing table, Lauren
loves gardening and playing around in the dirt.

MICK SCHUBERT
Comic book writer and letterer for FUBAR, OUTRÉ, and IGOR: OCCULT
DETECTIVE. He moonlights as a science consultant for Marvel Comics.
jeyradan.daportfolio.com

KEVIN M. STONE
Art director and comic book artist, he wrote, inked, and colored the series
OLD SOLDIERS. Kevin has also worked on other series such as
NEW OLYMPUS and CLOCK PUNCHER. kstonedesign.com

TOMASZ WITAS
An illustrator and comic book artist from Poland. His work has appeared in
THE GATHERING: SPIES (GrayHaven). tomaszwitas.blogspot.com

JUSTIN WOOD
A comic book line artist and colorist. He operates out of Virginia, currently
working on his creator-owned project GENESIS WALTZ.
linestothepaper.wix.com/theartofjustinwood

Corey Fryia @coreyfryia
Comic writer described as a stuck-up, half-witted, scruffy-looking nerf herder.

Jason Moning
Designer and illustrator from Saint Louis with an obsession for gummi worms.
jasonmoning.wix.com/moningdesign

Marcus Muller
Comics and video game concept artist operating on ambition and lack of sleep.
marcusmuller.blogspot.com

Marta Tanrikulu
Editor, comics writer, and reformed mad scientist.
vizyonentertainment.com

Image Chaz Simmons, Grade 7, NYC

For more information and to participate:
www.comicbookproject.org

The publisher and creators of this anthology believe in the power of comics to open minds and improve lives. Some proceeds from this book will be donated to The Comic Book Project, an innovative, worldwide literacy program. For over twelve years, the Comic Book Project has helped over 100,000 children write, design, and publish original comic books. The creators of this anthology are happy to support the next generation of comic creators, writers, and artists.

Stache encourages everyone to pick up a pen and

#makecomiX

www.makecomix.com